Palgrave Studies in Prisons and Penology

Series Editors
Ben Crewe
Institute of Criminology
University of Cambridge
Cambridge, UK

Yvonne Jewkes
School of Social Policy, Sociology
and Social Research
University of Kent
Canterbury, UK

Thomas Ugelvik
Department of Criminology and Sociology of Law
University of Oslo
Oslo, Norway

This is a unique and innovative series, the first of its kind dedicated entirely to prison scholarship. At a historical point in which the prison population has reached an all-time high, the series seeks to analyse the form, nature and consequences of incarceration and related forms of punishment. Palgrave Studies in Prisons and Penology provides an important forum for burgeoning prison research across the world.

Series Advisory Board
Anna Eriksson (Monash University)
Andrew M. Jefferson (DIGNITY—Danish Institute Against Torture)
Shadd Maruna (Rutgers University)
Jonathon Simon (Berkeley Law, University of California)
Michael Welch (Rutgers University)

More information about this series at
http://www.palgrave.com/gp/series/14596

Elizabeth Stanley
Editor

Human Rights and Incarceration

Critical Explorations

palgrave
macmillan

Editor
Elizabeth Stanley
Institute of Criminology
Victoria University of Wellington
Wellington, New Zealand

Palgrave Studies in Prisons and Penology
ISBN 978-3-319-95398-4   ISBN 978-3-319-95399-1   (eBook)
https://doi.org/10.1007/978-3-319-95399-1

Library of Congress Control Number: 2018947397

This Palgrave Macmillan imprint is published by the registered company Springer Nature Switzerland AG
The registered company address is: Gewerbestrasse 11, 6330 Cham, Switzerland

*This book is dedicated to all those who work to reform
and abolish carceral sites.*

Acknowledgements

This book has been supported by a Rutherford Discovery Fellowship (RDF-VUW1301), administered by the Royal Society of New Zealand. Among other benefits, this Fellowship provided finances for a nourishing symposium in Wellington. Over a couple of days in April 2017, authors presented draft papers and swopped ideas for this book. We were particularly fortunate to be joined by a small, stellar group of academics, students, practitioners and activists committed to reform and abolition. Our stimulating exchanges led to valuable chapters. To the top-notch scholars in this book: Thank you for all your inspirational teaching, research and activism over the years, and for writing so beautifully here.

Many people have helped me to produce this work. Thanks to Josie Taylor and the team at Palgrave Macmillan for their encouragement and assistance. I also thank Ben Crewe, Yvonne Jewkes and Thomas Ugelvik, editors of the *Prisons and Penology* series, for their support in taking this volume forward. Special mention also goes to Anne Holland for her meticulous formatting and referencing work, as well as Robin Briggs, for his indexing talents.

I am always thankful for my colleagues and students at the Institute of Criminology, Victoria University of Wellington. I consider it a great fortune to work alongside such talented and supportive people who are committed to critical research and social justice.

Thanks to my mum, Nick, Sue, Billy, JD and Sandra for their staunch support, and to Tippi for being Tippi. Finally, an extra special thank you to the marvellous Acky for his good humour, care and love. Thank you all.

Contents

Notes on Contributors

Thalia Anthony is an Associate Professor at the Faculty of Law, University of Technology Sydney. She has a high profile in contributing to research in Indigenous criminal justice issues, particularly through the critical lens of colonisation and Indigenous self-determination. Her research methodologies are underpinned by fieldwork in Indigenous communities and partnerships with Indigenous legal organisations in Australia and overseas.

Eileen Baldry is Deputy Vice Chancellor Inclusion and Diversity and Professor of Criminology, UNSW Sydney. She has taught social policy, social development and criminology over the past 30 years. She is a critical criminologist and her research focuses on social justice including mental health and cognitive disability in criminal justice systems, criminalised women, and Indigenous Australian women and youth. She was awarded the NSW Justice Medal and was recently named as one of Australia's 100 influential women.

Harry Blagg is a Professor of Criminology at the Faculty of Law, University of Western Australia. Harry has a national and international reputation as a leading criminologist specialising in Indigenous people and criminal justice, young people and crime, family violence, crime prevention, diversionary strategies, policing and restorative justice. He has an extensive fieldwork background in remote communities in Australia.

Bree Carlton is a Senior Lecturer in Criminology, School of Humanities and Social Sciences, Deakin University. Her politics and commitment to transforming structural injustice drives her research focus on documenting and resisting institutionally generated experiences of discrimination, harm and violence. Recent publications appear in the *Australian and New Zealand Journal of Criminology* and *Punishment and Society*. Her and E. K. Russell's forthcoming book is titled *Resisting Carceral Violence: Women's Imprisonment and the Politics of Abolition* (Palgrave Macmillan).

Michael Grewcock teaches criminal law and criminology at the Faculty of Law, UNSW Sydney. His main areas of research are border policing and State Crime. He is a member of the Editorial Board of the *State Crime* journal.

Deena Haydon is an independent researcher in Northern Ireland. Linking research, theory, policy and practice her main interests are childhood, family support, youth justice, and children's rights. Deena's publications include a co-authored book, journal articles, book chapters, reports, resources for children and practitioners, as well as submissions to the UN Committee on the Rights of the Child. She has presented to academic and public audiences in the UK, Europe, the US, Australia and New Zealand.

Nessa Lynch is a Senior Lecturer at the Faculty of Law, Victoria University of Wellington, where she teaches and researches in the areas of youth justice, criminal law and sentencing.

Margaret S. Malloch is Associate Professor in Criminology at the University of Stirling, and Associate Director with the Scottish Centre for Crime and Justice Research. Her work is focused on challenging the ongoing and international tendency to prioritise criminal justice solutions to the detriment of justice more broadly.

Tracey McIntosh (Ngāi Tūhoe) is a Professor of Indigenous Studies at the University of Auckland. Her research focuses on the incarceration of Indigenous peoples, inequality, poverty and justice. She is engaged in community work and served as co-director of Ngā Pae o te Māramatanga, NZ's Māori Centre of Research Excellence.

Riki Mihaere (Ngāti Kahungunu) engaged 'A kaupapa Māori analysis of the use of Māori cultural identity in the prison system' for his Ph.D. thesis at Victoria University of Wellington (VUW). From 2016–2017, he was a Post-Doctoral Fellow on a Rutherford Discovery Fellowship project at the Institute of Criminology, VUW.

Emma K. Russell is a Lecturer in Crime, Justice and Legal Studies at La Trobe University, Australia. Her research explores how social movements challenge, critique and shape systems and spaces of policing and punishment. She has a keen interest in activist histories and queer, feminist and abolitionist politics. Her recent publications appear in the journals *Crime Media Culture*, *Critical Criminology* and *Australian Feminist Law Journal*. With Bree Carlton, she is co-author of *Resisting Carceral Violence* (Palgrave Macmillan).

David Scott works at the Open University, UK. He has been directly involved in abolitionist and social justice activism for more than twenty years. He is the author of several books including the trilogy *Emancipatory Politics and Praxis* (EG Press, 2016), *Against Imprisonment* (Waterside Press, 2018) and *The Estranged Other* (Waterside Press, forthcoming 2019).

Phil Scraton is Professor Emeritus in the School of Law, Queen's University Belfast. His research includes controversial deaths and the state (Hillsborough Independent Panel) and the politics of incarceration (NI Human Rights Commission). Recent books include: *Power, Conflict and Criminalisation*; *The Violence of Incarceration*; *The Incarceration of Women*; *Hillsborough: The Truth*; and, *Women's Imprisonment and the Case for Abolition*.

Elizabeth Stanley is a Reader and Rutherford Discovery Fellow at the Institute of Criminology, Victoria University of Wellington. Her research focuses on state crimes, human rights, detention and social justice. Her publications include *Torture, Truth and Justice*; *State Crime and Resistance* (with Jude McCulloch); and *The Road to Hell: State Violence against Children in Post War NZ*.

List of Tables

1

Human Rights and Incarceration

Elizabeth Stanley

Introduction

We live in a carceral age. In Anglophone societies, many groups—offenders, 'non-citizens', people with disabilities, those with mental health problems, children 'in care', and others—are locked up. At the same time, carceral responses can only be regarded as demonstrating "the power of the imaginary to create acquiescence in the absurd" (Carlen 2008: 10). Incarceration never alleviates the harms that it purports to deal with or prevent. Prisons, for example, have no substantive bearing on crime rates, while immigration detention does not stem the conflicts or pressures from which migrants flow. The use of carceral institutions also makes social problems worse. The list is long but, among other outcomes, incarceration: routinises cultures of offending, violence and substance use; developmentally-damages children and

E. Stanley (✉)
Institute of Criminology, Victoria University of Wellington,
Wellington, New Zealand
e-mail: elizabeth.stanley@vuw.ac.nz

© The Author(s) 2018
E. Stanley (ed.), *Human Rights and Incarceration*, Palgrave Studies
in Prisons and Penology, https://doi.org/10.1007/978-3-319-95399-1_1

young people; preserves racialised power relations and bias; sustains gendered forms of regulation and violence; and leads to stigma, discrimination and poverty. These impacts are not individualised. They reach across generations, so much so that incarceration and its effects are normalised in some communities. In short, carceral sites indicate and perpetuate violations of human rights for vast numbers of people.

In many respects, human rights could be regarded as a 'failed project' for those incarcerated in neo-liberal states. As this chapter shows, their human rights are continually eroded by state power relations, criminalisation practices, legal processing and administrative agendas. In response, we might ask: are rights still worth prioritising in relation to incarceration? And, if so, how might we envision or strengthen them? These questions are the foundation for this book.

This introduction considers some of the legal frameworks through which human rights are established, debated and monitored. It sets out the landscape of protective 'carrots' and 'sticks' that may encourage or shame states into human rights conscious activity. And, it reflects upon the necessity of reaching beyond legal and institutional responses, towards new forms of justice. After all, the values of human rights deepen the chance of better lives. They herald opportunities for freedom, dignity, respect, peace, equity, compassion and shared humanity. And, in doing so, they present vital tools to the social problems of 'crime', harms and incarceration.

Human Rights Frameworks

Human rights have long guided the operation of prisons, justice residences, and other places of detention. Some detention-related rights—such as habeas corpus—are centuries old, and have formed the basis of our liberal democracies. However, from the mid-twentieth century in particular, the United Nations has progressed laws, rules and principles to underpin the fair treatment and dignity of all detainees, and they have established a parallel network of mechanisms for oversight and accountability. In some parts of the world, states are now bound by regional laws and bodies (such as the European Convention on Human

Rights and its corresponding Court). The Council of Europe, for example, has established that prison conditions should resemble those in the community with greater efforts being made to decriminalise and develop alternative responses to crime (Scharff-Smith 2016). Many states retain domestic human rights laws that codify civil and political rights. Protections for incarcerated people are promised across the world.

It is not within the scope of this introduction to chart the array of relevant laws or norms. However, UN instruments—like the *International Covenant on Civil and Political Rights* or the *Convention against Torture and Other Cruel, Inhuman or Degrading Treatment or Punishment*—set the ground for rights relating to incarceration. They establish that all those deprived of liberty shall be humanely treated, with respect for their inherent dignity. They spell out rights to privacy, family life, freedom of expression, liberty and security of the person, among other rights, that all incarcerated people should enjoy. They prohibit all torture, establishing that states should never return or extradite someone (non-refoulement) when there are grounds to believe they will be tortured on arrival. The *Basic Principles for the Treatment of Prisoners* assert that all prisoners should retain "the human rights and fundamental freedoms" set out in all UN Covenants and Protocols, "except for the limitations that are demonstrably necessitated by the fact of incarceration" (Principle 5).

Further directions are found in the UN's *Standard Minimum Rules for the Treatment of Prisoners*. The most recent 2015 Rules (aka the *Nelson Mandela Rules*) attend to the sharp end of imprisonment—such as prohibiting solitary confinement (defined as lock downs of 22 hours or more a day without meaningful human contact), painful restraints, or excessive 'discipline and order'. They provide practical guidelines on food, accommodation, clothing, and so on. However they also emphasise the need for authorities to be attentive to how imprisonment, in and of itself, produces violations. For example, Rules establish the need for prisoners to receive equitable health care, including care related to mental health problems that can be "brought on by the fact of imprisonment" (Rule 30(c)). Prisons should not "aggravate the suffering inherent in" situations of liberty deprivation (Rule 3).

Alongside these instruments lie a raft of UN Conventions and Declarations that prohibit harmful practices towards groups including Indigenous people, women, children, and persons with disabilities. As detailed in subsequent chapters, many provide explicit instructions to prevent discrimination, criminalisation and incarceration. They dovetail with the UN's guiding *International Covenant on Economic, Social and Cultural Rights* (ICESCR) that asserts "the ideal of free human beings enjoying freedom from fear and want" (Preamble). This instrument establishes numerous rights for all, including: to self-determination, to education, to work, to join a union and to strike, to receive fair wages for a decent living, to enjoy safe and healthy working conditions, and to receive social security. Everyone has rights to "adequate food, clothing and housing, and to the continuous improvement of living conditions" (Article 11) and to enjoy "the highest attainable standard of physical and mental health" (Article 12).

Signatory states to these international laws participate in regular oversight reporting on their rights progress. Alongside Universal Periodic Reviews from the UN Human Rights Council (UNHRC), all conventions are overseen by specific UN Committees that monitor, ensure compliance and promote preventative actions. On a cyclical basis, UN Committees visit states, engage with civil society groups, hear complaints, receive and produce reports on progress, and make recommendations for remedies and prevention. The UN has also established 'National Preventive Mechanisms' (NPMs) as part of the *Optional Protocol to the Convention Against Torture*. This means that independent NPMs now have a complementary mandate to make regular visits to places of detention, including unannounced visits. NPMs subsequently recommend improvements and measures to prevent ill-treatment, publish reports, and exchange information with their international counterparts. All of these Committees have a role in exposing the gaps between stated laws or policies and actual practice, and they regularly provide a litany of abusive treatments and harmful conditions across carceral sites.

Reporting mechanisms reflect ritualism but, in bringing increased scrutiny to rights-eroding practices, they shame states and mobilise communities by educating and agitating on human rights concerns. They lead civil society groups and activists to take an increased interest in monitoring standards and to create "new lines of accountability" that "promote the bottom-up development of a human rights culture" (Weber et al. 2014: 46). Committees may also be empowered to undertake inquiries of systemic violations of human rights, and to demand changes on those terms. And, it is clear that changes in one country create ripple effects across other jurisdictions (Barbaret 2014).

The judiciary may also act as a protective force of accountability (Naylor 2016) and, at certain junctures, has substantive impacts. For example, mass-imprisonment in the USA has been directly challenged by court decisions. In *Brown v Plata* [2011], judges found that state prisons were so overcrowded that they constituted "cruel and inhuman" conditions. And, in the face of extreme mental health and medical problems for prisoners, they upheld a "systemwide population-reduction order" (Simon 2014: 134). This provoked deep changes: not least a drop in the Californian prison population, "from its 2006 peak of 173,000 to 130,000" in 2014 (Schlanger 2016: 65). Court decisions also led to improved conditions of confinement for those with a range of medical or mental health needs, including those relating to disabilities. These emerged from a particular "eco-system"—the tenacity of empathetic lawyers, a hospitable bench and the development of "humanitarian anxiety" (ibid.; Simon 2014: 150). For Simon (ibid.: 137), such decisions represent a new "dignity cascade" in which "society recognizes that it has profoundly violated human dignity and in response expands its very understanding of what humanity includes and requires of the law". It also reminds us that—even in the most strident of carceral states—the administration of law offers useful scope for protections. Nonetheless, as the next section demonstrates, there are many factors that erode rights for those targeted for incarceration.

Incarceration and the Erosion of Rights

Incarceration always sustains harm—the denial of movement and the separation of individuals from their families and loved ones[1] challenge two of the most crucial aspects of human experience: to have freedom, and to be connected in close relationships. For some groups, like children, incarceration damages human development and personality, regardless of the quality of conditions, staff relationships or treatments on offer.

Yet, beyond these deprivations, incarcerated people regularly find that their access to established human rights is deeply challenged. Prisoners, for example, know that their access to multiple rights including rights to vote, to receive equivalent health care, to have a family life, to benefit from education, to work or to have personal safety are all deeply compromised. This section considers why this occurs in relation to issues of state legitimacy, criminalisation, managerialism and the law.

Legitimacy

Modern states have always relied upon violence, or its threat, to regulate economic, political, legal and socio-cultural life (Green and Ward 2004). And, given that states claim "the *monopoly of the legitimate use of physical force*" (Weber 1970: 77), they assert "an entitlement to do things which if anyone else did them would constitute violence and extortion" (Green and Ward 2004: 2–3). The act of incarceration—a violence in and of itself—is made legitimate under state governance. However, beyond the simple process of removing freedom of movement, states regularly engage with violations against incarcerated people as a means to assert state power (Stanley 2017a). For example, the egregious Australian abuses of 'non-citizens' held in offshore processing centres or the British refusal to allow prisoners to vote have been bolstered by state arguments of border protection, state sovereignty and the reassertion of government controls against 'interfering' outsiders.

Building legitimacy must, however, be carefully managed by states and powerful others. We frequently view human rights as vital for developing countries, whose deviance might be rehabilitated through well-meaning human rights monitoring and training (Jefferson 2005).[2] But, at home, human rights are usually minimised or silenced in education, media or politics (Boyle and Stanley 2017). Those who campaign for rights can also be quickly vilified and sometimes severely punished—for example, the *Australian Border Force Act 2015* enables the two-year imprisonment of "entrusted persons" who speak out about gross human rights violations in immigration detention centres. Such threats demonstrate that violence, by state agencies or their contractors, requires careful policing to retain popular legitimacy.

At the same time, Anglophone states are also well attuned to the merits of demonstrating allegiance to human rights. State legitimacy is simultaneously dependent upon human rights attainment or, at the very least, the marketing of human rights consciousness. States will often manage human right discourses to their own advantage: demonstrating "moral virtue" at certain times (McCulloch and Scraton 2009: 6), such as during interactions with UN agencies. There are therefore contradictory approaches in operation as states seek legitimacy by simultaneously asserting human rights engagement while providing the material, discursive and institutional conditions under which rights are violated. Under these circumstances, it pays to be attentive to inconsistencies in rhetoric, policy and practice, and to understand that any attempt to embed rights must confront and negotiate state politics.

Criminalisation

Criminalisation is crucial to perspectives on who 'should' be incarcerated or who 'deserves' violation. Anglophone countries have long histories of criminalisation on the grounds of invisibility or distancing—colonising and colonial states were built through the discursive and practical control of difference. Indigenous people have been killed, brutalised, assimilated and incorporated as a result, but colonial legacies remain through the ongoing mass incarceration of Indigenous peoples, black populations, and other minority groups. Representational distancing progresses further, such that incarceration is directed to welfare 'bludgers', to people with mental health 'disorders', to drug 'addicts', to the 'illegals' that arrive at borders, or to those deemed 'dangerous' on other grounds. Human rights protections are often dismissed by states in a bid to control, deter or punish 'them'—in the emphasis on threats, we lose sight of human plight (Simon 2014).

Criminalisation processes are often guided by highly politicised narratives of risk or securitisation that eclipse human rights values and commitments. These concepts are opaque, ever-changing, but very powerful in that they are used to legitimise violations without any real need for evidence of effectiveness or necessity. Many liberal democratic states are now dominated by an assumption that "we will somehow undermine our collective safety and security and the very foundations for social order" if we recognise rights (Drake 2012: 149). This has become so entrenched that violations, and the dismissal of fundamental legal rights or punishment principles, are increasingly normalised. The use of mandatory detention or civil detention, adult punishments imposed on children, 'three strikes' legislation or 'supermax' conditions are all invoked to neutralise threats (Simon 2014). Moreover, given the opacity of real or imagined threats, violations are also pre-emptively directed, on the grounds that some individuals may engage in criminality or 'risky' behaviour at some point (Stanley 2017b). Under these conditions, universal rights are replaced by a notion that human rights may only be accorded to those deserving (largely mythical) law-abiding citizens—not just now, but also in the imagined future (Genders and Player 2014; McCulloch and Wilson 2016).[3]

Criminalisation processes are also self-perpetuating—criminalisation sustains incarceration but the use of incarceration also reinforces criminalisation. To be incarcerated becomes a signifier of risk, so much so that in current managerialist and multi-agency working contexts, those who have experienced incarceration can be perpetually labelled as risky. Under these circumstances, any violations are also articulated as an individual's problem for being 'dangerous', 'threatening' or different in the first place. These redesignations have significant individual effects but they also reassert carceral legitimacy.

Managerialism

Under current conditions, the publicity of violations also brings risks to carceral institutions (Whitty 2011). Appearing to be human rights-compliant remains crucial to institutional "legitimacy, authority, and international reputation" (Hannah-Moffat 2012: 256). Yet, in an era in which managerialist frames dominate, many institutions prioritise tick-box compliance, producing significant gaps between human rights discourse and actual practice. For example, consider the 'right to life'. In a bid to prevent prisoner deaths, many facilities have introduced long lock-downs in barren cells, anti-rip gowns, continual observation through CCTV, waist restraints, and tie-down beds for those deemed 'at risk' of suicide. Such conditions and treatments, undertaken to ensure 'the right to life', are widely condemned for increasing fear, depression and despair among those already suffering great distress (Moore and Scraton 2013; Harris and Stanley 2017).

These examples remind us that while agencies adhere to the language of human rights in their brochures, training manuals, policy and guidelines, the translation of human rights into practice is, at best, "ambiguous and open to negotiation" (Aas and Gundhus 2015: 4). Compliance is a relatively elastic condition. And, under a managerialist logic— where, for example, deaths in custody are a key performance indicator (KPI) while prisoner despair is not—human rights can be successfully audited out (Carlen 2008).[4] This performance approach produces "paper accountability... rather than ethical accountability to professional standards" (Hannah-Moffat 2012: 256). It ensures that rights are restricted and co-opted in ways to provide "a new cloak of legitimacy for existing penal practices" (Scott 2013: 238; Carlen 2010).

Law

The law may further provide carceral legitimacy. While, as noted above, the law may facilitate protection to incarcerated people, this often does not happen. Part of the problem, here, relates to the inability of law to challenge the structural, institutional or socio-cultural conditions in which violations occur. The causal or cumulative effects of colonisation, criminalisation or inequalities go unaddressed by individualised legal processes. Some areas of international human rights law also need significant redevelopment to make them fit for contemporary purpose. For example, the *Convention Relating to the Status of Refugees* allows states to determine their own responses to individual claimants, and has no guide for responses to mass displacements. Correspondingly, many states have developed a network of dehumanising carceral sites for those arriving at their borders (Grewcock 2016).

Beyond this, securing human rights through legal cases is not easy (Easton 2013; van Zyl Smit and Snacken 2011). Within Anglophone countries, statutory organisations that monitor detention facilities do not have adequate resources or power to identify problems or compel change. Legal aid funding is limited, it is hard to gather evidence, and successful cases (that rely on professionals with significant legal expertise) can take years (Parkes 2007). Given that rights laws are also commonly viewed as "charters for villains, career criminals, and terrorists" (Easton 2013: 487), most countries have instituted measures to reduce opportunities for prisoners or other detainees to seek redress—by blocking available remedies, removing entitlements to legal costs, barring compensation, or even stopping claimants from taking complaints altogether. Even if a case gets to court, the rights of incarcerated people are regularly read down as judges defer to state arguments that violations are necessary for reasons of security, order, safety or crime prevention (Drake 2012). While, even in successful cases, judicial judgments have limited trickle down effects. Courts subsequently indicate "considerable tolerance" for systemic problems in detention, such that inadequate treatments, poor facilities and physical harms go unchallenged (Scott 2013: 246).

In summary, human rights for incarcerated people are established and downgraded in highly politicised environments. In Anglophone states, where penal punitiveness has captured political imaginations, rights are quickly silenced, minimised, devalued or dismissed by official authorities. These distorted versions of rights allow states to build power, redraw sovereign boundaries, and reassert who 'belongs' and who does not. Despite the development of laws and regulations, state institutions (and contractors) have become increasingly adept at managing human rights.

Human Rights and Social Justice

There is, clearly, a chasm between human rights laws or values and the experiences of those incarcerated (or those being propelled into detention). Part of the problem is that, over the last quarter-century, mainstream human rights have consolidated at the same time as neo-liberal economic structures that have exacerbated social injustice. Violations of economic, social and cultural rights—including insecure working conditions, growing health inequalities, educational deficits, or the denial of welfare protections—are commonplace across Anglophone states and they have dramatically influenced the growth of punishment systems (Beckett and Western 2001; Bell 2013; De Giorgi 2013; Wacquant 2009). Such injustices are, of course, not new. In (neo)colonial societies, the dispossession of land, combined with discriminatory laws and controls, racism, punitive welfarism, socio-cultural identity loss, and economic marginalisation have propelled Indigenous people into courts and carceral institutions (Anthony 2013; Cunneen and Tauri 2017; McIntosh 2011). They are joined by other disadvantaged groups. In these circumstances, prisons, youth justice residences and immigration detention facilities are dramatic indicators of state failures to provide rights for multiple populations.

Sustaining all of this is a dominant human rights approach that concentrates almost exclusively upon 'civil and political rights' while ignoring the 'social, economic or cultural' (or other) rights that are regularly violated through the normal inequitable workings of colonial, patriarchal and market-led state systems (Stanley 2007). In reality, these sets of human rights are interlinked, and they each give rise to binding obligations.[5] The current unpicking of mainstream rights ('civil and political rights') from social justice ('economic, social and cultural rights') does not make sense in an international rights framework. The disconnection of these Covenants demonstrate Anglophone statehood and political interests rather than any codified hierarchy of rights.

There are ramifications to all of this. First, the carceral 'industry' mirrors social injustice. More people are imprisoned, and an increasing number of agencies are granted the power to incarcerate—seen, for example, in the rise of immigration-based detention centres (Stanley 2017b). Expanding the use of incarceration ensures that disadvantage is maintained, normalised and extended. This is a circular relationship, as increased spending on carceral sites (as well as community supervisions, testing regimes, electronic monitoring and so on) ensures tighter purse-strings on social spending that would alleviate economic, social and cultural violations that give rise to so much incarceration in the first place. Meanwhile, incarceration amplifies violations, extending and creating new relationships of colonisation, patriarchy, adultism and other structural inequalities (McCulloch and Scraton 2009).

Second, some individuals and groups become carceral subjects. That is, while we often reflect upon incarceration as an isolated event (a period of time, in a specific carceral space), some populations are continuously targeted for incarceration across life-times and generations, in ways that can only be regarded as self-sustaining. Some people spend years ricocheting through the system—from care residences to youth justice residences to prisons to mental health institutions, and so on. Their incarceration is often deemed to be the consequence of 'bad' individual choices, rather than social problems. Yet, those enmeshed in this transcarceration, and the "liminal spaces between prison and 'community'" (Cunneen et al. 2013: 183), endure multiple disadvantages and victimisations. Their criminalisation is developed through insecure human rights in the community.

Third, under such conditions, incarceration is often marketed as an opportunity to meet needs—allowing individuals to take a break from poverty, drug use or violence. Incarceration is even recast as a time for 'therapy', enabling people to reconnect with their culture, or to undertake beneficial programmes. Incarceration can be "reinvented as an *appropriate* response" to a whole host of structural, social and institutional failings towards people (Cunneen et al. 2013: 109). In these circumstances, apparently progressive rights-based reforms may even "become part of the problem" (Malloch 2013: 37).[6] While it is enticing to accept 'rehabilitation services', 'community custody', 'gender responsive approaches' or 'indigenous units' as human-rights conscious changes, critical examinations remind us that they entrench systems of punishment, lead to repressive conditions, and remove our attention from the structural and socio-cultural shifts necessary to challenge social justice (Cohen 1988). Apparently progressive reforms can consolidate carceral systems (Blagg 2008; Brown and Schept 2017; Gottschalk 2013) and "cement" the use of criminal justice (over social justice) responses to those who are "deemed as high risk" or "high need" (Cunneen et al. 2013: 191). They provide the illusion of change (Hannah-Moffat 2012).

The task, for many of us, is to identify and pursue the culturally "transformative work that [is] required to meaningfully alter" carceral dynamics (McLeod 2015: 1207). It requires multiple initiatives. It demands cultural reforms in carceral institutions, such that institutions are led by relational rights cultures that are empathetic, supportive, kind and that foster equal standing (Genders and Player 2014). It requires that governments act on their rights obligations, to ensure incarcerated people have everything they need to flourish (including education, employment, healthcare, counselling, access to family or social life, and leisure opportunities). It needs human rights to become more than "a metric and something to react against" (Piacentini and Katz 2017: 9). But, it also necessitates the advancement of true alternatives to detention. This includes social policies to lessen the criminogenic elements of institutions and societies, and to seriously limit the use of incarceration. It entails abolitionist strategies that galvanise structural and socio-cultural change through the attainment of human rights, including anti-discrimination initiatives, quality education or accessible health care within communities (Brown and Schept 2017; Davis 2003). The ability of populations to access social, economic and cultural rights (together with their group rights) would have profound effects on the broader forces of crime, migration and deviancy that sustain carceral states.

These processes require positive imaginations to reconstruct social-cultural, political and economic arrangements (McLeod 2015) in ways that displace the inequitable power relations that propel certain populations into the criminal justice system and that undermine the standing of incarceration. They invariably require us to advance new institutions and social projects, and to progress "communities of warmth" that empower and protect people through political arrangements that emphasise welfare, environmental and personal health, education, housing, cultural celebrations, gender safety, and human spirit (Sim 2008: 155). Within colonial contexts, these developments have to be further "aligned with Indigenous struggles for freedom, self-determination, and social justice" (Baldry et al. 2015: 183). It means that states would need to move away from "governing through crime" (Simon 2006) in favour of governing through rights.[7]

This Collection

Building upon the above debates—as well as previous criminological work (such as Brown and Wilkie 2002; Drenkhahn et al. 2016; Jefferson and Gaborit 2015; Naylor et al. 2015; Weber et al. 2014, 2017)—the following chapters develop our thinking on the connections between human rights and incarceration across carceral sites in Australia, New Zealand and the UK. In relation to case-study material focused on groups that are disproportionately affected through incarceration—including Indigenous populations, children, women, those with disabilities, and 'non-citizens'—contributors spell out the ways in which carceral conditions, treatments and practices persistently violate human rights laws and norms.

Importantly, this book does not just consider how and why human rights are eroded but what might be done in response. Contributors consider how individuals and groups have engaged and demanded rights, often in the most difficult situations. They chart the community activism, media engagement, legal changes and international campaigning that have propelled progressive shifts for those incarcerated, and they establish useful frameworks to continue these strategies. Beyond this, contributors reflect on how our human rights thinking and approaches can move beyond carceral options and logics. In short, they spell out some of the decarceral and abolitionist strategies that are necessary to invigorate humanity-enriched, socially just responses to the problems of crime and harms.

Chapter 2, by Deena Haydon, examines children held in secure accommodation on welfare grounds. Drawing on research with 21 children in a Northern Irish secure care centre, she meticulously records how childrens' 'best interests' are regularly dismissed in favour of pragmatic criminalisation, risk management and institutional expediencies that breach rights standards. Haydon highlights the real potential of legal and policy standards to advance childrens' rights in secure care, but she prioritises a critical agenda that emphasises socially just measures to prevent criminalisation and incarceration for children in the first place.

Haydon's approach of contextualising international and national legal standards in a structural and institutional context is continued by

Eileen Baldry, in Chapter 3. Baldry examines the work of the UN Committee on the Rights of Persons with Disabilities [UNCRPD] in Australia and, in doing so, highlights the potential of international interventions to place obligations on states to pursue systemic changes. She shows how, under neoliberalism, diversionary and therapeutic measures have done little to stop large numbers of people with mental or cognitive disability from being funnelled through the criminal justice system. In response, Baldry prioritises a disability social justice framework to improve services and treatments while embedding equitable arrangements to ensure those with disabilities can enjoy access to and enjoyment of rights, including the right not to be criminalised.

The potential of UN engagements is a focus for Elizabeth Stanley and Riki Mihaere, in Chapter 4. They examine the nature and impact of UN interventions to the (neo)colonial criminalisation and 'over-representation' of Māori in New Zealand prisons. Using extensive documentary analysis and interview data, they unpick how the NZ state engages in pervasive ritualism to deflect scrutiny and secure state legitimacy through performative reporting to UN agencies. Despite this, UN engagement remains a necessary tool for Māori to develop evidence, contest state-led myths, consolidate Indigenous networks and affirm Indigenous rights. Any justice for Māori must, they note, prioritise rights in ways that propel self-determination and challenge the normalisation of the prison.

In Chapter 5, Michael Grewcock exposes the endemic violations by the Australian state against 'non-citizens'. Charting the extensive violence, degradations and harms from offshore processing and indefinite mandatory detention policies, he shows how border controls are constituted in law as legitimate expressions of sovereign interest. He details how the Australian state employs human rights laws to justify violations against adult and child refugees. Such actions have faced long-standing resistance from international and national bodies, activists, academics and civil society. Grewcock illustrates the value of this resistance to develop networks of solidarity, mobilise demands, and build an ethos of humanity beyond borders.

The potential of civil society resistance is further developed by David Scott, in Chapter 6. Scott addresses the deaths that permeate the prison experience in England and Wales. Arguing that the right to life is extinguished through forms of civil, social and corporeal death, he shows how penal abolitionists contest the 'spirit of death' through the strategies of speaking, naming and making something happen. Among other outcomes, activism by prisoners, family members and advocates can expose the nature of violence, provide collective remembrance, re-establish humanity, and sometimes guide political, media and public debates. In conjunction with official reports from Inspectors, Ombudsman and others, they build an *agora* in which the right to life is prioritised.

In Chapter 7, Nessa Lynch reflects upon the opportunities that still exist to change criminalisation and incarceration practices through legal and policy action. With a focus on the youth justice system in New Zealand, she shows how and why 'serious' young offenders continue to be sentenced to long sentences of imprisonment, administered through adult correctional systems. These responses are at distinct odds with international and national rights standards towards children. Lynch envisions a human rights model (encompassing seven key principles) that would allow age-appropriate accountability through national youth justice systems for all young offenders.

The opportunities to develop new rights-reflecting practices is the focus of Bree Carlton and Emma Russell's Chapter 8. Working from archival and documentary research, alongside interviews and focus groups, they explore the early 1980s campaigns to improve conditions for female prisoners in Victoria, Australia. They show how reform projects exposed women's carceral experiences of violence, discrimination and degradation in ways that, while radical at the time, brought short-term gains. Carlton and Russell highlight how these projects provided the rationales and justifications for the expansion of imprisonment for women, and failed to shift many long-standing violations in the prison estate. The problem, they note, is that activists focused on reform, not abolition.

The problems that ensue from failing to prioritise abolition are further considered by Phil Scraton in Chapter 9. He draws upon the changing dynamics of imprisonment (against wide-scale violations during 'the Troubles'), to show how reform-based approaches have failed to challenge egregious breaches of international and national human rights in Northern Irish prisons. Compelling reports from human rights agencies, inspectorates and other bodies, have been vigorously resisted by prison managers and workers. Scraton shows that while rights-based reforms may bring individualised change, they also operate to provide a veneer of legitimacy, and can be quickly incorporated into correctional talk. He argues that we must keep a focus on abolitionist strategies that attend to the structural conditions and social consequences of marginalisation, disadvantage and criminalisation.

In Chapter 10, Margaret Malloch demonstrates how seemingly progressive rights reforms also require clear sightedness about wider community injustices if they are to be successful. Considering recent developments to reduce the number of women in Scottish prisons, she reflects upon proposals to develop community custody units that appear to be benevolent spaces in their intensive supports, family connectedness, and appeals for 'recovery'. Malloch spells out how these approaches remain highly individualised in their therapeutic and trauma-informed focus; they do not translate into a social or community rights agenda that can ease circumstances of violence, poverty, extreme disadvantage and criminalisation processes that impact on women before, during and after incarceration. She prioritises a social equality approach, to stop criminal justice as the 'go-to solution' for social distress.

The continuities of violence and social injustice are further considered by Harry Blagg and Thalia Anthony in Chapter 11. Drawing upon recent testimonies to the Royal Commission into Child Protection and Youth Detention in the Northern Territory, they demonstrate how racist violence and subordination in Australian prisons is part of a carceral continuum for Indigenous people. Violations (including stolen land, forced labour, child removals and military interventions into Indigenous communities) reflect ongoing colonising processes in which the prison is just one site of sovereign elimination. Indigenous rights require, therefore, the abolition of prisons but also a paradigm shift in the state relations that underpin racism, dispossession and subordination. Without Indigenous sovereignty, rights for those incarcerated can never be fully realised.

In the final Chapter 12, Tracey McIntosh engages with the poetry of a young Māori woman, who is currently incarcerated in New Zealand.

In doing so, McIntosh reflects upon the role of creative, intellectual, emotional, cultural and spiritual energies to destabilise the normalisation of the prison, and to develop ourselves as agents of transformative change. Outlining the limitations of liberal democratic human rights to empower Indigenous peoples, or to confront the realities of incarceration developed upon colonisation and complex social problems, she asserts the ground for Indigenous sovereignty, rights and justice. To unmake the prison, we must commit to *mauri ora*, to human flourishing.

Taken together, these vibrant chapters reiterate that human rights have to be developed, prioritised and engaged with; they are not static. While human rights protections are state managed and deeply precarious, rights principles remain vital to progressive change. Prioritising rights, and the values that propel them, requires us to deepen actions that propel humane responses to crimes and harms. At the centre of these endeavours—as many contributors assert—is the need for a decolonising and feminist social justice through which human needs are met. This work is certainly "unfinished" and "uncertain", and it requires short and long-term struggles (Cohen 1988: 111–112). However, human rights values are, now more than ever, crucial to shifting many social problems, including that of incarceration.

Notes

1. In some circumstances, the 'right to family' is used to justify the detention of children in extremely damaging environments (see Grewcock, this volume).
2. In this respect, human rights interventions may be little more than colonising controls that distract attention from global inequalities (Jefferson 2005).
3. Alternatively, it is proposed that, in protecting rights for one person or group (such as offenders), the rights of others (such as victims) will be diminished. But, human rights are not a finite resource and offenders are not a mutually exclusive category from victims (Stanley 2017a).

4. Carlen (2010) notes that KPIs impede human rights progress by: undermining innovative leadership and strategy, limiting the debates on what could change, doing little to advance multicultural organisations, and reprioritising prison programmes and services over those in the community.

5. Under Article 2.1 of the *Covenant of Economic, Social and Cultural Rights*, rights may be progressively realised according to the maximum available resources. This tempering of obligations is not evident in the *Covenant of Civil and Political Rights*.

6. Reformers can contribute to this, especially if they are incorporated into the carceral system. Under a remit of engagement and inclusivity, carceral institutions can strategically manage the agenda of steering or advisory groups, delineating the boundaries of what might be discussed or acted upon (Carlen 2010).

7. The most progressive programmes can quickly evaporate under renewed emphases on risk, security, cost-effectiveness or political capital (Piacentini and Katz 2017). To achieve longer-term shifts, further cultural and discursive changes are required, not least to move away from a 'war' footing on crime and migration, and towards values of inclusion, egalitarianism, education, or human security (McCulloch and Scraton 2009; Pratt and Eriksson 2013).

References

Aas, K., & Gundhus, H. (2015). Policing humanitarian borderlands: Frontex, human rights and the precariousness of life. *British Journal of Criminology, 55*(1), 1–18.

Anthony, T. (2013). *Indigenous People, Crime and Punishment*. London: Routledge.

Baldry, E., Carlton, B., & Cunneen, C. (2015). Abolitionism and the paradox of penal reform in Australia: Indigenous women, colonial patriarchy, and co-option. *Social Justice, 41*(3), 168–189.

Barbaret, R. (2014). *Women, Crime and Criminal Justice: A Global Enquiry*. London: Routledge.

Beckett, K., & Western, B. (2001). Governing social marginality. *Punishment & Society, 3*(1), 43–59.

Bell, E. (2013). The prison paradox in neoliberal Britain. In D. Scott (Ed.), *Why Prison?* (pp. 44–64). Cambridge: Cambridge University Press.

Blagg, H. (2008). *Crime, Aboriginality and the Decolonisation of Justice*. Annandale, NSW: Hawkins Press.

Boyle, O., & Stanley, E. (2017). Private prisons and the management of scandal. *Crime, Media, Culture*. [Online]. https://doi.org/10.1177/1741659017736097. Accessed March 22, 2018.

Brown, D., & Wilkie, M. (2002). *Prisoners as Citizens. Human Rights in Australian Prisons*. Annandale, NSW: Federation Press.

Brown, M., & Schept, J. (2017). New abolition, criminology and a critical carceral studies. *Punishment & Society, 19*(4), 440–462.

Carlen, P. (2008). Imaginary penalties and risk-crazed governance. In P. Carlen (Ed.), *Imaginary Penalities* (pp. 1–25). Cullompton: Willan.

Carlen, P. (2010). *A Criminological Imagination: Essays on Justice, Punishment and Discourse*. London: Ashgate.

Cohen, S. (1988). *Against Criminology*. London: Transaction Publishers.

Cunneen, C., & Tauri, J. (2017). *Indigenous Criminology*. Bristol: Policy Press.

Cunneen, C., Baldry, E., Brown, D., Brown, M., Schwartz, M., & Steel, A. (2013). *Penal Culture and Hyperincarceration: The Revival of the Prison*. Farnham: Ashgate.

Davis, A. (2003). *Are Prisons Obsolete?* New York: Seven Stories Press.

De Giorgi, A. (2013). Prisons and social structures in late-capitalist societies. In D. Scott (Ed.), *Why Prison?* (pp. 25–43). Cambridge: Cambridge University Press.

Drake, D. (2012). *Prisons, Punishment and the Pursuit of Security*. Basingstoke: Palgrave Macmillan.

Drenkhahn, K., Dudeck, M., & Dunkel, F. (Eds.). (2016). *Long-Term Imprisonment and Human Rights*. London: Routledge.

Easton, S. (2013). Protecting prisoners: The impact of international human rights law on the treatment of prisoners in the United Kingdom. *The Prison Journal, 93*(4), 475–492.

Genders, E., & Player, E. (2014). Rehabilitation, risk management and prisoners rights. *Criminology and Criminal Justice, 14*(4), 434–457.

Gottschalk, M. (2013). The politics of the carceral state: Yesterday, today and tomorrow. In D. Scott (Ed.), *Why Prison?* (pp. 233–258). Cambridge: Cambridge University Press.

Green, P., & Ward, T. (2004). *State Crime: Governments, Violence and Corruption*. London: Pluto Press.

Grewcock, M. (2016). Australian border policing, the detention of children and state crime. In L. Weber, E. Fishwick, & M. Marmo (Eds.), *The Routledge International Handbook of Criminology and Human Rights* (pp. 157–168). Abingdon: Routledge.

Hannah-Moffat, K. (2012). "Knowledge, politics, and penal reform": Book Review Symposium on Pat Carlen's "A Criminological Imagination". *Punishment & Society, 14*(2), 254–257.

Harris, A., & Stanley, E. (2017). Exacerbating risks and diminishing rights for "at risk" prisoners. *Criminology & Criminal Justice*. [Online]. https://doi.org/10.1177/1748895817739666. Accessed March 22, 2018.

Jefferson, A. (2005). Reforming Nigerian prisons: Rehabilitating a "deviant" state. *British Journal of Criminology, 45*(4), 487–503.

Jefferson, A., & Gaborit, L. (2015). *Human Rights in Prisons: Comparing Institutional Encounters in Kosovo, Sierra Leone and the Philippines*. New York: Palgrave Macmillan.

Malloch, M. (2013). Crime, critique and utopian alternatives. In M. Malloch & M. Munro (Eds.), *Crime, Critique and Utopia* (pp. 21–43). Basingstoke: Palgrave Macmillan.

McCulloch, J., & Scraton, P. (2009). The violence of incarceration. In P. Scraton & J. McCulloch (Eds.), *The Violence of Incarceration* (pp. 1–18). London: Routledge.

McCulloch, J., & Wilson, D. (2016). *Pre-crime: Pre-emption, Precaution and the Future*. London: Routledge.

McIntosh, T. (2011). Marginalisation: A case study: Confinement. In T. McIntosh & M. Mulholland (Eds.), *Māori and Social Issues* (pp. 263–282). Wellington: Huia/Ngā Pae o te Māramatanga.

McLeod, A. (2015). Prison abolition and grounded justice. *UCLA Law Review, 62,* 1156–1239.

Moore, L., & Scraton, P. (2013). *The Incarceration of Women: Punishing Bodies, Breaking Spirits*. Basingstoke: Palgrave Macmillan.

Naylor, B. (2016). Human rights and their application in prisons. *Prison Service Journal, 227,* 17–22.

Naylor, B., Debeljak, J., & Mackay, A. (2015). A strategic framework for implementing human rights in closed environments. *Monash University Law Review, 41*(1), 218–270.

Parkes, D. (2007). A prisoners' charter? Reflections on prisoner litigation under the Canadian Charter of Rights and Freedoms. *UBC Law Review, 40,* 629–676.

Piacentini, L., & Katz, E. (2017). Carceral framing of human rights in Russian prisons. *Punishment & Society, 19*(2), 221–239.

Pratt, J., & Eriksson, A. (2013). *Contrasts in Punishment: An Explanation of Anglophone Excess and Nordic Exceptionalism*. London: Routledge.

Scharff-Smith, P. (2016). Prisons and human rights: Past, present and future challenges. In L. Weber, E. Fishwick, & M. Marmo (Eds.), *The Routledge International Handbook of Criminology and Human Rights* (pp. 525–535). London: Routledge.

Schlanger, M. (2016). The just barely sustainable California prisoners' rights ecosystem. *Annals of the American Academy of Political and Social Science, 664*(1), 62–81.

Scott, D. (2013). Unequalled in pain. In D. Scott (Ed.), *Why Prison?* (pp. 301–324). Cambridge: Cambridge University Press.

Sim, J. (2008). Pain and punishment: The real and the imaginary in penal institutions. In P. Carlen (Ed.), *Imaginary Penalities* (pp. 135–156). Cullompton: Willan.

Simon, J. (2006). *Governing Through Crime: How the War on Crime Transformed American Democracy and Created a Culture of Fear*. Oxford: Oxford University Press.

Simon, J. (2014). *Mass Incarceration on Trial: A Remarkable Court Decision and the Future of Prisons in America*. New York: The New Press.

Stanley, E. (2007). Towards a criminology for human rights. In A. Barton, K. Corteen, D. Scott, & D. Whyte (Eds.), *Expanding the Criminological Imagination* (pp. 168–197). Cullompton: Willan.

Stanley, E. (2017a). Human rights as a protective force. In L. Weber, E. Fishwick, & M. Marmo (Eds.), *The Routledge International Handbook of Criminology and Human Rights* (pp. 503–512). London: Routledge.

Stanley, E. (2017b). Expanding crimmigration: The detention and deportation of New Zealanders from Australia. *Australian & New Zealand Journal of Criminology*. [Online]. https://doi.org/10.1177/0004865817730858. Accessed March 22, 2018.

van Zyl Smit, D., & Snacken, S. (2011). *Principles of European Prison Law and Policy*. Oxford: Oxford University Press.

Wacquant, L. (2009). *Punishing the Poor: The Neoliberal Government of Social Insecurity*. London: Duke University Press.

Weber, M. (1970). *From Max Weber: Essays in Sociology* (H. J. H. Gerth & C. W. Mills, Trans. & Eds.). London: Routledge.

Weber, L., Fishwick, E., & Marmo, M. (2014). *Crime, Justice and Human Rights*. Basingstoke: Palgrave Macmillan.

Weber, L., Fishwick, E., & Marmo, M. (Eds.). (2017). *The Routledge International Handbook of Criminology and Human Rights*. London: Routledge.

Whitty, N. (2011). Human rights as risk: UK prisons and the management of risk and rights. *Punishment & Society, 13*(2), 123–148.

Table of Cases

Brown v Plata [2011] 563 US 493.

2

Children Deprived of Their Liberty on 'Welfare' Grounds: A Critical Perspective

Deena Haydon

Introduction

Children deprived of their liberty are "an invisible and forgotten group in society" (OHCHR 2017).[1] Despite concerns about illegal, arbitrary or unnecessary detention, and human rights violations, minimal verifiable information or research data exists about them (UNCRC 2014). Children held in secure accommodation on 'welfare' grounds, for their own or others' protection, typically have multiple complex needs as a consequence of poverty, family instability, domestic violence, parental rejection, neglect, abuse or bereavement. Their non-attendance or exclusion from school is common (Gough 2016; Hart and La Valle 2016; RQIA 2011). Many also have inherent developmental, physical or mental health problems (Barry and Moodie 2008; Justice Studio 2014; Sinclair and Geraghty 2008). Generally known to Social Services since early childhood, they are often placed in residential

D. Haydon (✉)
Belfast, Northern Ireland, UK

© The Author(s) 2018
E. Stanley (ed.), *Human Rights and Incarceration*, Palgrave Studies
in Prisons and Penology, https://doi.org/10.1007/978-3-319-95399-1_2

care as the challenges posed by their behaviour increase. For some, living in a group setting can act "as a conduit to … being bullied, sexual exploitation and predatory adult networks, suicide pacts, and exposure to increased criminalisation" (RQIA 2011: 43).

Their level of vulnerability, due to this "broad range of difficult and traumatic life experiences", has a "significant influence on their engagement with the world around them" (RQIA 2011: 47). Exposed to "extreme danger" and "very unsafe situations … likely to cause them serious harm" (Gough 2016: 6), they may have been offered services by various agencies but provision is "fragmented" with a "lack of continuity" as they move around the care system (Sinclair and Geraghty 2008: 4). Secure accommodation is perceived as providing "the opportunity to 'hold' them" so that engagement work can begin (Hart and La Valle 2016: 46).

Provision is diverse within the UK. In England and Wales children who receive a custodial sentence from the criminal court or are remanded to secure local authority accommodation, or those placed by local authorities on welfare grounds, can be detained in one of fifteen Secure Children's Homes (fourteen in England, one in Wales), some of which mix welfare and justice referrals. In March 2017, 51% of those in secure homes were placed on welfare grounds (Department for Education 2017). Scotland has five Secure Care Units dedicated mainly to welfare referrals, with 75–80% being detained for their own safety rather than having been remanded or sentenced (Gough 2016: 6). In Northern Ireland, a single Secure Care Centre consists of two small units for welfare placements with a separate Juvenile Justice Centre (JJC) for those on remand or sentenced through the youth justice system.

Across the jurisdictions there is inconsistency in the use of secure placements and a lack of consensus about the purpose or function of secure care (Gough 2016; Hart and La Valle 2016; RQIA 2011). Use of secure accommodation is ultimately determined by the availability of a placement. Goldson (2002: 91) notes that when the "welfare route … is obstructed, some placing authorities will be inclined to explore the justice route in respect of the same children"; this is a form of "pragmatic criminalisation" to address their "manifest welfare needs".

According to Northern Ireland's Criminal Justice Inspectorate, "the gatekeeping process for secure care could actually lead to children being placed in the JJC if they did not meet the strict secure care criteria", with "trivial offences" providing "the opportunity to use custody as quasi-care" (CJINI 2008: 5; RQIA 2011).

Contextualised within an overview of international children's rights standards, this chapter draws on consultation with children in Northern Ireland's Secure Care Centre to explore institutional violations. It argues that children's rights standards provide the foundation on which to develop a framework for policies and practices which prioritise 'protection' and 'participation'. Full implementation of children's rights can only be achieved, however, by identifying and challenging the structural inequalities that affect *all* children but particularly the most disadvantaged and vulnerable.

Promoting and Protecting Children's Rights

Children's rights were first codified in the *Geneva Declaration of the Rights of the Child* (1924) adopted by the League of Nations, consolidated in the *United Nations Declaration on the Rights of the Child* (1959). Thirty years later the UN *Convention on the Rights of the Child* (CRC) (1989) was opened for signature and subsequently ratified by every member of the United Nations except the United States. Kilkelly (2008: 188–191) considers that the CRC offers "the most comprehensive, legally binding document on the treatment of children". Arguing that the CRC consists of "legal rights or norms which anticipate (or dictate) laws which in many countries do not yet exist", King (1994: 388–390) suggested that it also provides a "powerful moral force which can be deployed to raise the level of awareness about factors affecting children's well-being and ways of improving their welfare and autonomy" without use of direct legal coercion.

The Convention's Articles articulate the principles, provisions and protections to which all under-18s are entitled. Four general principles are fundamental to implementation: (i) non-discrimination; (ii) the 'best interests' of the child as a primary consideration, with provision of the protection and care necessary to secure their well-being; (iii) the right to life, survival and development; and (iv) the right of the child to express their views in all matters affecting them, with their views given due weight in accordance with their age and maturity.

The CRC recognises important civil and political rights—including rights to privacy, to access appropriate information, and to not be subjected to torture, cruel or inhuman or degrading treatment or punishment—alongside freedoms such as to expression, to thought, conscience and religion, and to association and peaceful assembly. Social and economic rights include: a standard of living adequate for the child's physical, mental, spiritual, moral and social development; the highest attainable standard of health; rest, leisure, age-appropriate play and recreational activities. The right to accessible education includes measures to encourage regular school attendance and to reduce drop-out rates.

Parents or legal guardians retain primary responsibility for the child's upbringing and development, but states should provide appropriate assistance to support child-rearing and ensure development of facilities and services for the care of children. Specific Articles focus on the state's role in providing alternative care where necessary, and the regular review of placements. States are expected to take legislative, administrative, social and educational measures to protect children from physical or mental violence, injury or abuse, neglect or negligent treatment, maltreatment or exploitation while they are in the care of parents or legal guardians. They should also establish measures to protect children from sexual exploitation or abuse, and from using narcotic drugs or psychotropic substances. The Convention prioritises the promotion of recovery and social reintegration, asserting that any restriction of liberty should be a measure of last resort which enables maintenance of family contact.

The UN General Assembly (2010) has produced *Guidelines for the Alternative Care of Children* detailing state obligations to support families, protect children's rights and, where appropriate, provide alternative care which ensures the safety, well-being and development of the child. There are also international standards specific to children deprived of their liberty. The *United Nations Standard Minimum Rules for the Administration of Juvenile Justice—[the Beijing Rules]* (UN General Assembly 1985)—emphasise that states should further the well-being of children and families through social policy that promotes their welfare. Those in institutions are expected to receive care and protection as well as social, educational, vocational, psychological, medical and physical assistance commensurate with their age, sex and personality. The UN *Guidelines for the Prevention of Juvenile Delinquency*—[*the Riyadh Guidelines*] (UN General Assembly 1990a)—emphasise "a child centred orientation" (Guideline 3), stressing the importance of policies which provide opportunities to meet the varying needs of young people and their personal development, particularly for those who are "demonstrably endangered or at social risk" (Guideline 5a). Affirming that placement in an institution should be a last resort and for the minimum necessary period, these Guidelines establish the criteria that should be applied to authorise institutionalisation (Guideline 46).

The Special Rapporteur on Torture has raised concerns regarding children deprived of their liberty. Noting that "children experience pain and suffering differently to adults owing to their physical and emotional development and their specific needs", he states that even "very short periods of detention can undermine the child's psychological and physical well-being and compromise cognitive development" (Méndez 2015: para 33). The UN *Rules for the Protection of Juveniles Deprived of the Liberty*—[*the Havana Rules*] (UN General Assembly 1990b)—explicitly state that deprivation of liberty should be "limited to exceptional cases" (Rule 2). Aimed at "countering the detrimental effects of all types of detention" and "fostering integration" (Rule 3), they establish: educational, health, personal and social entitlements for those detained; requirements governing the use of restraint, discipline and sanctions; and expectations regarding independent inspection, requests, complaints and resettlement processes.

These internationally agreed standards provide the foundation for holding states to account while positively influencing the jurisprudence of international and national courts. Together with secondary sources derived in the jurisprudence of the UN Committee on the Rights of the Child (e.g. in General Comments or Concluding Observations following periodic reviews), these non-binding "soft law" Rules and Guidelines "raise standards through persuasive force, their use in advocacy and campaigning, and by aiding the interpretation of the Convention and other legally binding instruments" (Hollingsworth 2017: 191). Analysing legal implementation of the CRC in 12 states, Lundy et al. (2012: 4) note that, where the Convention was incorporated into domestic law, interviewees felt "children were more likely to be perceived as rights-holders and that there was a culture of respect for children's rights". Significant drivers included a strong NGO sector, key children's rights advocates and supporters in government or public office, and the process of periodic reporting to the UN Committee (ibid.: 8).

The UK Context

Devolution within the UK has led to jurisdiction-specific legislation and policy. In the mid-2000s, promotion of children's rights was evident in the strategic frameworks of the devolved administrations in Wales (Welsh Assembly Government 2004), Northern Ireland (OFMDFM 2006) and Scotland (Scottish Government 2008). The precise wording differs in more recent legislation, with Welsh Ministers expected to have "due regard" to the CRC when exercising their functions while their Scottish counterparts have a duty to "give better or further effect to the requirements" of the Convention. Consultation with children is central, together with the promotion of public awareness and understanding about children's rights, and regular reporting on compliance. However, this political commitment does not fully incorporate the CRC into domestic legislation.

Across UK jurisdictions, specific criteria dictate the use of secure accommodation. A child who has a history of 'absconding' and is likely to run away from any other type of accommodation and, if s/he runs away, is likely to suffer significant harm could be placed in a secure facility. Similarly, a child who is likely to self-harm or injure others if in any other form of accommodation fits the criteria.[2] The Health and Social Care Trust in Northern Ireland, local authority in England or Wales, determines whether these criteria are met and a secure placement is necessary. If the placement exceeds 72 hours the case is referred to the Family Proceedings Court, which may authorise a placement for up to three months in the first instance and up to six months at any one time in subsequent applications. In Scotland, social workers or other lead professionals considering secure accommodation have to investigate options and discuss these with a named Unit and the local authority Chief Social Work Officer prior to seeking authorisation at a Children's Hearing. Once an order has been issued by the Hearing, the Chief Social Work Officer and the Head of Unit have certain powers and duties regarding whether the secure authorisation is actually implemented.

The statutory framework for restriction of liberty in a secure facility is specified in accompanying regulations.[3] In England, Wales and Northern Ireland, these establish that children under the age of 13 cannot be placed in secure accommodation on welfare grounds without Ministerial approval. Taking into account the wishes and feelings of the child (as well as their parents/guardians, the child's independent visitor, and the person managing the secure accommodation), it is expected that regular reviews will consider whether the criteria for a secure placement continue to apply and the placement remains "necessary" or, in Scotland, "in the child's best interests".

Additional guidance clarifies interpretation of the legislation and associated regulations. However, in England, Hart and La Valle (2016: 33–34) found "differences in perception—not just across but within authorities—about when it is time to draw the line" in determining thresholds for secure placements. Northern Ireland guidance stresses that the restriction of liberty must be a last resort, having considered and rejected all else—it should never be used because there is no other placement available, as a result of staffing inadequacies, because the child is being a nuisance, or as a form of punishment (DHSS 1996b: para 15.5). Scotland's guidance emphasises that depriving a child of their liberty "infringes on one of their most fundamental human rights" and "impinges on associated rights to freedom of association and family life", thus placement in secure accommodation "can only be justified because it is in their best interests and/or because it will protect the rights of others" (Scottish Government 2013: para 1.3).

Listening to Children's Voices

Beyond consideration of the 'legal' validity of rights implementation, *critical* analyses also focus on social, cultural, political, economic conditions and how particular circumstances or relationships influence behaviours and attitudes. A key issue is whether rights discourses and implementation have the potential to address structural inequalities rooted in the determining contexts of class, gender, sexuality, age, ethnicity, culture, and abilities. It is within these contexts that differential responses, limited opportunities and the marginalisation of *all* children prevail, but particularly for those in state care or in conflict with the law. Central to understanding the impact of determining contexts are the views and experiences of individuals and specific groups. Qualitative research with children deprived of their liberty on welfare grounds has been minimal. Yet, as the following sections demonstrate, it reveals consistent deficiencies in the implementation of rights.

Secure Accommodation in Britain

Children in secure accommodation in Britain describe experiencing discrimination on the basis of being 'looked after' (Goldson 2002). Some have poor relationships with social workers and feel judged. They consider that they should be able to make personal choices but are disengaged from decision-making processes such as reviews, hearings and care planning. Lack of participation and preparation are common, with children not informed about where they are being taken and then traumatised by admission to secure care. Some are located a considerable distance from their families and local communities, including 'cross border' placements in other jurisdictions, which affects family relationships and contact (Barry and Moodie 2008; Gough 2016, 2017).

While some enjoy the educational provision in secure accommodation—both in its own right and because it relieves boredom—others consider the curriculum too simplistic, repetitive, unlikely to help them gain qualifications and inappropriate to their immediate needs (Barry and Moodie 2008; Children's Rights Director for England 2009).

Leisure opportunities are insufficient, with access to activities restricted by budgets or staff availability and the withdrawal of activities used as a sanction (Barry and Moodie 2008). Professionals have significant concerns about the quality and/or sufficiency of therapeutic provision and Child and Adolescent Mental Health Services [CAMHS] (Gough 2016, 2017; Hart and La Valle 2016; Held 2006; Mooney et al. 2012).

Many young people perceive and experience secure accommodation as punitive, describing isolation on arrival as frightening and distressing. Overly restrictive rules, alongside inconsistencies in approach between staff within units, provoke frustration and anger. Children report a lack of privacy during family visits, limited telephone access, and restrictions on their use of the internet or social media. They express confusion about sanctions, criticising the approaches used—particularly the inconsistent or frequent use of 'time out' and 'single separation', which they consider counterproductive. Some raise concerns over the unjustifiable use of physical intervention and restraint, expressing a lack of confidence that complaints will be satisfactorily addressed. Inadequate preparation and support as they move on from secure accommodation is also an issue, especially if this contributes to subsequent placement breakdowns or repeat admissions (Barry and Moodie 2008; Children's Rights Director for England 2009; Gough 2016, 2017).

The Experiences of Children in Northern Ireland

Within Northern Ireland, the independent Regulation and Quality Improvement Authority [RQIA] is responsible for monitoring the availability and quality of health and social care services. However, its inspection reports on children's homes, including the Secure Care Centre, are not published. This compromises public accountability regarding regime management and operation. As part of the process of periodic review, preparation for the 2015 *Northern Ireland NGO Alternative Report* to the UN Committee on the Rights of the Child included consultation with children held in the Centre during Spring 2015 (Haydon 2016). Group discussions and interviews with a total of 21 children aged 12–17 (15 females, 6 males) illustrated rights violations as a result of the socio-cultural and institutional contexts in which decisions about their care were made. In these, their entitlements to 'participation' and actions being taken in their 'best interests' were undermined by a perceived over-emphasis on protection and risk management.

The Culture of Risk Management

The culture of risk identification, reduction and avoidance underpins policy and practice within health, social care and youth justice—from 'early intervention' based on assessment of 'risk factors' (Haydon 2014) to patient, client, or offender management. As 'looked after' children, those consulted were more closely monitored than their peers, leading to harsher responses:

> If you're in care, you're treated differently. Your social worker's onto you if you take drugs. Then you're sent here. Other people are taking drugs, all your mates are taking drugs, and nothing happens to them. They wouldn't end up in here.

The issue of child sexual exploitation [CSE] was particularly pertinent. According to Marshall (2014: 67), the CSE debate is "skewed" towards a perception that it primarily concerns young people in residential care who go missing, mainly because their activities are so closely monitored and recorded. This can lead to humiliating interventions for young women:

> Staff follow you and get the cops to stop your bus. They say things like "This person's high risk, code red, sexual exploitation". That's not right. That should be private, not said in front of everyone on the bus. It's embarrassing.

Verifying such experiences, care staff reported to Northern Ireland's CSE Inquiry how they followed young people, stopped buses or trains to remove them, and contacted the police when they felt they had no other option or that the risk was sufficient (Marshall 2014: 84).

Other care experienced young people have discussed being classed as 'missing' when they failed to return to their children's home at the agreed time, or were absent without permission. Understanding the need for police involvement in 'high risk' instances, they noted that the police were "called too often and too readily", believing "there must be more effective ways of managing absconding and risk-taking behaviour" (VOYPIC 2014: 24). A young person's working group informing the Northern Ireland CSE Inquiry commented that "over-reactions" by staff in a care setting "could be interpreted as a worker doing what was best for themselves (e.g. ensuring all possible measures were taken should there be a later investigation) rather than what was best for the young person", proposing that a greater balance should be achieved between bureaucratic reporting and young person-centred responses (Neill and Moffett 2014: 10).

A few of the consulted young women did not agree with their social workers' assessment of risk. Disputing the likelihood of sexual exploitation occurring while she was using 'legal highs', one commented:

> They think you'll drop you knickers when you're out of it. People say "When you're conked out, you're a high risk". But who's gonna see you lyin' there, out of it, and want sex with ya? Na, that's not gonna happen.

Another stated:

> I know the risks, but I don't feel they are risks. Social workers are nosy. They use information against you. You can't trust them. I understand they're worried, but they feel everything I do is risky. [A secure placement is] more for my own safety from others than for *my* behaviour.

Some young people considered that social workers exaggerated the level of risk to gain a secure accommodation placement. One commented: "Stuff in LAC [Looked After Children] reviews is pure crap—if they can't manage you, they'll do everything in their power to get you in secure". Another affirmed: "They say you've been worse to get you in here, to meet the criteria to get into [Secure Care Centre]." They were acutely aware that secure care was restricted to under-18s: "When you get to 18 you're thrown out, so they need to think about other ways to manage risk".

These quotes illustrate a clear disconnect between young people's perceptions of risk and the responses of the professionals working with them. While they may have under-estimated potential risk of harm, young people questioned what they considered 'over-reactive' and intrusive interventions. Their comments highlight how professional emphasis on risk management procedures can appear to take precedence over discussion with the young person about how their needs, and concerns about their safety, could best be addressed.

Determining the 'Best Interests' of the Child

It is evident that the nebulous concept of 'best interests' is difficult for state agencies to implement when children do not share the same level of concern for their personal well-being as that identified by those responsible for their care:

> Decisions are made for you about *everything*. But I don't think they're made in my best interests. I wasn't even allowed to go to the shop. I was always reported as missing.

Some young people resented not being able to make the choices they wanted—including decisions that were potentially harmful:

> They should listen to me. It's not best for me to be in here ... If I want to go back on herbal ['legal high'], I'll go back on it.

> Adults can try and help you, but if you don't want help you should be able to say "Fuck you". I'd rather be outside [the Secure Care Centre], with someone nagging me, than be in here.

Secure care was perceived as a punishment: "There shouldn't be a place like this. We're not bad people". This was particularly significant when children who had suffered sexual exploitation were deprived of their liberty while perpetrators remained free. Some argued that secure care should be abandoned: "You should have meetings … where secure is off the list of options … What you need is a support worker, someone to talk to".

Those consulted clearly articulated the support required. They recognised the impact of 'evolving capacities' and the fact that adolescents require assistance: "If they're under 13 … they don't have the ability to make their own decisions. If they're 13–16 they still need help". They considered early intervention a priority: "They need support and help earlier—when they're still a child … It's too late when you're 16 or 17, you don't want help then". Also vital to them was identification of the underlying causes of 'problematic' behaviour:

> Children are called "brats" if they're behaving badly. They're punished. But there's a reason why they're behaving badly. People should find out the reason. I wasn't bad because I wanted to be. There was stuff going on. I couldn't talk to teachers.

Noting the potential negative impacts of available placements, one young woman talked about being in an intensive residential care home: " … with six other young people who've all got loads of problems—all being together in one place, you're bound to go mad".

International standards assert that deprivation of liberty should be used only as a measure of last resort and for the shortest appropriate period of time. Understandably, children in secure care resented their confinement. They also questioned the value and success of short-term responses to risky behaviour: "They say to me in here that using drugs is a short-term solution. But being put in here is a short-term solution. And it doesn't work".

Young people can spend long periods in secure accommodation, either on consecutive Orders or aggregated over a period of time: "I've been in [Secure Care Centre] 18 months on and off, with 3 months outside altogether". This young woman admitted that she would "go on the herbal and can't cope" when outside, concluding: "If I wasn't in here, like, I'd be dead". However, another perceived repeat admissions as clear evidence that individuals' needs remained unaddressed: "If a young person ends up in [Secure Care Centre] once, I can understand that. But if they keep coming, it obviously isn't working".

Noting the lack of support available during their childhoods, those consulted described how their needs could have been more appropriately addressed through earlier intervention and individualised support in their communities. While temporarily providing a safe, stable environment and access to specialist support, "the timetable for a secure placement is driven by the reduction in risk, not the child's needs, which means that more fundamental—and lengthy—work on the underlying causes of the child's difficulties cannot be undertaken" (Hart and La Valle 2016: 9). As those consulted pointed out, secure accommodation is therefore an ineffective short term response. However, children's perspectives are routinely not sought, or ignored, within policy and practice.

Limited 'Participation'

All children and young people are affected by limited opportunities for participation, but care experienced children are consistently denied this entitlement. Many of those consulted gave examples concerning their experiences of LAC reviews: "You're not listened to. I'd get pissed off—people just write stuff down but say nothing". They were frustrated about the minimal interaction and information sharing:

> I didn't feel listened to, not even a wee bit. You go into a room full of people and they're talking about you and writing stuff down, and you're sitting there like a dick. They're sharing information that I thought was classified—"She's [having sex] with this one and she's with that one", and I'm not with any of them. But that's my private business, they're talking about my private business.

Young people were regularly not informed in advance about meetings regarding their referral to secure accommodation:

> There had been a lot of talk about secure, but I didn't know I was coming when I did. It was almost a threat: "If you don't … you'll be going to secure".

> I came into secure on my 17th birthday and didn't know I was coming in. I didn't know my case was going to the [Restriction of Liberty] Panel.

They felt their views were not heard in court: "If the social worker says they want you to get three months, you get what the social worker said". A move could subsequently happen very quickly, and a young man described his distress:

> I had no idea. I was arguing with staff in [residential care home] about phone top-ups and was told "You're going to secure". I said "When?" and was told "Now". I was greetin' [crying] all the way here. I didn't even cry when I was told I was adopted. But I cried in the car all the way here, for about an hour and a half, in the police car that brought me here. That says something.

Once placed in secure accommodation, their autonomy was minimal: "Every decision is made for you—where you go, when you eat, when you go to bed". Questioning the imposition of bedtimes, one young woman stated:

> You should have the right to make decisions for yourself, within boundaries. Like what time you go to bed. In here, if you're 13, your bedtime's half nine. But I wouldn't usually go to bed 'til half 11. That's way too early.

Having commented that his bedtime (10 o'clock) was "the time I'd be going out half the time if I was outside", a 15 year old young man stated wryly: "I don't know why it's so early—it's a secure unit!".

Some considered that while in secure care there was no choice over engagement with youth justice agencies or specialist services such as drug and mental health services or projects for those at risk of sexual exploitation. Usually this was included in their 'exit plan': "You have to work with them to come out".

Not generally involved in the decision-making processes leading to their placement in secure care, young people's participation in defining routines and required interventions while detained was also minimal. Contributing to high levels of frustration, this undermined their capacity to consider the support they needed to understand the impacts of difficult or traumatic experiences, manage their feelings and behaviour, stay safe and cope with everyday life.

Lack of Civil Rights and Freedoms

Basic civil rights were consistently violated within secure care. Freedom of association was undermined in a building where doors to every room were locked on entry and exit, despite rooms being off a locked corridor within a secure building. Expressing frustration, one young man commented that he would rather be in the JJC because it was less restrictive:

> No-one should be here … Staff coming to work here should have to spend a day living how we live, so they know what it's like. They should have their keys taken off them so other staff have to let them in and out of rooms. They should know what it's like to have to ask for a key to go for a crap.

In 2015, the Special Rapporteur declared: "the imposition of solitary confinement, of any duration, on children constitutes cruel, inhuman or degrading treatment or punishment or even torture", whether as a disciplinary or "protective" measure (Méndez 2015: para 44). However, the first 24 hours in secure care were spent "on your own in your room, to settle in—you're kept apart from the others, you're eased into the group". Those consulted explained that this produced an emotional mix of fear and anger:

> When I arrived here I was put into a room. I thought "What have I done to be put out of the group?"

> For the first 24 hours you don't have a clue. You go in, you get locked in your room and you're like "What the fuck!"

Isolation was also used in response to challenging behaviour:

> You can be put in an empty room—a completely empty room without your clothes or anything, no TV, no radio. They just keep you in there and don't take you out to education or anything. I was in there for eight days once. It does your head in.

Contact with family and friends was limited. There was no access to the internet and mobile phones were confiscated. Staff justified this policy on the basis of protecting young people from harm. Telephone calls were restricted to two per evening and each young person had a contact list drawn up by their social worker. One young woman expressed annoyance that "You can't phone your mates … someone who doesn't even know you decides who you can talk to". Constant monitoring and observation inhibited privacy:

> There's no privacy at all in here. Staff sit in the room while you're on the phone. You can't whisper to each other, or draw pictures, or pass notes, or anything.

> Currently, all my family contact time is supervised by a Social Worker who constantly takes notes while we are talking and, on occasion, interrupts our conversations.

Acknowledging that evening group meetings provided opportunities to raise issues, these were considered an inappropriate forum to make complaints. Some young people were aware of an Independent Representation Scheme operated by an NGO. However, doubts were raised about the effectiveness of complaints procedures: "frankly, they do fuck all" or "they'd make a joke of it".

Listening to the voices of these young people reveals how measures intended to 'protect' them regularly led to breaches of their rights—not only through deprivation of their liberty but also within interactions and interventions which did not prioritise their participation or best interests.

Reaffirming Commitment to Children's Rights

This overview highlights endemic breaches of international laws, Rules and Guidelines despite independent inspections, the existence of human rights organisations and Children's Commissioners, a UK National Preventive Mechanism, and periodic reviews by UN Treaty bodies. The following provides the basis for considering the significance of children's rights discourses.

Rights-Based Interventions: A Critique

According to Hollingsworth (2017: 192), the non-binding Concluding Observations produced by Treaty bodies can "play an important role within domestic political accountability processes". Courts have, albeit rarely, given "indirect legal effect to concluding observations with which the government had previously failed to comply". Enforcement mechanisms, however, are weak and compliance is dependent on "diplomacy and political pressure rather than legal sanction", thus, on "issues about which the government is resolute, or which would be politically unpopular … the monitoring process can appear futile" (Hollingsworth 2017: 191). For example, Concluding Observations of the UN Committee on the Rights of the Child [UNCRC] (2016) concerning the UK government's most recent—*fifth*—periodic report include recommendations focusing on measures to reduce the inequalities, discrimination and stigmatisation experienced by children and specific groups (including children in care). While re-affirming the CRC's general principles, the Committee's recommendations include reference to: mental and adolescent health, child poverty, school exclusion, child sexual exploitation and abuse, alternative care, secure accommodation, and the use of restraints, detention and solitary confinement.

Debate also continues regarding the strength and effectiveness of the CRC. This concerns the lack of its incorporation into domestic law within the UK and devolved administrations. The only statutorily available human rights instrument which may currently be used in cases of alleged rights violations is the *European Convention on Human Rights* [ECHR], given domestic effect by the *Human Rights Act 1998* and enforceable through the European Court of Human Rights. Hollingsworth (2017: 193) argues that "international standards can be used in litigation to secure immediate advances in children's rights by providing the basis for legally binding remedies for individuals or groups of children and, when used strategically, systemic change". As Stanley (2007: 176–177) notes, however, "the broader political context in which rights operate in law cannot be disregarded" and specific groups may have neither the knowledge nor the finances to progress legal proceedings. This is particularly pertinent for children. In addition, "demand for *legal* remedies for children may provide little more than formalistic responses from governments" which have limited impact on children's suffering and powerlessness (King 1994: 386), since governments may simply declare their policies as "lawful" within the terms of the CRC (King 1994: 398).

The UN Development Group (2003) affirms that a 'rights-based' approach requires building the capacity both of duty-bearers to fulfil their obligations and of rights-holders to claim their rights. As King noted soon after ratification of the CRC, the existence of legislation may not result in significant improvement in children's lives—especially if "custom, cultural norms or moral principles" undermine the potential for children to be treated equally and with dignity. Within the UK, unequal power relations exist interpersonally (in relationships between children and parents, community members or adult workers), institutionally (where social and material inequalities are reproduced in services and institutions), and societally (where children's views are disrespected or marginalised). Their subordination to adults, as individuals and as a social group, operates at all levels (see Scraton 1997). Physically and psychologically dependent on adults due to lack of experience (inherent vulnerability), children and young people are ignored, their perspectives are not valued, and they are excluded from decision-making processes (structural vulnerability). Despite the increasingly fashionable use of terms such as 'agency' and 'empowerment' to describe the resistance of individuals or specific groups to these dynamics, children's actions are invariably mediated by adult control of time, space, access to resources, and decision-making.

Children in care are generally from the most economically deprived families and communities. While children and parents in these circumstances may benefit from family support initiatives, interventionist emphasis on 'protection' and 'resilience' cannot overcome persistent, severe, and multiple adversities manifested in on-going family conflict and long-term poverty (Devaney et al. 2012). Labelled 'deficient', 'lacking capacity', 'at risk' or 'vulnerable', these children's routine experiences, capacity to negotiate 'choices', and future life chances are restricted by their socio-economic location. At the same time, as shown above, gendered expectations about sexual behaviour result in different thresholds of concern and judgement regarding 'risk'. While male sexual vulnerability is under-recognised (Roesch-Marsh 2014), greater anxiety about girls' vulnerability to risk of sexual exploitation leads to those who 'go missing' being more likely than boys to be placed in secure accommodation on welfare grounds. Boys are more often detained through the youth justice system for behaviour defined as posing a threat to others or related to potential involvement in 'disorder' or 'criminal behaviour' (Held 2006; Hart and La Valle 2016). Girls who commit offences or are deemed to be at considerable risk move more quickly through the welfare and justice systems towards secure care or custody (Gough 2016).

Thus the determining contexts of age, class, gender and sexuality influence perceptions of, and presumptions about, those who engage in 'risky' behaviours as well as responses focused on protection and risk avoidance or reduction. Challenging this emphasis on the responsibilisation of individual young people, an alternative approach is the promotion of rights as a political strategy—encouraging and enabling children as rights-holders to claim the social, cultural, economic, civil and political entitlements specified in the CRC and elsewhere while also holding the state and its agencies to account for implementation of their obligations.

In 2017 the UN Secretary General commissioned a global study: "Children Deprived of Liberty" to document the current situation, in all its forms. Having assessed the implementation of applicable international laws and standards, and the effectiveness of existing approaches, this study is intended to identify good practice. Recommendations for action will focus on meeting international obligations, reducing the number of children deprived of liberty, and implementing alternative responses (see OHCHR 2017).

Current reviews in England, Scotland and Northern Ireland into the need for, and use of, secure accommodation within the range of provision for 'looked after children' include consideration of the links between secure care, mental health and youth justice. While providing an opportunity for reflection and positive developments, there is a danger that managerialist agendas—revision of legislation, regulations, guidance, policy, inspection frameworks and standards; the roles and responsibilities of government departments and agencies; relative costs and commissioning processes for different forms of provision; modification of existing facilities and services; staff training, development, terms and conditions—will dominate. In terms of professional practice, establishing appropriate processes for assessment and intervention, or effective 'behaviour management' approaches within open and secure accommodation, are important issues. However, it is essential that the reviews focus on determining best practice for addressing the needs *and* *rights* of children considered highly 'vulnerable' and involved in potentially harmful behaviours.

Ways Forward

In addition to considering the interpersonal and institutional contexts in which potentially harmful behaviours occur, policy priorities must be re-framed to emphasise the promotion of social justice through intrinsic changes to the distribution of social and economic resources. The CRC and other international human rights standards provide a significant framework for articulating and implementing policy and practice which is inclusive; overtly challenging negative stereotypes, discrimination and stigmatisation while explicitly promoting and protecting children's individual and collective rights.

Childrens' rights should be regarded as entitlements for all under-18s. Neither conditional on adults 'conferring' them, nor transactional through notions of responsibility, they are intended to address the disadvantages, vulnerabilities and unmet needs of individuals and specific groups. Negative stereotypes and assumptions about 'children' (under-12s) and 'young people' (13–18 years old) must be contested. While recognising their need for care and protection, under-18s should be viewed as social actors in all aspects of their lives. Their inherent *and* structural vulnerabilities should be acknowledged. Rather than defining them 'incompetent' or 'irrational', adults need to comprehend children's understanding of their worlds and support them in developing necessary skills to express their views, negotiate relationships and decisions, 'claim' their entitlements and seek redress for rights violations.

Children's perspectives provide significant insight into what is needed for successful implementation of rights standards and should inform understanding about whether duty-bearers are fulfilling their obligations. Meaningful participation is dependent on the adults living and working with children really listening to them, taking them seriously and acting on their views. There are inevitable tensions involved in achieving a balance between 'participation' and 'best interests' when a child does not recognise potential harms to their own or others' well-being. In discussing these issues, the adults involved need to understand the child's perspectives concerning the role of social workers and other professionals, their comprehension of 'risks', their judgement about potentially harmful activities or situations, and their suggestions regarding appropriate responses when they consistently engage in unsafe practices. As Marshall (2014: 94) states: "children have a right to be protected and … this will be most effectively secured if their views are taken into account about how matters of care and control should be addressed".

It is vital that children's understanding about, and acceptance of responsibility for, 'unacceptable' or potentially harmful behaviour is distinguished from shaming and punishment. Avoiding stigmatisation and criminalisation, policies should "explicitly recognise that the most challenging young people … are those requiring the most nurturing" (McAra and McVie 2010: 200). Harmful behaviour by a relatively small number of children and young people can cause concern, fear, intimidation and suffering in communities, including harm to other children and young people. Recognising that challenging behaviour is often symptomatic of unmet needs and/or negative experiences with peers, parents and other community members, the adults involved in children's care, health, education and socialisation are responsible for identifying and addressing the causes of such behaviour. These may include social 'norms' and *adult* behaviours observed and learned by children concerning drink, drug use, sexual harassment, inter-personal and inter-community violence. Also relevant is the broader context of the child care system, including the role and practices of social workers and the quality of their relationships with children (particularly their capacity to develop trusting relationships while providing regular contact and support). The culture of 'open' residential settings and access to resources are significant (Goldson 2002), as is the scope of provision—from earlier intervention to maintain children in their families and communities to specialist placements and long-term support to meet the needs of vulnerable individuals (see Hart and La Valle 2016; Mooney et al. 2012; RQIA 2011; Sinclair and Geraghty 2008).

For children experiencing multiple disadvantages, the circumstances of their lives can be changed only through supportive policies and practices that extend to their families and communities. This includes access to essential services and an adequate standard of living. Child-centred, holistic, non-stigmatising provision for 'vulnerable' children who require additional support to fulfil their potential and avoid social exclusion is crucial. Community based, this should include practical support and guidance in relation to personal development. Access to education, training and employment opportunities is vital, as is information about welfare benefits and accommodation. Services to address physical and mental ill-health (including substance misuse), and family support to ensure children's care and protection, are basic requirements. Also necessary are adequate play, leisure, youth and community facilities.

Co-ordinated, multi-agency support is required to address the chronic and serious problems experienced by children defined 'in need', alongside intensive specialist interventions for those recovering from the impact of difficult childhoods and traumatic life experiences. Such interventions should involve positive role models and 'significant adults' to support children through the difficulties they experience as they transition to adulthood, rather than short-term interventions (see Martynowicz et al. 2012). Discourses of individual pathology and responsibilisation, exemplified by the rhetoric of young people 'not putting themselves at risk' or 'keeping themselves safe', should be avoided and replaced by a commitment to ensuring each individual's personal, social and educational development. Also significant is the recognition and regulation of adults who encourage harmful behaviours, exploit young people's vulnerabilities, and perpetrate abuse or exploitation.

It is clear that a small number of children will require a 'safe space' during periods when they experience extreme vulnerability. They should be fully involved in all decisions concerning their care, protection and resettlement, with their needs agreed and prioritised. Marshall (2014: 8) concludes that the "challenge for society is to provide the kind of structure, safety and quality of care" provided by secure facilities "without depriving young people of their liberty and of the opportunity to develop into individuals who can cope with freedom". Detention should be exceptional—a last resort to protect the child or others from harm. Otherwise, as international standards establish, it represents an unequivocal breach of children's rights.

Notes

1. In accordance with Article 1 of the UN *Convention on the Rights of the Child* (CRC), the term "children" is used throughout the chapter to define "every human being below the age of eighteen years". Children deprived of their liberty include those detained: in custody, for their own/others' protection, as a consequence of physical or mental disability/ill-health, in immigration detention, or because they are considered a threat to national security.
2. See: *Children Act, 1989*, Section 25(1) in relation to England; the *Social Services and Well-being (Wales) Act 2014*, Section 119; the *Children (Northern Ireland) Order 1995*, Article 44(2); and the *Children's Hearing (Scotland) Act 2011*, Section 83(6).
3. See Department of Health (1991), DHSS (1996a), Welsh Ministers (2015), and Scottish Ministers (2013).

References

Barry, M., & Moodie, K. (2008). *This Isn't the Road I Want to Go Down. Young People's Perceptions and Experiences of Secure Care*. Glasgow: Who Cares? Scotland.

Children's Rights Director for England. (2009). *Life in Secure Care*. London: OFSTED.

Criminal Justice Inspection Northern Ireland [CJINI]. (2008). *Inspection of Woodlands Juvenile Justice Centre, May 2008.* Belfast: CJINI.

Department for Education. (2017). *Children Accommodated in Secure Children's Homes at 31 March 2017: England and Wales.* SFR 23/2017. London: Department for Education.

Department of Health. (1991). *The Children (Secure Accommodation) Regulations 1991.* London: Department of Health.

Department of Health and Social Services [DHSS]. (1996a). *Children (Secure Accommodation) Regulations (Northern Ireland) 1996.* Belfast: DHSS.

Department of Health and Social Services [DHSS]. (1996b). *Children (NI) Order Guidance and Regulations, Volume 4: Residential Care.* Belfast: DHSS.

Devaney, J., Bunting, L., Davidson, G., Hayes, D., Lazenbatt, A., & Spratt, T. (2012). *Still Vulnerable. The Impact of Early Childhood Experiences on Adolescent Suicide and Accidental Death.* Belfast: Northern Ireland Commissioner for Children and Young People [NICCY].

Goldson, B. (2002). *Vulnerable Inside. Children in Secure and Penal Settings.* London: The Children's Society.

Gough, A. (2016). *Secure Care in Scotland: Looking Ahead. Key Messages and Call for Action.* Glasgow: Centre for Youth and Criminal Justice.

Gough, A. (2017). *Secure Care in Scotland: Young People's Voices.* Glasgow: Centre for Youth and Criminal Justice.

Hart, D., & La Valle, I. (2016). *Local Authority Use of Secure Placements.* London: Department of Education.

Haydon, D. (2014). Early intervention for the prevention of offending in Northern Ireland. *Youth Justice, 14*(3), 226–240.

Haydon, D. (2016). *Promoting and Protecting the Rights of Young People Who Experience Secure Care in Northern Ireland.* Belfast: Children's Law Centre.

Held, J. (2006). *Qualitative Study: The Use by Local Authorities of Secure Children's Homes.* London: Department for Education and Skills.

Hollingsworth, K. (2017). The Utility and Futility of International Standards for Children in Conflict with the Law. The Case for England. In L. Weber, E. Fishwick, & M. Marmo (Eds.), *The Routledge International Handbook of Criminology and Human Rights* (pp. 190–199). London: Routledge.

Justice Studio. (2014). *They Helped Me, They Supported Me: Achieving Outcomes and Value for Money in Secure Children's Homes.* London: Justice Studio.

Kilkelly, U. (2008). Youth justice and children's rights: Measuring compliance with international standards. *Youth Justice, 8*(3), 187–192.

King, M. (1994). Children's rights as communication: Reflections on autopoietic theory and the United Nations convention. *The Modern Law Review, 57*(3), 385–401.

Lundy, L., Kilkelly, U., Byrne, B., & Kang, J. (2012). *The UN Convention on the Rights of the Child: A Study of Legal Implementation in 12 Countries.* London: UNICEF-UK and Centre for Children's Rights, Queens University Belfast.

Marshall, K. (2014). *Child Sexual Exploitation in Northern Ireland. Report of the Independent Inquiry.* Belfast: CJINI/RQIA/ETI Northern Ireland.

Martynowicz, A., Moore, L., & Wahidin, A. (2012). *'She's a Legend'. The Role of Significant Adults in the Lives of Children and Young People in Contact with the Criminal Justice System.* Belfast: Northern Ireland Commissioner for Children and Young People (NICCY).

McAra, L., & McVie, S. (2010). Youth crime and justice: Key messages from the Edinburgh Study of Youth Transitions and Crime. *Criminology and Criminal Justice, 10*(2), 179–209.

Méndez, J. E. (2015). *Report of the Special Rapporteur on Torture and Other Cruel, Inhuman or Degrading Treatment or Punishment, Juan E. Méndez.* A/HRC/28/68. Geneva: UNHRC.

Mooney, A., Statham, J., Knight, A., & Holmes, L. (2012). *Understanding the Market for Secure Children's Homes. Summary Report.* London: Childhood Wellbeing Research Centre.

Neill, G., & Moffett, K. (2014). *Child Sexual Exploitation—Young Person's Working Group Report.* Belfast: Include Youth.

Office of the First Minister and Deputy First Minister [OFMDFM]. (2016). *Our Children and Young People—Our Pledge: A Ten Year Strategy for Children and Young People in Northern Ireland 2006–2016.* Belfast: OFMDFM.

Office of the High Commissioner for Human Rights [OHCHR]. (2017). *Children Deprived of Liberty—The United Nations Global Study.* [Online]. Available http://www.ohchr.org/EN/HRBodies/CRC/StudyChildrenDeprived Liberty/Pages/Index.aspx. Accessed June 6, 2017.

Roesch-Marsh, A. (2014). Risk assessment and secure accommodation decision-making in Scotland: Taking account of gender? *Child Abuse Review, 23*(3), 214–226.

Regulation and Quality Improvement Authority [RQIA]. (2011). *A Report on the Inspection of the Care Pathways of a Select Group of Young People Who Met the Criteria for Secure Accommodation in Northern Ireland.* Belfast: RQIA.

Scottish Government. (2008). *Getting It Right for Every Child (GIRFEC)*. Edinburgh: Scottish Government.

Scottish Government. (2013). *Good Practice Guidance. The Children's Hearings (Scotland) Act 2011 (Implementation of Secure Accommodation Authorisation) (Scotland) Regulations 2013*. Scottish Government: Edinburgh.

Scottish Ministers. (2013). *The Children's Hearings (Scotland) Act 2011 (Implementation of Secure Accommodation Authorisation) (Scotland) Regulations 2013*. Edinburgh: Scottish Government.

Scraton, P. (Ed). (1997). *'Childhood' in 'Crisis'?* London: UCL Press.

Sinclair, R., & Geraghty, T. (2008). *A Review of the Use of Secure Accommodation in Northern Ireland*. London: National Children's Bureau.

Stanley, E. (2007). Towards a criminology for human rights. In A. Barton, K. Corteen, D. Scott, & D. Whyte (Eds.), *Expanding the Criminological Imagination. Critical Readings in Criminology* (pp. 168–197). Cullompton: Willan Publishing.

UN Committee on the Rights of the Child [UNCRC]. (2014). *Letter to Secretary-General of the United Nations recommending that a study be undertaken on the Issue of children deprived of their liberty, 19 May'*. KS/CRC. [Online]. Available http://www.ohchr.org/Documents/HRBodies/CRC/StudyChildrenDeprivedLiberty/Committee_on_CRC_letter_to_SG_19May2016.pdf. Accessed March 22, 2018.

UN Committee on the Rights of the Child [UNCRC]. (2016). *Concluding Observations on the Fifth Periodic Report of the United Kingdom of Great Britain and Northern Ireland*. CRC/C/GBR/CO/5. Adopted June 3, 2016.

UN Development Group. (2003). *The Human Rights Based Approach to Development Cooperation. Towards a Common Understanding Among UN Agencies*. New York: United Nations Development Group.

UN General Assembly. (1985). *United Nations Standard Minimum Rules for the Administration of Juvenile Justice [Beijing Rules]*. A/RES/40/33. Adopted November 29, 1985.

UN General Assembly. (1990a). *United Nations Guidelines for the Prevention of Juvenile Delinquency [Riyadh Guidelines]*. A/RES/45/112. Adopted December 14, 1990.

UN General Assembly. (1990b). *United Nations Rules for the Protection of Juveniles Deprived of their Liberty [Havana Rules]*. A/RES/45/113. Adopted December 14, 1990.

UN General Assembly. (2010). *Guidelines for the Alternative Care of Children.* A/RES/64/142. Adopted December 18, 2009.

Voice of Young People in Care [VOYPIC]. (2014). *Independent Inquiry on Child Sexual Exploitation in Northern Ireland. Consultation with Care Experienced Young People.* Belfast: VOYPIC.

Welsh Assembly Government. (2004). *Children and Young People: Rights to Action.* Cardiff: Welsh Assembly Government.

Welsh Ministers. (2015). *The Children (Secure Accommodation) (Wales) Regulations 2015.*

3

Rights of Persons with Disability Not to Be Criminalised

Eileen Baldry

Introduction

On 10 October 2016, the United Nations Committee on the Rights of Persons with Disabilities [UNCRPD] released its full findings in relation to the complaint lodged by Mr. Marlon Noble, regarding his indefinite prison detention for ten years in Western Australia (WA).[1] Mr. Noble is an Aboriginal man with a cognitive disability who had been deemed unfit to stand trial but was held without conviction for an alleged offence. The Committee found that the WA government had failed to fulfil its obligations to Mr. Noble under the Convention, particularly in relation to "Articles 5 (1) and (2), 12 (2) and (3), 13 (1), 14 (1) (b) and 15" (UNCRPD 2016: para. 9). These articles emphasise the rights of persons with disability to equality before, and equal protection of, the law as well as access to justice and substantial equality in law requiring procedural adjustments and training for legal officers.

E. Baldry (✉)
University of New South Wales, Sydney, NSW, Australia
e-mail: e.baldry@unsw.edu.au

© The Author(s) 2018
E. Stanley (ed.), *Human Rights and Incarceration*, Palgrave Studies in Prisons and Penology, https://doi.org/10.1007/978-3-319-95399-1_3

The Committee went on to require the state (Western Australia) to make reparation to Mr. Noble, to release him from any justice related orders, and to publish the Committee's views. Very importantly, the Committee went on to state:

> In general, the State party is under an obligation to take measures to prevent similar violations in the future. In this regard, the Committee refers to the recommendations contained in its concluding observations. (CRPD/C/AUS/CO/1, para. 32) (UNCRPD 2016: para. 9[b])[2]

These findings and recommendations are crucial to future applications and understandings of the Convention in relation to persons with disabilities and their involvement in criminal justice systems in Australia and elsewhere. The Committee recognised both the *individual* person's right to be treated in accordance with the articles of the Convention and also importantly the State's obligation to make *legislative and systemic* changes to ensure persons with disabilities do not endure such treatment in the future. In this instance, that meant that there should be a change to the way in which the Western Australian government ensured that preventive remedies were available for a whole class or group of people, and not just one individual.

This chapter will argue that these findings and recommendations should be applied not only to formal criminal justice settings in Western Australia but to every jurisdiction in Australia as well as to community contexts in which the behaviours of persons with disability may be criminalised. This would assist in disrupting the creation of pathways into formal criminal justice settings.

The Committee's findings on Mr. Noble's case followed over a decade of research projects, reports and submissions lodged with various Australian state, territory and Commonwealth government departments and agencies (Sotiri et al. 2012; New South Wales Law Reform Commission 2013; Victorian Law Reform Commission 2013; Baldry et al. 2015). These works have outlined injustices and breaches of human rights in the treatment of persons with mental and cognitive disability including those with complex support needs (persons with

multiple disabilities and social needs requiring multiple interactive sup-
port services) in criminal justice systems across Australia. They noted
particular concerns regarding the treatment of Indigenous Australians.
Similar matters have been raised internationally for example in the
UK and the USA (Lamb and Weinberger 1998; Bradley 2009; Her
Majesty's Inspectorate of Probation 2014; Giraud-Saunders 2013).[3]

Mr. Noble's case is not isolated with dozens of persons, many of them
Indigenous Australians, held in similar circumstances every year (Sotiri
et al. 2012; Senate Standing Committee on Community Affairs 2016).
Nor is it unique to Australia. In many countries, there are persons with
disabilities, especially those with multiple disabilities who are severely
disadvantaged, who cannot access their rights to community support
and protection from criminalising practices or to fair and equitable
treatment under the law, often resulting in long-term criminal justice
involvement (see, for example, Shakespeare 1994; Draine et al. 2002;
McCausland and Baldry 2017). There are also persons with cognitive
disabilities who are denied their right to liberty by judicial determinations regarding detention after a finding of unfitness. The continuing detention of those found unfit to plead in prisons or other secure
facilities may be viewed as a system of preventive detention based on
the premise that because they have been charged with an offence and
because they have cognitive disabilities, they pose a risk to others.[4] Their
detention is said to be justified on the basis of community protection
(Arnstein-Kerslake et al. 2017).

It is important to note that Mr. Noble's case is not representative
of the thousands of socially disadvantaged persons with disability who
are accused of minor (non-indictable) offences and left to the management of the police and other criminal justice agencies each year (Baldry
and Dowse 2013). Individuals in this group are picked up frequently
by the police, often held overnight in police cells and their cases heard
in the Magistrates' court. They are frequently incarcerated on remand
and then given short sentences, cycling in and out of custody, effectively in serial detention. So, there are two groups of persons of concern:
(i) those accused of a serious offence and found unfit and held indefinitely (like Mr. Noble) and (ii) those enmeshed in minor offending,

cycling in and out of detention and being managed by the criminal justice system. This latter group's circumstances will also be explored as this chapter progresses.

These ways of treating persons with disabilities would appear to be in contravention of a number of UN rights instruments and, given that Australia and comparable nations are signatories to the relevant Conventions, it must be asked why it is that these circumstances have gone uncorrected?

Disregard for Aspects of Human Rights in the Neo-Liberal State

One factor that may help explain this disregard for human rights is the rise of the neo-liberal state. Criminal law in Western countries is inherently individualistic and this feature has been emphasised during the neo-liberal turn of the past thirty years which has also devalued social justice principles and the social democratic polity. In his discussion of international criminal justice, Findlay (2008: 15) succinctly summarises the values and principles of neo-liberalism that have reshaped criminal justice, including: the individualisation of rights and responsibilities; the valorisation of individual autonomy; a belief in free and rational choice which underpins criminal liability and penality; a denial of welfare as central state policy; the valorisation of a free market model and profit motivation as a core social value; and the denial of cultural values which stand outside of, or in opposition to, a market model of social relations.

In these "Western" neo-liberal states, Norrie (2014: xviii) has argued that there is greater emphasis on, and reinterpretation of, criminal law as an authoritarian means by which to maintain order and, by extension it can be argued, to manage difference. In this framework, the need for social and structural responses to crime such as reducing unemployment rates, improving educational outcomes, increasing wages, ensuring proper welfare support, improving housing and urban conditions is swept to the side (Brown 2009: 456). This devaluing of difference and diversity further entrenches individual choice and responsibility no matter the context or background that a person or groups of people experience.

While in the past decade since the adoption of the *UN Convention on the Rights of Persons with Disabilities* there has been increasing commitment to the rights of people with disabilities by governments globally, the over-representation of people with mental and cognitive disability in criminal justice systems has received comparatively little attention. Nevertheless, some headway is being made in Australia with the development, by some state governments, of a Disability Justice Plan or Strategy as urged by Australia's Disability Discrimination Commissioner within the Australian Human Rights Commission (2014; see, for example, Attorney-General's Department, South Australia 2014). To date, these disability rights-conscious developments include diversionary and therapeutic measures, such as mental health courts, enactment of provisions of sentencing legislation allowing diversion, and provision of mental health nurses in courts and 'responding to persons with disability' training for police, that are designed to accommodate a person's disabilities. These appear to have had little impact on reducing the large numbers of disadvantaged people with mental and cognitive disability being managed by and entrenched in criminal justice systems across Australia's six states and two territories. For example, whilst the number and rate of adolescents in youth detention have decreased substantially in recent years, the rate of those with mental health disorder (87%), extremely low IQ in the Intellectually Disability range (14%) and with Attention Hyper-Activity or other behavioural disorder (70%) in detention have increased. Adult detention numbers and rates have soared since the mid-1990s and 63% of adults in prison have been diagnosed with a mental illness. These are significantly above the rates in the comparable community populations (Justice Health & Forensic Mental Health Network, New South Wales Government 2016: 13, 17).

Criminal legal systems recognise the potential injustice that can occur in the management of persons with disability by criminal justice agencies. These systems provide some mechanism for mitigation of the impact that mental and cognitive disability can have on persons' behaviours and capacity (such as 'fitness to plead' legislation, 'problem solving courts' and mental health acts and tribunals). In some cases though, these can and do have pernicious effects such as persons with disability being incarcerated indefinitely, being subject to more stringent sanctions or requirements than their peers or being managed in the criminal justice system because apparently there are no suitable community support options (Gooding et al. 2016). These mitigations are also individualistic and 'at the bottom of the cliff' so to speak, and do not address the causal and cumulative factors argued to be associated with criminalisation of persons with disability. These factors highlight the importance of a justice disability rights framework being founded *outside* the criminal justice system to ensure that criminal justice agencies do not remain the default management options for persons with disability. To date most of the little work that has been done on exploring the interactions between human rights, disability and criminal justice has been focused on assisting individuals with disability to access their rights as victims or offenders (on a case by case basis) once *in* the criminal justice system. Important though this is, it is only one side of a multifaceted 'coin'.

The Nature of Criminalisation in Relation to Disability

In a formal sense, to criminalise a behaviour or act is to make it a criminal offence by making it illegal; making a person's or group of people's particular behaviour or activity illegal criminalises the person or group of people. These formal understandings of criminalisation, although important and relevant to the discussion in this chapter, are by no means sufficient to assist this examination of why so many people with mental and cognitive disability are incarcerated. The position taken here is that criminal justice is a social construct, comprising the formal attributes of criminal laws but more substantively made up of a myriad of historical and proximate influences and conditions and that the practices which constitute it are inconsistent, sometimes contradictory and influenced by personal biases and cultural and political contexts

(Brown 2013; Hogg 1983; Lacey 2009; Norrie 1996). Criminalisation is not just a function of applying a law so as to make a particular behaviour illegal but also of a multitude of practices by workers inside and outside criminal justice agencies and across criminal, civil and administrative law systems. Brown points to the "mishmash, a blurring of forms, agents, subjects and modes of regulation and power" (2013: 616) in relation to the contextual nature of and front line practices that characterise contemporary forms of criminalisation. This is nowhere more evident than in the practices that swirl around and accumulate to enmesh particular groups of persons with disability in the orbit of criminal justice agencies.

There are well-documented criminalising practices by some workers and carers in out of home care (OOHC) facilities[5] and psychiatric units, such as calling the police to report minor 'offences' of throwing crockery or punching a wall. Although strictly speaking these are offences, were these to happen in a family home, parents or others in the family would deal with the matter and discipline the child or young person. But in an institutional setting such behaviour is criminalised often leading to young persons or persons with mental illness being charged, removed from the residence or unit and sometimes held in custody (Ashford and Morgan 2004; McFarlane 2010). There is also a wealth of documentation regarding criminalisation of persons with mental health disorders, particularly of those who are homeless. For example, over thirty years ago, Teplin (1984) demonstrated that people with mental illness in the US were significantly more likely than those without such illness to be charged and arrested for identical offences.

As is now recognised in relation to many justice systems (Bradley 2009; KPMG 2007; New South Wales Law Reform Commission 2012),[6] the majority of people with disability who are managed by and in criminal justice systems have more than one impairment, often have been or are homeless, have a substance abuse problem, are poor and come from disadvantaged areas and backgrounds. That is, they have multiple and complex needs (Baldry and Dowse 2013: 222; Riches et al. 2006: 388). In Australia recent state law reform commission papers have recognised that a large proportion of people with disability charged with and convicted of offences have more than one disability

(New South Wales Law Reform Commission 2012, 2013; Victorian Law Reform Commission 2013). They also note that the law does not deal well with complex support needs, with 'upstream' interventions and supports to prevent persons with disability ending up in prison being far more appropriate than the criminal law (Baldry 2014).

The ways in which persons with disability are caught up and funnelled into offending and criminal justice management are often complicated and many layered. Those persons with disability who enter criminal justice management as children or young people have almost always had very difficult and disadvantaged childhoods. They have not enjoyed access to their rights as children or as persons with disability to a safe and secure loving childhood with appropriate services and supports for their disabilities. The Mental Health Disorders and Cognitive Disabilities in the Criminal Justice System (MHDCD) dataset contains detailed lifecourse data for a cohort of 2731 persons who had been in prison in New South Wales at some point between 2001 and 2008 (Baldry et al. 2015). Approximately 40% had been in juvenile justice as young persons and every one of them had either mental or cognitive disability or both (Baldry 2014: 375). Of the 12% who had been in OOHC, 90% had a cognitive disability (ibid.). Those who had complex support needs (two-thirds of the cohort) were significantly more likely than those with no disability or one disability to have had earlier and greater contact with police, be a victim of abuse or a crime, have had more arrests, convictions and prison episodes; they were also more likely to have had more remand and shorter prison stays (ibid.: 375–376). According to police records, when they were young these persons with multiple disabilities were significantly more likely to be left to the police to be managed when their families were unable to do so or were absent. These young persons were also significantly more likely than their peers in the community to have been expelled or excluded from school and not to have completed any formal school certification and, across their lives (as adults), to have come from and returned to a very small number of very disadvantaged towns and suburbs (Baldry et al. 2015).

These findings echo observations in Australia on the 'OOHC to prison pipeline' (McFarlane 2010; Australian Institute of Health and Welfare 2016) and on the development of similar pathways of developmental disadvantage elsewhere, such as the 'school to prison pipeline' in the US (Langberg and Fedders 2013: 653–655), the 'looked after children (LAC) to criminal justice' pipeline in the UK (Hayden 2010; Fitzpatrick and Williams 2017; Howard League for Penal Reform 2016) and the 'care to custody' pipeline in Aotearoa-New Zealand (Stanley 2016). This neglect of young persons with disabilities who are disadvantaged accumulates to create complex support needs and can enmesh these persons in a vicious criminal justice management cycle which, for by far the majority of them, continues into adult prison (Baldry and Dowse 2013).

Police are the gatekeepers to the criminal justice system and are often the avenue to criminalisation. Persons with disability who are very socially disadvantaged and become known to the police as young persons at risk, as individuals with publicly challenging behaviours due to their mental or cognitive disability, as victims of violence, as persons who are homeless or have alcohol or other drug problems, and who do not have family or community capacity to support them, are at very high risk of being managed by the police regularly and of custody becoming a normal way of life (Baldry and Dowse 2013). The MHDCD findings provide many examples of police trying to find appropriate support and safe accommodation for young persons with complex support needs and being frustrated at the lack of such support. In some cases, police use overnight police custody as a 'safe' alternative and even if the person with disability is not charged, once this way of managing that person with disability has occurred reasonably often, criminal justice management becomes normalised and the person is criminalised (Baldry et al. 2015).

Similarly, the absence of early and appropriate diagnosis and adequate social support for socially disadvantaged children with cognitive disability or for those who develop a mental illness or acquire a cognitive disability as an adult means that criminalisation and management by criminal justice agencies can be the default 'care' pathway (Baldry and Dowse 2013; Hayden 2010). This is particularly the case for Indigenous Australians with disability. The research cited above provides evidence that persons in these groups are being systematically criminalised.

Incarceration and Further Criminalization and Punishment

At least half of the adults imprisoned across Australia have mental or cognitive disability or both (Australian Institute of Health and Welfare 2015) and these are in addition to high rates of other disabilities such as hearing impairment amongst Indigenous prisoners (Vanderpoll and Howard 2011) and chronic diseases (Indig et al. 2010). Indications are that children and young people in Australian youth detention have even higher rates of disability (Indig et al. 2011). Previous reports such as the *Burdekin Report* (1993) in the 1990s documented the widespread over-arrest and incarceration of persons with mental illness in Australia. The contemporary evidence is overwhelming that persons with mental and cognitive disabilities continue to crowd prisons (Steinberg et al. 2015; Ollove 2017; Prison Reform Trust 2016).

The case is similar across other Western jurisdictions such as in the USA where researchers have observed that prisons comprise the largest psychiatric institution in the nation (Lamb and Weinberger 1998; 2014). They also provide evidence of the over-incarceration of persons with cognitive and other disabilities (Bronson et al. 2015). Research and reports reveal similar concerns and prevalence in the UK (Equality and Human Rights Commission 2016), in Aotearoa-New Zealand (Indig et al. 2016) and Canada (Centre for Addiction and Mental Health 2013).

Those found unfit to plead may face indefinite detention in prison or other secure settings; potentially for longer than if they had in fact been convicted and sentenced (Arnstein-Kerslake et al. 2017). This should be understood as cruel and unusual punishment, as an outcome not intended in fitness to plead legislation and as a breach of the rights of persons with disability (Gooding et al. 2017). As has been shown to be the case in institutional settings generally, persons with disability, especially those with cognitive disability, are likely to be subjected to torture, abuse and violations (from extreme physical restraints to sexual assault) and not to be afforded protection (Nowak 2008).

Although various UN bodies have criticised these many breaches of the rights of persons with disabilities, including criticisms of Australian criminal justice jurisdictions (UNCRPD 2016), abuses continue. Torture and cruel and unusual punishment in Australian juvenile detention and adult prisons have been revealed over many decades in media reports and Royal Commissions (see Royal Commission into NSW Prisons 1978; Royal Commission into the Detention and Protection of Children in the Northern Territory 2017), indicating institutional cultures of abuse are structurally embedded. Indigenous Australians with cognitive disabilities appear to face particular disadvantage in this area of criminal law (Baldry et al. 2015). For example, the recent case of Dylan Voller, an Aboriginal boy with disability who was subjected to restraint in a restraint chair and a spit hood, in a juvenile detention centre in the Northern Territory, has been condemned as cruel and unusual punishment and as torture (McCausland and Baldry 2017). The indefinite detention of Mr. Malcolm Morton, an Aboriginal man with profound cognitive disability, in a Northern Territory maximum security prison for over six years, since he was a juvenile, is another such case. Mr. Morton was regularly subjected to cruel and unusual punishment by being strapped in a restraint chair, injected with sedating medications, and being so distressed that he banged his head until it bled (Robinson and Branley 2016). After years of advocacy Mr. Morton has finally been released into a secure disability unit with appropriate supports and contact with his family. Ms. Roseanne Fulton is yet another Aboriginal person with significant cognitive impairment (foetal alcohol spectrum disorder) who has been serially imprisoned in Western Australia and the Northern Territory (Baldry 2014). All are examples of Indigenous persons whose disability behaviours have been criminalised and negatively affected by an unfitness to plead finding. In the context of the *Convention on the Rights of Persons with Disabilities*, unfitness to stand trial laws in Australia have been assessed as potentially violating the rights of persons with disabilities to equal recognition before the law, access to justice, and liberty and security of the person (Arnstein-Kerslake et al. 2017; Gooding et al. 2017).

Relevant Legal Rights

The *Convention on the Rights of Persons with Disabilities* proclaims human rights for persons with disabilities, some of which mirror rights in other UN instruments, such as in the *International Covenant on Civil and Political Rights* and the *International Covenant on Economic, Social and Cultural Rights*. The *Convention on the Rights of the Child* is also relevant because many persons with disability who are funnelled into prison as adults were criminalised as children with disability.

Key rights enshrined in the *Convention on the Rights of Persons with Disabilities* that are particularly relevant to those who are at risk of being, or are, criminalised and are managed by criminal justice agencies are:

- the right to protection from adverse stereotyping (Article 8);
- the right to protection and safety in situations of risk (Article 11);
- the right to equal recognition before the law (Article 12);
- the right to equal and effective access to justice (Article 13);
- the right to life and security of the person, and to treatment in accordance with the principles of international humanitarian law when deprived of liberty and for the existence of a disability not in any case to justify a deprivation of liberty (Article 14);
- the right to freedom from torture or cruel, inhuman or degrading treatment or punishment (Article 15);
- the right to freedom from violence, exploitation and abuse (Article 16);
- the right to respect for physical and mental integrity on an equal basis with others (Article 17);
- the right to access appropriate support (Article 19);
- the right to education without discrimination and with equal opportunity (Article 24); and
- the right to habilitation and rehabilitation (Article 26);

Had these rights been available and accessible in the community to the people with complex support needs in the MHDCD cohort prior to their contact with criminal justice agencies, they may not have been criminalised.

The Optional Protocol to the UNCRPD is an associated agreement which allows its parties to recognise the competence of the Committee on the Rights of Persons with Disabilities. Under the Optional Protocol, individuals are able to bring petitions to the Committee claiming breaches of their human rights, and the Committee is empowered to undertake inquiries of grave or systematic violations of rights under the Convention. In its report to the UN General Assembly in 2015 the Committee commented on global systematic violations and the lack of legislation, policy and procedures to ensure implementation of the UNCRPD, and urged the member states to remedy these issues (UNCRPD 2015). In general comments, the Committee expressed serious concerns regarding the treatment of persons with disability in criminal justice systems. To date there is no information on steps taken by UN member states to remedy these concerns. The Committee has heard and made determinations on numerous individual complaints since 2006, but the majority of these have not involved criminal justice matters. However, of the complaints regarding mistreatment of a person with disability in the criminal justice system, most appear to be against Australia.[7] Australia is a signatory to both the Convention and the Optional Protocol and it was under the protocol that the above complaints concerning Mr. Noble and Mr. Morton were made.

The *Convention Against Torture and Other Cruel, Inhuman and Degrading Treatment* is also particularly relevant and is referred to by the UNCRPD in its reports and findings.[8] This Convention prohibits any act of torture (Article 2) and ensures state parties take effective measures to prevent torture. It requires:

- keeping interrogation rules, instructions, methods and practices under systematic review regarding individuals who are in custody or physical control in any territory, in order to prevent torture (Article 11);
- making torture a criminal offence (Article 4);

- training and educating relevant people and officials regarding the prohibition of torture (Article 10); and
- preventing all acts of cruel, inhuman or degrading treatment or punishment in any territory (Article 16).

The bans on torture (proclaimed in Article 2) and other acts of cruel, inhuman or degrading treatment or punishment are both absolute and non-derogable—there are "no exceptional circumstances whatsoever" that are deemed to justify limiting or overriding this prohibition. This is most relevant in the context of the use of restrictive practices on persons with disability in Australia (Arnstein-Kerslake et al. 2017; Gooding et al. 2017). The use of restraint chairs, spit hoods, forcible injections, physical bashings, tear gassing, long periods in sensory deprived isolation cells are all abusive restrictive practices that are or have been used recently in some Australian custody settings to restrain or restrict persons with disability (Royal Commission into the Protection and Detention of Children in the Northern Territory 2017; Senate Standing Committee on Community Affairs 2015). They were of extreme concern to an Australian Parliamentary Committee investigating violence, abuse and neglect against persons with disability, which concluded that persons with disability should not be subjected to restrictive practices and that prisons and other places of detention are not suitable for persons with mental and cognitive disability (Senate Standing Committee on Community Affairs 2015). A key mechanism to prevent and monitor the use of torture is the *Convention Against Torture's Optional Protocol* (OPCAT). It requires states that have ratified it, to establish a national preventive mechanism to conduct random inspections of places of detention. Australia ratified the OPCAT only in late December 2017.

The arguments made and examples given to this point in this chapter reveal the lack of access for poor, disadvantaged and Indigenous Australians with disability to rights under the UNCRPD and other Conventions. Were these persons afforded their rights to disability support in a timely and appropriate manner their criminalisation may have been prevented. Were they afforded their rights once in the criminal justice system they may have been diverted or at least not been subjected to torture or cruel and unusual punishment.

Towards a Disability Social Justice Rights Framework

The integration of human rights within prisons has emphasised international legal standards, rules and guidelines. For example, Coyle proposes a comprehensive framework applying the various UN Conventions starting with the fundamental right of all persons to be treated with respect and for the inherent dignity of the human person (Coyle 2002). This framework requires human rights training for all who work in prisons and the proper oversight of treatment of prisoners to ensure their rights are upheld.

In 2012, Chan et al. argued for the use of the UNCRPD in the development of a human rights framework for persons with disability who are in contact with the criminal justice system. Three foundation principles for this framework were proposed: the inherent dignity of the person; the accommodation and inclusion of the needs of persons with disabilities in the physical and social environment; and the addressing of underlying social factors that predispose persons with disabilities to have contact with criminal justice systems (Chan et al. 2012: 560). They pointed out in particular that Article 14:

> … provides that the existence of disability cannot justify a deprivation of liberty. This speaks loudly to the institutionalization and restraint of people with disabilities in the absence of explicit and justifiable legal sanctions that are based on factors other than the mere existence of impairment and disability. (ibid.: 561)

In a case study of a person with complex support needs held indefinitely they illustrated how their framework could be applied. Nevertheless, they did not expand on their third principle to address the structural, social and other factors that funnel persons with disability into the criminal justice systems.

Similarly, disability justice strategies or plans (Attorney-General's Department, South Australia 2014) being developed by some Australian States, positive though they are, tend to focus on the individual once in contact with the criminal justice system. Guidance on the relevant principles and actions that should be included in such strategies is set out in the Australian Human Rights Commission's *Equal Before the Law: Towards Disability Justice Strategies* report (2014). These strategies provide direction for criminal justice agencies to improve the way they interact with and treat persons with disabilities and to avoid the pernicious effects detailed earlier. They include training for staff in understanding disabilities, how persons with disabilities might behave when confronted by criminal justice staff (such as police) and how staff might respond appropriately to such behaviour. It emphasises potential diversionary avenues and disability rights.

These approaches are illustrative of a common bias in the way human rights conventions and protocols are often interpreted and applied. This is, in this current case, that they are individualised and focused on the context of the criminal justice system without attention being given to the equally important structural and systemic elements of the UNCRPD. These include the right to appropriate supports and services being available in the community in an equitable manner to prevent involvement in criminal justice systems in the first place. It is argued here that implicit in the *Convention on the Rights of Persons with Disabilities* is the right *not* to be criminalised and that measures to protect this right need to be embedded structurally and not just applied to each individual on a case by case basis once such an individual is in contact with a criminal justice agency.

Access to rights by persons with disability once in criminal justice systems, including within carceral institutions, is necessary but not sufficient to enable them to activate their rights at the earliest relevant stage. Those who are vulnerable to criminalisation due to their inequitable circumstances should be able to access their rights not to be criminalised from the outset. Key to the "structure and animus [of the CRPD] are issues of discrimination and reasonable accommodation to ensure that rights may be enjoyed on an equal basis with others" (Bartlett 2012: 755 (footnote omitted)). In other words, the intent of the Convention is that *equitable* arrangements should be made to enable disadvantaged persons to access their rights, not just that people are treated equally. The substantive matter here is "how society can make rights real for people with disability" (Bartlett 2012: 759).

An outcome of "equal before the law" is not sufficient because this entails a situation where a disadvantaged person with disability coming before the law is equal to all other people coming before the law and will be treated equally. This is plainly unacceptable in view of the problems noted earlier in relation to the application of criminal law on the basis of individual circumstances alone without reference to the broader social context in which that individual is located. There is a long and deep literature debating and discussing the relationship between equity and equality and what the necessary conditions for equality are, but there is not the space to rehearse these discussions here. Of import to the argument in this chapter is an understanding of equity as the quality of being fair or socially just in a structural and societal sense, and equality as the condition of being equal in the sense of individuals and groups (Herrera 2007). Vertical inequity, that is, maldistribution according to differences in relevant circumstances (Calhoun 2002), cannot be addressed individually; it is a matter of just or fair social arrangements, that is, of social justice. Although we may be born equal in principle, in reality and practice we are not equal. Compared with their disabled but socially advantaged peers or with those without disability, disadvantaged persons with disabilities do not have equal access to opportunities, resources, habilitation, education, and so on. These inequities are compounded by factors such as racism and sexism, and have significant consequences in terms of criminalization and criminal justice processing.

Conclusion

Addressing individual circumstances and rights one at a time and when a person is already involved in the criminal justice system does not deal with the structural inequities driving criminalisation of disadvantaged people with disability in the first place. This requires action to address equity (forms of affirmative action), such as making additional support, accommodation and resources systemically available for people in these groups to arrive at equality of outcome. Here it is appropriate to return to the recommendations of the Committee on the Rights of Persons with Disabilities in regard to the case of Mr. Noble, discussed above. The Committee recommended legislative and systemic change to ensure that persons such as Mr. Noble are not criminalised. It is also appropriate to return to the critical assessments of the criminal law by Norrie (1996, 2014), as well as by numerous other criminologists, as ignoring context and structural disadvantages that lead to criminalisation of particular groups of people. If the principles of the *Convention on the Rights of Persons with Disabilities* are applied in the same narrow and individualistic way as the criminal law itself to persons with disabilities in relation to their contact with the criminal justice system, the same unsatisfactory and substantively unjust outcomes will occur. Those more advantaged persons with disability are likely to receive support early and have access to protective factors and resources and so be unlikely to be criminalised, and those from disadvantaged and racialised backgrounds are unlikely to have access to such resources and so be more likely to be criminalised.

Rights that are enunciated but are applied without governments and societies embedding social justice principles and practices to ensure equitable distribution are inaccessible to the most disadvantaged and excluded persons in our communities. If persons with mental and cognitive and other disabilities are to gain access to their right not to be criminalised, a disability justice rights framework is needed to provide a holistic life-course assurance of fair distribution of the resources needed to ensure access to and enjoyment of these rights. Such a framework would mean far fewer people with disabilities being funnelled into criminal justice agencies for management because they would instead be supported in the community from a stage prior to that involvement in the criminal justice system occurring. They would live equal, engaged and included lives.

Notes

1. These findings were stated by the UN Committee on the Rights of Persons with Disabilities [UNCRPD] (2016), in a communication dated 12 April 2012 pursuant to the Optional Protocol to the Convention on the Rights of Persons with Disabilities (UNCRPD 2006).
2. For these concluding observations see Committee on the Rights of Persons with Disabilities [UNCRPD] (2013).

3. See also Revolving Doors Agency (2016) and Howard League for Penal Reform (2017).
4. On preventive detention regimes in general, see McSherry (2014).
5. Being in OOHC means a child or young person has been removed from their family for their protection or because their family has no capacity to care for them.
6. See also the discussion of the issues and initiatives being pursued in the voluntary sector set out in "Multiple and Complex Needs" (Clinks 2017).
7. See UN Committee on the Rights of Persons with Disabilities [UNCRPD] reports.
8. As above at 7.

References

Arstein-Kerslake, A., Gooding, P., Andrews, L., & McSherry, B. (2017). Human rights and unfitness to plead: The demands of the Convention on the Rights of Persons with Disabilities. *Human Rights Law Review, 17*(3), 399–419.

Ashford, B., & Morgan, R. (2004). Criminalising looked-after children. *Criminal Justice Matters, 57*(1), 8–38.

Attorney-General's Department, South Australia. (2014). *Disability Justice Plan 2014–2017*. [Online]. Available https://www.agd.sa.gov.au/projects-and-consultations/disability-justice-plan. Accessed February 5, 2018.

Australian Human Rights Commission. (2014). *Equal Before the Law: Towards Disability Justice Strategies*. [Online]. Available https://www.humanrights.gov.au/equal-law-towards-disability-justice-strategies. Accessed February 5, 2018.

Australian Institute of Health and Welfare. (2015). *The Health of Australia's Prisoners 2015*. Canberra: Australian Institute of Health and Welfare.

Australian Institute of Health and Welfare. (2016). *Young People in Child Protection and Under Youth Justice Supervision 2013–2014*. Canberra: Australian Institute of Health and Welfare.

Baldry, E. (2014). Disability at the margins: Limits of the law. *Griffith Law Review, 23*(3), 370–388.

Baldry, E., & Dowse, L. (2013). Compounding mental and cognitive disability and disadvantage: Police as care managers. In D. Chappell (Ed.), *Policing *the Mentally Ill: International Perspectives* (pp. 219–234). Boca Raton: CRC Press.

Baldry, E., McCausland, R., Dowse, L., & McEntyre, E. (2015). *A Predictable and Preventable Path: Aboriginal People with Mental and Cognitive Disabilities in the Criminal Justice System.* [Online]. Available https://www. mhdcd.unsw.edu.au/a-predictable-and-preventable-path-iamhdcd-report. html. Accessed February 5, 2018.

Bartlett, P. (2012). The United Nations Convention on the Rights of Persons with Disabilities and mental health law. *Modern Law Review, 75*(5), 752–778.

Bradley, K. (Lord). (2009). *The Bradley Report: Lord Bradley's Review of People with Mental Health Problems or Learning Disabilities in the Criminal Justice System.* London: Department of Health.

Bronson, J., Maruschak, L. M., & Berzofsky, M. (2015). *Disabilities Among Prison and Jail Inmates, 2011–2012.* [Online]. Available https://www.bjs. gov/index.cfm?ty=pbdetail&iid=5500. Accessed February 5, 2018.

Brown, D. (2009). Searching for a social democratic narrative in criminal justice. *Current Issues in Criminal Justice, 20*(3), 453–456.

Brown, D. (2013). Criminalisation and normative theory. *Current Issues in Criminal Justice, 25*(2), 605–625.

Burdekin, B. (1993). *Report of the National Inquiry into the Human Rights of People with Mental Illness* (Burdekin Report). Canberra: Australian Government Printer.

Calhoun, C. (Ed.). (2002). *Dictionary of the Social Sciences.* Oxford: Oxford University Press.

Centre for Addiction and Mental Health [CAMH]. (2013). *Mental Health and Criminal Justice Policy Framework.* Toronto: Centre for Addiction and Mental Health.

Chan, J., French, P., Hudson, C., & Webber, L. (2012). Applying the CRPD to safeguard the rights of people with a disability in contact with the criminal justice system. *Psychiatry, Psychology and Law, 19*(4), 558–565.

Clinks. (2017). *Multiple and Complex Needs.* Available http://www.clinks.org/ criminal-justice/multiple-and-complex-needs. Accessed August 31, 2017.

Coyle, A. (2002). *A Human Rights Approach to Prison Management: Handbook for Prison Staff.* London: International Centre for Prison Studies.

Draine, J., Salzer, M. S., Culhane, D. P., & Hadley, T. R. (2002). Role of social disadvantage in crime, joblessness, and homelessness among persons with serious mental illness. *Psychiatric Services, 53*(5), 565–573.

Equality and Human Rights Commission. (2016). *Strategic Plan 2016–2019*. [Online]. Available https://www.equalityhumanrights.com/en/publication-download/strategic-plan-2016-19. Accessed February 5, 2018.

Findlay, M. (2008). *Governing Through Globalised Crime: Futures for International Criminal Justice*. Cullompton: Willan Publishing.

Fitzpatrick, C., & Williams, P. (2017). The neglected needs of care leavers in the criminal justice system: Practitioners' perspectives and the persistence of problem (corporate) parenting. *Criminology and Criminal Justice, 17*(2), 175–191.

Giraud-Saunders, A. (2013). *Making the difference: The role of adult social care services in supporting vulnerable offenders* (Briefing Paper). London: Prison Reform Trust.

Gooding, P., Mercer, S., Baldry, E., & Arstein-Kerslake, A. (2016). Unfitness to stand trial: The indefinite detention of persons with cognitive disabilities in Australia and the United Nations Convention on the Rights of Persons with Disabilities. *Courts of Conscience, 10, 6*.

Gooding, P., Arstein-Kerslake, A., Andrews, L., & McSherry, B. (2017). Unfitness to stand trial and the indefinite detention of persons with cognitive disabilities in Australia: Human rights challenges and proposals for change. *Melbourne University Law Review, 40*(3), 816–866.

Hayden, C. (2010). Offending behaviour in care: Is children's residential care a "criminogenic" environment? *Child and Family Social Work, 15*(4), 461–472.

Her Majesty's Inspectorate of Probation. (2014). *A Joint Inspection of the Treatment of Offenders with Learning Disabilities Within the Criminal Justice System—Phase 1 from Arrest to Sentence*. London: Her Majesty's Inspectorate of Constabulary and Fire & Rescue Services [HMICFRS].

Herrera, L. M. (2007). Equity, equality and equivalence. *Revista Española de Educación Comparada, 13,* 319–340.

Hogg, R. (1983). Perspectives on the criminal justice system. In M. Findlay, S. Egger, & J. Sutton (Eds.), *Issues in Criminal Justice Administration* (pp. 3–19). Sydney: Allen and Unwin.

Howard League for Penal Reform. (2016). *Criminal Care: Children's Homes and Criminalising Children*. London: Howard League for Penal Reform.

Howard League for Penal Reform. (2017). *Prisons and Criminal Justice, Briefings and Submissions*. [Online]. Available http://howardleague.org/our-expertise/briefings-and-submissions/. Accessed February 5, 2018.

Indig, D., Gear, C., & Wilhelm, K. (2016). *Co-morbid Substance Abuse Disorders and Mental Health Disorders Among New Zealand Prisoners*. Wellington: New Zealand Department of Corrections.

Indig, D., Topp, L., Ross, B., Mamoon, H., Border, B., Kumar, S., et al. (2010). *2009 NSW Inmate Health Survey: Key Findings Report*. Sydney: Justice Health.

Indig, D., Vecchiato, C., Haysom, L., Beilby, R., Carter, J., Champion, U., et al. (2011). *2009 NSW Young People in Custody Health Survey: Full Report*. Sydney: Justice Health and Juvenile Justice.

Justice Health & Forensic Mental Health Network. (2016). *2015/2016 Year in Review*. Sydney: NSW Ministry of Health.

KPMG. (2007). *Evaluation of Multiple and Complex Needs Initiative* (Final Report). Melbourne: Government of Victoria, Department of Human Services.

Lacey, N. (2009). Historicising criminalisation: Conceptual and empirical issues. *Modern Law Review, 72*(6), 936–960.

Lamb, H. R., & Weinberger, L. E. (1998). Persons with severe mental illness in jails and prisons: A review. *Psychiatric Services, 49*(4), 483–492.

Lamb, H. R., & Weinberger, L. E. (2014). Decarceration of US jails and prisons: Where will persons with serious mental illness go? *Journal of the American Academy of Psychiatry and the Law, 42*(4), 489–494.

Langberg, J. B., & Fedders, B. A. (2013). How juvenile defenders can help dismantle the school-to-prison pipeline: A primer on educational advocacy and incorporating clients' education histories and records into delinquency representation. *Journal of Law and Education, 42*(4), 653–690.

McCausland, R., & Baldry, E. (2017). "I feel like I failed him by ringing the police": Criminalising disability in Australia. *Punishment & Society, 19*(3), 290–309.

McFarlane, K. (2010). From care to custody: Young women in out-of-home care in the criminal justice system. *Current Issues in Criminal Justice, 22*(2), 345–353.

McSherry, B. (2014). *Managing Fear: The Law and Ethics of Preventive Detention and Risk Assessment*. London: Routledge.

New South Wales Law Reform Commission. (2012). *People with Cognitive and Mental Health Impairments in the Criminal Justice System: Diversion* (Report 135). Sydney: New South Wales Law Reform Commission.

New South Wales Law Reform Commission. (2013). *People with Cognitive and Mental Health Impairments in the Criminal Justice System: Criminal Responsibility and Consequences* (Report 138). Sydney: New South Wales Law Reform Commission.

Norrie, A. (1996). The limits of justice: Finding fault in the criminal law. *Modern Law Review, 59*(4), 540–556.

Norrie, A. (2014). *Crime, Reason and History: A Critical Introduction to Criminal Law* (3rd ed.). Cambridge: Cambridge University Press.

Nowak, M. (2008). *Interim Report of the Special Rapporteur of the Human Rights Council on Torture and Other Cruel, Inhuman or Degrading Treatment or Punishment, Manfred Nowak*. A/63/175. New York: United Nations General Assembly.

Ollove, M. (2017, April 7). Getting the mentally ill out of jails. *Stateline*. [Online]. Available http://www.pewtrusts.org/en/research-and-analysis/blogs/stateline/2017/04/07/getting-the-mentally-ill-out-of-jails. Accessed February 5, 2018.

Prison Reform Trust. (2016). *No One Knows*. [Online]. Available http://www.prisonreformtrust.org.uk/ProjectsResearch/Learningdisabilities anddifficulties. Accessed February 5, 2018.

Revolving Doors Agency. (2016). *Criminal Justice and Policing*. [Online]. Available http://www.revolving-doors.org.uk/changing-policy/changing-policy. Accessed February 5, 2018.

Riches, V. C., Parmenter, T. R., Wiese, M., & Stancliffe, R. J. (2006). Intellectual disability and mental illness in the NSW criminal justice system. *International Journal of Law and Psychiatry, 29*, 386–396.

Robinson, N., & Branley, A. (2016, August 3). Northern Territory prison's treatment of intellectually disabled Aboriginal man referred to UN. *ABC News*. [Online]. Available http://www.abc.net.au/news/2016-08-03/unhrc-asked-to-probe-nt-man-restraint/7683346. Accessed February 5, 2018.

Royal Commission into New South Wales Prisons & Nagle, J. (1978). *Report of the Royal Commission into New South Wales Prisons*. Sydney: Government Printer.

Royal Commission into the Protection and Detention of Children in the Northern Territory, White, M., & Gooda, M. (2017). *Report of the Royal Commission and Board of Inquiry into the Protection and Detention of Children in the Northern Territory*. Darwin: Commonwealth Government. [Online]. Available https://childdetentionnt.royalcommission.gov.au/Pages/Report.aspx. Accessed February 5, 2018.

Senate Standing Committee on Community Affairs. (2015). *Report on Violence, Abuse and Neglect Against People with Disability in Institutional and Residential Settings, Including the Gender and Age Related Dimensions, and the Particular Situation of Aboriginal and Torres Strait Islander People with Disability, and Culturally and Linguistically Diverse People with Disability*. Canberra: Parliament of Australia.

Senate Standing Committee on Community Affairs. (2016). *Indefinite Detention of People with Cognitive and Psychiatric Impairment in Australia.* Canberra: Parliament of Australia.

Shakespeare, T. (1994). Cultural representation of disabled people: Dustbins for disavowal? *Disability and Society, 9*(3), 283–299.

Sotiri, M., McGee, P., & Baldry, E. for The National Justice Chief Executive Officers Working Group. (2012). *No End in Sight: The Imprisonment and Indefinite Detention of Indigenous People with a Cognitive Impairment.* Sydney: Aboriginal Disability Justice Campaign. [Online]. Available https://www.pwd.org.au/documents/pubs/adjc/NoEndinSight.pdf. Accessed February 5, 2018.

Stanley, E. (2016). From care to custody: Trajectories of children in post-war New Zealand. *Youth Justice, 17*(1), 57–72.

Steinberg, D., Mills, D., & Romano, M. (2015). *When Did Prisons Become Acceptable Mental Healthcare Facilities?* [Online]. Available https://law.stanford.edu/publications/when-did-prisons-become-acceptable-mental-healthcare-facilities-2/. Accessed February 5, 2018.

Teplin, L. A. (1984). Criminalizing mental disorder: The comparative arrest rate of the mentally ill. *American Psychologist, 39*(7), 794–803.

UN Committee on the Rights of Person with Disabilities [UNCRPD]. (Various). [Online]. Available http://tbinternet.ohchr.org/_layouts/treatybodyexternal/TBSearch.aspx?Lang=en&TreatyID=4&DocTypeID=27. Accessed February 5, 2018.

UN Committee on the Rights of Persons with Disabilities [UNCRPD]. (2006). *Convention on the Rights of Persons with Disabilities (CRPD).* A/RES/61/106. Adopted December 13, 2006.

UN Committee on the Rights of Person with Disabilities [UNCRPD]. (2013). *Concluding Observations on the Initial Report of Australia, Adopted by the Committee at Its Tenth Session (2–13 September 2013).* CRPD/C/AUS/CO/1. [Online]. Available http://undocs.org/CRPD/C/AUS/CO/1. Accessed February 5, 2018.

UN Committee on the Rights of Person with Disabilities [UNCRPD]. (2015). *Report of the Committee on the Rights of Persons with Disabilities, Supplement No. 55.* A/70/55. [Online]. Available http://undocs.org/A/70/55. Accessed February 5, 2018.

UN Committee on the Rights of Person with Disabilities [UNCRPD]. (2016). *Views Adopted by the Committee Under Article 5 of the Optional Protocol, Concerning Communication No. 7/2012.* CRPD/C/16/D/7/2012. [Online]. Available http://undocs.org/en/CRPD/C/16/D/7/2012. Accessed February 5, 2018.

Vanderpoll, T., & Howard, D. (2011). *Investigation into Hearing Impairment Among Indigenous Prisoners Within the Northern Territory Correctional Services*. Darwin: Northern Territory Correctional Services.

Victorian Law Reform Commission. (2013). *Review of the Crimes (Mental Impairment and Unfitness to Be Tried) Act 1997: Consultation Paper*. Melbourne: Victorian Law Reform Commission.

4

Challenging Māori Imprisonment and Human Rights Ritualism

Elizabeth Stanley and Riki Mihaere

Introduction

United Nations' (UN) reports have long shown concern over the high levels of Māori imprisonment in New Zealand (NZ). Recent data demonstrates that young and adult Māori are more likely to be apprehended by police, sentenced to remand, be held in youth justice residences, be imprisoned and re-imprisoned than all other populations in NZ (Department of Corrections 2007, 2017; JustSpeak 2014; New Zealand Police 2017). While Māori account for just over 15% of New Zealand's total population, over 55% of prisoners are Māori. The general rate of imprisonment is high, at 210 per 100,000 population. However, for Māori, this intensifies to 655 per 100,000 (Salvation Army 2017). Almost 60% of adult Māori prisoners are likely to be re-imprisoned within five years, and the Department of Corrections

E. Stanley (✉) · R. Mihaere
Institute of Criminology, Victoria University of Wellington,
Wellington, New Zealand
e-mail: elizabeth.stanley@vuw.ac.nz

© The Author(s) 2018
E. Stanley (ed.), *Human Rights and Incarceration*, Palgrave Studies
in Prisons and Penology, https://doi.org/10.1007/978-3-319-95399-1_4

has faced significant criticism for its lack of attention towards the prevention of re-offending by Māori. Developed in a context of neo-colonialism and advanced neo-liberalism, this chronic colonial penal capture has remained in place for over four decades.

Against this backdrop, it is important to identify the factors that sustain 'hyperincarceration' but also to advance processes that might challenge the prison as an institution of colonial rule. This chapter considers therefore the past and potential challenges to Māori imprisonment through engagement with United Nations' human rights laws and mechanisms. It charts how UN processes (involving UN treaty bodies, the NZ government and civil society representatives) have engaged with the concern of Māori imprisonment, and it reflects on the potential of international reporting mechanisms to advance decarceration.

The chapter is based on extensive primary research, involving three strands of work. First, a documentary analysis of reports, submissions and other process papers written by United Nations Committees, and subsequent responses from the NZ government as well as civil society. This analysis covers 211 reports, written between 2000 and 2015. Second, a corresponding stock-take of political commentary from Hansard and media reports, relating to UN human rights activity between 1997 and 2017. And, third, interviews (conducted from February to April 2017) with 12 senior Māori professionals (lawyers, academics and civil servants), all of whom have engaged with the UN over many years and/or have deep knowledge of Māori imprisonment.[1] To ensure confidentiality, interviewees are identified by the te reo Māori term Kaikōrero, or 'speaker'.

The chapter demonstrates that, in relation to Māori imprisonment, NZ has been reluctant to advance human rights in a way that moves beyond ritualism. Within international human rights reporting, NZ has sought to deflect scrutiny, accountability and progressive change, while affirming the country's reputation as a human rights conscious country. Despite this political management, the chapter shows that engagement with the UN is still useful and necessary for Māori. UN treaty bodies have the ability to place pressure upon governments and recommend change within structural or institutional processes. Further, Māori engagement with UN human rights bodies brings important outcomes to challenge myths, propel Indigenous understandings, and develop significant networks. Given this, Kaikōrero outline that further engagement with international human rights mechanisms is vital to counter increasing levels of Māori imprisonment. However, such bureaucratic activities must be dovetailed with other crucial aspects, including attempts to envision decolonising responses to 'crime' and social harms that move beyond the prison.

Māori Imprisonment

Chronic levels of Māori imprisonment are normalised in New Zealand. Notwithstanding the scale of the problem, there have been relatively few government reports on the issue (see Department of Corrections 2007; Morrison 2009). The Department of Corrections has tended to invisibilise Māori issues—from 2008 to early 2017, no Departmental briefings "made any mention of Māori or the need to reduce overrepresentation in prison" (Workman, cited in McLachlan 2017). There has not been a single Parliamentary debate on over-representation over the last twenty years.

In terms of formal politics, the topic of Māori imprisonment has emerged within broader debates about specific legislation or social issues. On rare occasions, politicians (notably from the Māori Party) have reflected concerns of colonisation, discrimination and hardship. Yet, dominant debate has emphasised perceptions on the individual or collective failings of Māori (Jackson 1988). For example, Ron Mark (NZ First Party) expressed:

> … the reason Māori are in jail is that they break the law. As Māori, we have to accept that we have a culture of violence that starts in the family … Māori themselves need to accept their responsibility for their culture of violence. (Hansard 23 November 2005: 445)

Similarly, Chris Tremain (National Party) stated that over-representation was the result of Māori who treat gang members "as though they are … part of our community … Māori need to break free from the shackles of gang thuggery, to disown gangs, and to stop making excuses for them" (Hansard 12 February 2009: 1238). His colleague, Hon Judith Collins, Minister of Police and Corrections for many years, regarded over-representation as the result of "crime becoming a way of life" for Māori, something that was developed "from the time that an offender is born or probably even before the offender is born" (Hansard 27 July 2010: 12,731–12,733). These politicians saw penal capture as the inevitable result of pathological and socio-cultural deficits among Māori. Even the late Parekura Horomia, the Labour Minister of Māori Affairs, saw that social problems for Māori reflected a negative "woe is me" agenda, with Māori refusing to take responsibility for their own failings (Hansard 14 March 2006: 1707).[2]

Indigenous and critical academic research has offered a rather different interpretation. It has connected Māori imprisonment to a series of historical and contemporary practices that have entrenched disadvantage, discrimination, violence and social harms towards Māori. This has included:

- The British control and imprisonment of Māori who rebelled against coercive land acquisitions, the development of colonial laws, and other discriminatory incursions (Bull 2001; Quince 2007; Walker 1990);
- Overt racism, bias and discriminatory practices embedded within social, educational, welfare, policing and justice institutions (Andrae et al. 2017; Cunneen and Tauri 2016; Jackson 1988; McIntosh 2011; Mihaere 2015; Quince 2007; Tauri and Webb 2012);
- The mass removal of Māori children from whānau into state 'care', especially from the 1960s, and the impacts of subsequent physical, sexual and psychological abuse on those children (Stanley 2016);
- Structurally-embedded disadvantage within NZ society such that Māori have continually been at the forefront of increasingly negative statistics on inequalities, poverty, unemployment, wages, home ownership, retirement income, and so on (Mihaere 2015).

It seems obvious to state that Māori have not yet felt the full benefits of multiple international human rights laws, including the *International Bill of Human Rights*.

Ritualism and Human Rights

Beyond generic international human rights standards, two specific UN instruments are useful to consider. First, the *Convention on the Elimination of All Forms of Racial Discrimination* [CERD] (1965). Under this Convention, state parties must "condemn racial discrimination" and pursue policies to eliminate "racial discrimination in all its forms" (Article 2(1)). They "shall take effective measures to review governmental, national and local policies, and to amend, rescind or nullify any laws and regulations which have the effect of creating or perpetuating racial discrimination wherever it exists" (Article 2(1)(c)). Further, they must "guarantee the right of everyone, without distinction as to race, colour, or national or ethnic origin, to equality before the law" (Article 5). Second, the *Declaration on the Rights of Indigenous Peoples* (2007: 4) establishes 46 articles, "to be pursued in a spirit of partnership and mutual respect". Among others, the Declaration includes the rights of Indigenous people: to "be free from any kind of discrimination" (Article 2); to "self-determination" (Article 3); "to maintain and strengthen their distinct political, legal, economic, social and cultural institutions" (Article 5); "to participate in decision-making in matters which would affect their rights" (Article 18); and, to give "their free, prior and informed consent before adopting and implementing legislative or administrative measures that may affect them" (Article 19). This Declaration also asserts that Indigenous people have rights to "the improvement of their economic and social conditions" (Article 21) and to "the highest attainable standard of physical and mental health" (Article 24). These instruments establish rights that, if implemented, would fundamentally change the prospects for Indigenous peoples.

Internationally, New Zealand holds a positive status for Indigenous rights. In 1971, the NZ government introduced the *Race Relations Act*, to give force to elements of the UN's CERD. In 1975, the government also took significant action to address 'historical' grievances by establishing the Waitangi Tribunal. Many claims to the Tribunal have since been settled, Māori have received apologies from the Crown, and a body of historical research that illustrates colonial atrocities has developed. At the same time, Māori have continued to make advances to the ongoing survival of Māori culture (Walker 1990), and have actively engaged with Indigenous rights by publicly criticising the NZ government in human rights terms, engaging the language of self-determination, and developing extensive links with other Indigenous peoples (Iorns Magallanes 1999).

Notwithstanding these developments, the NZ state has engaged a "selective endorsement" of Indigenous rights (Lightfoot 2012). For example, alongside other (neo)colonial states of Australia, Canada and the United States, New Zealand initially refused to sign the *Declaration on the Rights of Indigenous Peoples* in 2007. Following an international campaign of shaming and criticism, the government relented. The final endorsement was cautious: the government focused on the "aspirational" nature of the Declaration and viewed all provisions as being solely consistent with current Treaty of Waitangi provisions and other domestic laws—no further implementation was necessary (Lightfoot 2012; Toki 2011). While "offering relief from transnational and domestic political pressure", this response allowed New Zealand to celebrate "the normative value of and their commitment to Indigenous rights" while taking no further actions (Lightfoot 2012: 119; Toki 2011).

Such an approach reflects a "pervasive" human rights ritualism (Charlesworth and Larking 2015: 10; Adcock 2012). While New Zealand goes through the motions of reporting to the UN, and receiving reports, it also goes to some lengths to "deflect real human rights scrutiny and to avoid accountability" for the lack of human rights protections towards Māori (Charlesworth 2010: 11). Part of the reason for ritualism is that the UN reporting system is deeply technocratic with formalised processes that are "highly orchestrated", following repetitive scripts from one year or treaty body to the next (Cowan 2015: 51–52). States can hide behind mechanical reports and, while they may "agree to the language and techniques of regulation", they also rely on the inability of regulators to monitor or follow-up plans and policies (Charlesworth and Larking 2015: 11). Thus, state engagement with human rights language and processes can bring reputational benefits and sustain dominant power relations, while deflecting increased scrutiny (Charlesworth and Larking 2015). This is evident in NZ's responses to UN concerns about Māori imprisonment.

The State-Managed Performance
of UN Reporting

From the turn of the century, UN human rights reports have made consistent mention of Māori over-representation across carceral sites. In 2006, a UN Special Rapporteur, Rodolfo Stavenhagen (2006: para. 57), expressed that "this pattern [of over-representation] arguably represents the underlying institutional and structural discrimination that Māori have long suffered". Five years later, another Special Rapporteur, James Anaya (2011: para. 62), noted that "regrettably, there has been little change in the incarceration rate of Māori since the previous Special Rapporteur's visit". In 2016, the UN Human Rights Committee outlined continued concerns about "the disproportionately high rates of incarceration and overrepresentation of Māori and Pasifika, particularly women and young people, at all levels of the criminal justice process" (para. 25). Similar concerns have been raised by many other UN Committees.

In response, the NZ government has employed a language of action. While the issue of over-representation is "a significant challenge" (UNCERD 2012: para. 98) and "an ongoing concern for the Government" (UNCERD 2016: para. 145), NZ will take action. It has "approved a range of other research and practical initiatives" (UNCERD 2007a: para. 87), has "set ambitious targets" and is "committed to addressing disparities" (UNCERD 2013: para. 9).

The government also promotes the language of commitment to rights, and heralds its achievements along this path. In "the task of reducing inequalities … good progress has been made" (UNCERD 2007b: 2). "New Zealand is strongly committed to the protection and promotion of international human rights" and "every effort is made to ensure that all services reach vulnerable Māori and Pasifika families" (UNHRC 2015: paras. 7 and 108). NZ takes pride that "significant progress has been made to improve the responsiveness of the criminal justice system to Māori and Pacific peoples" (UNCERD 2016: para. 145). In turn, UN Committees tend to produce encouraging noises. They are "encouraged to learn that the Government is taking targeted action to address this distressing situation" (Anaya 2011: para. 63) and they "note the efforts made" by NZ "to address the issue of the overrepresentation of Māori and Pasifika in the criminal justice system" (UNHRC 2016: para. 25).

This symbiotic performance emerges over multiple reporting cycles. For example, in 2009, the Committee against Torture asked for a response into "persons deprived of their liberty, notably women, indigenous peoples" (UNCAT 2009a: para. 22). The Government's reply described how "the Department of Corrections has developed a separate Māori Strategic Plan a primary focus of which is to reduce Maori offending" (UNCAT 2009b: para. 101). The Committee described "taking note of the Maori Strategic Plan … as well as the various initiatives undertaken by the Ministry of Justice to reduce Maori offending" but continued to be "alarmed at the disproportionately high number of Maoris and Pacific Islands [sic] people incarcerated, in particular women" (UNCAT 2009c: para. 5). During the next reporting cycle, the UN expectantly asked for an "update on the implementation of the Maori Strategic Plan developed by the Department of Corrections" (UNCAT 2012: para. 18). Rather than stating that the Plan had failed (like its predecessors), the Government illustrated the ever-changing nature of policy in the area. They reported new strategies "to reduce Māori offending, reoffending and victimisation"—"The Turning of the Tide" and "Creating Lasting Change 2011-2015", that would replace "all previous strategic documents, including its Māori Strategic Plan 2008-2013" (UNCAT 2014: para. 141, para. 147). While demonstrating concern on how "indigenous people continue to be disproportionately affected by incarceration", the UN declared satisfaction with the "efforts and subsequent measures taken by the State party to address the situation of indigenous people" (UNCAT 2015: para. 14). Despite some effort by UN Committees to query over-representation, this bureaucratised monitoring offers limitless scope for states to focus on policies and strategies, and to reiterate individualised problems rather than reflect on outcomes for Māori.

Clearly, the NZ state works to secure legitimacy through the strategic management of UN reporting processes. A key approach is to emphasise short-term targets, policies or strategies but, as noted above, NZ also seeks to divert responsibility for human rights problems. For instance, in reporting to the Committee on the Elimination of Racial Discrimination, New Zealand asserted that mass Māori imprisonment was the result of "the relative youth of the Maori population … risk factors associated with anti-social and criminal behaviour, including … poor achievement at school … low income, poor skills … and living in a neighbourhood that is poor, disorganised and overcrowded, with high rates of crime" (UNCERD 2006: para. 158). Following the lead of senior politicians, then, the government attributed Māori over-representation to Māori age, socio-psychological deficit and community dysfunction. The concerns of bias, or the multi-generational and systemic impacts of colonisation, were strategically ignored. The Committee politely reiterated concerns regarding racial basis, and recommended that NZ should "enhance its efforts to address this problem … as a matter of high priority" (UNCERD 2007c: para. 454).

In sum, with regards to the concern of carceral over-representation, NZ relies on the ritualism of "ceremonial moves" within UN reporting (Adcock 2012: 118). There is a symmetry in the language between NZ and UN agencies—concerns, challenges and commitments are mirrored within and across each reporting cycle. With limited institutional memory, each set of Committee reports tend to be regarded within the context of that period—accountability for the poor performance of states in relation to previously exposed concerns is rare. Given the emphasis on policies and strategies, all parties are also able to downplay the reality of outcomes. Thus, while reports reiterate concerns across decades they simultaneously provide an opportunity for NZ and the UN to legitimise continued state action and administrative achievements. When UN Committees have pointedly engaged with the state's role in Māori imprisonment levels, the NZ response has illustrated deflection, away from neo-colonising institutional practices and towards individual or community failings. All of these issues reflect an international human rights ritualism that is inherently state-serving and state-legitimising.

Māori Perspectives on Rights Ritualism

Human rights ritualism is well understood by Māori working in the fields of human rights, imprisonment and justice. Within interviews, Kaikōrero highlighted three issues that sustained this ritualism: bureaucratic limitations; illusionary consultation; and, the state management of criticism.

First, all Kaikōrero saw deep limitations with the administrative approach offered through UN reporting processes. In line with previous data, they identified that NZ used international human rights engagements as an opportunity to market New Zealand as a rights conscious country:

> Very rarely will you see New Zealand actually front up and admit that it has done this or that to Indigenous peoples, in the international sphere. It's all peas and gravy and unicorns and rainbows, like "Come, smiley people, they let us speak our language"! They roll that out but then … they tend to … fudge actually what's happening. (Kaikōrero 8)

Kaikōrero were attuned to the government strategy of focusing on policy and strategy, while downplaying outcomes or realities on the ground. One outlined:

> [We] are witnessing this tick-boxing formulaic commitment to ideas and norms but with the kind of complete lack of true commitment to the substance of those norms. So … [our] state might … make this grand public statement, you know that "We've signed up to this … these are the standards la la la", but it would make no commitment to actually give life to the standards that are in that instrument. (Kaikōrero 5)

Several Kaikōrero also identified that international human rights processes re-legitimised state authority, during a period in which the mass imprisonment of Māori has consolidated neo-colonial relations of power. Part of the problem, here, is that the UN human rights framework unconditionally accepts prisons and never seriously questions their use.

Second, Kaikōrero acknowledged a problem in the NZ state consultation with Māori. As Treaty partners, Māori should take a partnership role within UN reporting processes. In practice, Kaikōrero reflected that Māori tended to be either sidelined completely or strategically chosen. For example, in discussing the introduction of the UN Declaration, one Kaikōrero lamented:

> MFAT [Ministry of Foreign Affairs and Trade] didn't have proper lines of … consultation … Māori needed to be involved in it in a substantive way. And, given that the Declaration was about Indigenous rights, certainly Māori weren't involved enough in a formal way. And it was so antagonistic with the MFAT people … they didn't support the right of Indigenous peoples' self-determination! (Kaikōrero 1)

Kaikōrero discussed how, in relation to other treaty body reporting, both MFAT and the Ministry of Justice (central authorities in NZ reports to the UN) had focused 'consultation' towards Māori who either directly worked for them or were funded by them to provide services. Consulted Māori were not independent as they relied on state money. Such an approach was seen as a violation of the "Treaty relationship between the state and Māori" as the state has "an obligation to actually engage widely with Māori on issues that pertain to them directly" (Kaikōrero 2).

Third, Kaikōrero identified that the state pre-empted and silenced criticisms of human rights violations. This emerged through false assertions, threats, as well as limited supports for Māori. For example, Kaikōrero viewed that, within UN reporting, the NZ government represented programmes (such as 'Māori Focus Units' within NZ prisons) as promoting Indigenous rights when these reflect Pākehā initiatives (Mihaere 2015):

> [The Units involve] taking the core psycho criminogenic concepts … and Māori-fying them … I mean that is an attempt at window dressing, adding a bit of Māori on … That's not respectful of the Māori voice or experience or anything like that. (Kaikōrero 2)

Without independent Māori input, UN Committee members would not be well positioned to question such programmes. Given that civil society groups receive limited financial assistance or supports to participate in UN activities, there is an inevitable dominance of the state's perspective. Kaikōrero were also attentive to the capacity of state departments to threaten or enact funding cuts of domestic critics. In short, Māori professionals thought that NZ ensured ritualism by removing the ability of Māori to have a say about human rights protections. This has occurred as a result of insufficient resources for Māori to participate, the stringent state control of consultation processes, as well as the weaknesses of a technocratic human rights framework.

Political Representations of UN Interventions

Alongside this careful management of state-UN interactions, NZ politicians rarely allow UN comments or reports to gain traction within public debates. The NZ Parliament has no duty or impetus to discuss reports emerging from the UN. For example, in the wake of the critical report by UN Special Rapporteur Rodolfo Stavenhagen (2006), the Māori Party sought a debate. The Speaker of the House denied the request, on the basis that she was not convinced that the report "is a matter for which there is ministerial responsibility, even though the subject matter … clearly relates to matters of obvious interest to the Government" (Hansard 4 April 2006: 2414). Any mention of UN reporting (like the issue of over-representation) tends to emerge, therefore, as part of wider political debates. Further, when this commentary does occur it tends to diminish UN activities.

One common refrain from NZ politicians is that the UN should just leave New Zealand alone. For example, in a reading for the legislation which allowed NZ to implement the *Optional Protocol* to the Torture Convention, Ron Mark (NZ First) argued that "We do not need to hold ourselves ultimately accountable to some little tinpot committee inside the United Nations … It is all "touchy-feely", feel-good nonsense … The point is that we are not the problem" (Hansard 28 March 2006: 2177). Similarly, Tim Groser (National) recorded that the

UN Subcommittee on Torture would "be wasting its time" in visiting NZ, reasoning "I do not quite know what it is that they will be investigating. Somebody in a prison might have been given a cold hamburger, which some civil liberties lawyer has thought, perhaps, to be inhuman treatment" (Hansard 21 November 2006: 6680).

The implementation of the UN Declaration on the Rights of Indigenous People uncovered similar responses. For example, Rodney Hide (then ACT Party leader) regarded the UN Declaration as being "divisive". He continued that it "sets us up to enable foreigners from the UN to come to New Zealand to pontificate and to criticise New Zealand's race relations, policies, laws, and processes" (Hansard 20 April 2010: 10,227). Warming to the theme, Hon Jim Anderton (then Progressive Party leader) asserted that "We need no lessons whatever" on "how to treat indigenous peoples" (Hansard 20 April 2010: 10,227).

A second approach from NZ politicians is to diminish the UN's capabilities and to condemn critical reports. In response to the report by Special Rapporteur Rodolfo Stavenhagen, Ministers—including the Deputy Prime Minister—took various strategies. They argued that the Special Rapporteur was "captured by those entrenched in a grievance mentality" (Hansard [Winston Peters] 5 April 2006: 2536–2538) and influenced by "academic radicals at Auckland University" (Hansard [Michael Cullen] 5 April 2006: 2485–2487).[3] They declared the report to be "disappointing, unbalanced, and narrow" (Hansard [Michael Cullen] 5 April 2006: 2485–2487) and containing "spectacular idiocies" (Hansard [Tim Groser] 7 November 2006: 6275–6276).[4]

Similar disparaging words have been directed to the UN Committee on the Elimination of Racial Discrimination [UNCERD]. In response to a critical report in 2005 (in which the Committee recorded that the Foreshore and Seabed Act was discriminatory to Māori), then Prime Minister Helen Clark argued the report was from a "committee that sits on the outer edge of the UN", and that had followed "a most unsatisfactory process" (*NZ Herald* 2005). A couple of years later, a further UNCERD report was declared, by then Minister of Foreign Affairs, Winston Peters, to be "meddlesome", written by individuals with no expertise (cited by Te Ururoa Flavell, Hansard 22 August 2007: 11,357).

A final stance from politicians is to announce that the UN will have no impact on the nation's activities. This approach became very clear when NZ belatedly signed the UN Declaration. Then Prime Minister John Key consoled his distraught peers, who worried that Māori would take "control of the entire country" with the words that the Declaration "will have no impact on New Zealand law and no impact on the constitutional framework" (Hansard 20 April 2010: 10,229–10,237). Such displays have also been demonstrated by the Labour Party. Following the Stavenhagen report, the Labour government clarified that while they would "listen carefully to any recommendations", changes to law and policy would occur only "If the recommendations are consistent with Government policy … If they are not it is most unlikely" that the government would act (Hansard [Michael Cullen] 15 November 2005: 96–98). Māori Party politicians reflected that the government's admission that "nothing much will happen" was "now on public record" (Hansard [Tariana Turia] 5 April 2006: 2497).

Responses from NZ politicians have largely served to undermine international human rights engagements. UN Committees have been represented as partial and incapable. UN norms towards Indigenous people will have, as detailed above, no impact on a state that is depicted as having no human rights problems. Within the context of these debates on rights for Indigenous or incarcerated people, as well as the ritualism demonstrated through practical UN reporting on these issues, what hope might there be to engage human rights for Māori in NZ?

The Benefits of UN Engagement

Given the weaknesses of reporting processes and the state reluctance to positively engage with human rights, Māori have historically been wary about UN engagement. In 2007, Ani Mikaere (2007: 53) reflected that the international human rights framework tended to marginalise Indigenous populations and their values. And, even when culturally relativist practices are advanced, they often emphasise Western concepts as "the norm" while providing "allowances" for Indigenous cultures. For Māori, as Jackson (2007: 62) noted, "any discussion of human rights has seen our tikanga, which gives expression to the fullness of our humanity, redefined, squashed, or squeezed".

However, during interviews, all Kaikōrero saw value in drawing upon international human rights laws, norms and bodies to secure progressive outcomes for Māori. The state is not monolithic and they identified national bodies that also have capacity to advance rights protections (the Waitangi Tribunal being one example). Further, they thought that UN engagement brought several positive impacts that could not be underestimated.

UN criticisms are symbolically important. They embarrass the NZ government, provide moral leverage for rights campaigners and create opportunities for continued domestic and international pressure. One Kaikōrero commented that the recording of rights breaches has "value" in building an international record that "will at some stage come back to bite them [the government]" (Kaikōrero 3). Moreover, the involvement of Māori and others, in UN processes—providing independent written evidence and participating in Committee meetings—is significant in contesting the myths of state achievements. One Kaikōrero remembered how the weight of submissions started to change perspectives at the UN:

> ... it started to dawn on members of other states that actually things were not quite as rosy ... and that perception issue is something that [senior civil servants] do take very seriously. Any kind of potential damage to the image of New Zealand Incorporated! (Kaikōrero 1)

In building a stronger presence within UN meetings and reporting mechanisms, Māori can challenge ritualism. Engagements ensure that the issues that directly affect Māori are acknowledged and further prioritised (Charters 2010). They are also useful to Māori in consolidating local and international Indigenous networks. It allows campaigners, who are often "working in hard spaces", the opportunity to "hear positive stories of change" and to have inspiring conversations with other Indigenous activists from around the world (Kaikōrero 5). Such repeated engagements are vital to contesting and influencing state activities (Cowan 2015).

Despite these opportunities, Kaikōrero thought that Māori had not yet begun to fully use UN laws and processes to change the landscape of Māori imprisonment. They identified numerous levers to facilitate progressive human rights shifts in these areas, some at the domestic level[5] but most within the international arena. One key focus was that Māori should increasingly participate with the UN human rights system and affirm Indigenous rights wherever possible. Kaikōrero discussed the importance of articulating the Treaty as an international human rights instrument. However, most stressed the value of the Declaration on the Rights of Indigenous Peoples:

> A declaration will only gather the force of customary international law if people use it ... So in relation to Corrections ... if our people want to argue about ... a particular issue or policy, then I think we should begin not just with the Treaty but with the UN Declaration. And the second thing I tell our people is to start talking about the Treaty as a human rights instrument. (Kaikōrero 3)

The Declaration offers opportunities to advance not just human rights, but also Indigenous peoples' entitlements to "their inherent sovereign status" (Erueti 2017: 25). Alongside rights entitlements, it is powerfully imbued with principles of self-determination and decolonisation. Currently, "there is a significant political disjuncture between the [Declaration] rights ... and the operation of criminal justice systems" (Cunneen and Tauri 2016: 155). However, the Declaration has significant potential to challenge the structural, institutional and socio-cultural conditions that lead to prison. Engagement requires clear strategies, and Kaikōrero identified several levels of necessary action. First, Māori must further develop and sustain formal support mechanisms for those who work with the UN. In recent years, the 'Aotearoa Indigenous Rights Trust' and the Law Foundation has been able to support Māori who engage with international rights reporting. This has been important to the development of more effective interventions, by building confidence and sharing knowledge between actors on what works to advance change. Second, Māori should actively provide more informal supports, to ensure that those taking rights-based actions are helped and nourished. This is vital to avoid burn out for those on 'the front line' of rights work. Third, Māori must create an ongoing loop of feedback, between those working within international human rights organisations or government bodies and those working within Māori communities, such as those working with whānau or support organisations or prisoners. This feedback is vital to ensure that rights are continually questioned and positioned as valuable tools for all Māori, and to ensure that Māori do not become incorporated into state-focused agendas. And, fourth, Māori should demand resources, from national and international bodies, so that Māori can operate as 'peers' within the UN process.

These strategies for action reflected a common, broader concern for Kaikōrero: that rights cannot be attained for Māori without full partnership, as established under the Treaty. One Kaikōrero remarked:

> I think it's about looking at this word partnership and actually interrogating what that means. And, it not being just Māori can provide advice or we will consult with Māori, but actually who's making the decisions at the end of the day. And, are Māori just writing a paper and Pākehā having a look at it and making the decision, or is that decision being made by Māori and Pākehā? (Kaikōrero 10)

This focus on partnership raised many questions, such as: What would full consultation and partnership on criminal justice decision-making actually look like? How might things be different if Māori (whānau, hapū, and iwi) took a central role in legal changes, or in the design and implementation of responses to offenders? What impact would Māori culture and knowledge have on how we respond to violence or harms? And, how might true engagement with Māori impact upon the nature of NZ's human rights reporting to the UN? Several Kaikōrero imagined that criminal justice responses would irrevocably change if international human rights laws and norms were fully realised.

Conclusion: Beyond the Prison

The UN human rights bureaucracy can never provide the kinds of economic, political, social and cultural shifts that are necessary to undermine the high levels of Māori imprisonment and the institutional
processes that sustain them. International human rights instruments are
just one necessary part of the broader picture. Kaikōrero acknowledged,
therefore, the need to devote energies to subverting ritualism, by imag-
ining and propelling new worlds of Indigenous justice, and nourishing
Māori communities:

> It's really important that we keep trying to hold the government account-
> able and we keep writing reports about how what they're saying isn't actu-
> ally what the reality is, but where the real change and where the real hope
> is fostered is actually at the very local level … [besides] whoever can give
> you your rights can also take them away and so the best place then to get
> them is from ourselves in what we're doing. (Kaikōrero 10)

While most Māori have not spent time in prison, a life beyond prisons
needed to be both imagined and enacted in all communities. Among
other things, this requires significant shifts in how we speak about
harms, justice, or punishment:

> At the moment incarceration is virtually the only thing we think of as a
> punishment form … It is *the* form … Such is our reliance on that con-
> ceptually and actually is that we can't imagine a world without prison
> … So what would you need to have to not imagine a prison as a central
> institutional society? What would it mean at the education level, what
> would it mean in terms of the stories we tell our children? (Kaikōrero 4)

For many Kaikōrero, the knee-jerk reliance on imprisonment has to
be unpicked from every level of society—within UN agencies, government bodies, political parties, media, courts, schools and universi-
ties, churches, around the family table, everywhere. Within a "colonial
carceral landscape", a challenge to the normalisation of prison must
dovetail with national and international struggles for self-determination

and social justice (Baldry et al. 2015: 183). For Kaikōrero, such strategies would involve centralising the Treaty, embedding Mātauranga Māori perspectives into government law and policy, and giving life to the UN Declaration. Unsettling this carceral state requires the development of social, economic and cultural justice in ways that prioritise Indigenous rights.

Notes

1. The authors would like to thank all interviewees for their valuable kōrero, and to Sally Day for her research on political commentaries. We also acknowledge the Royal Society's Rutherford Discovery Fellowship that has enabled this research.

2. Following a critical US State Department Special Report in March 2006, that recorded social problems for Māori, Labour Party Minister Mita Ririnui saw that such criticisms were part of a "negative agenda", and that over-representation reflected a "woe is me" agenda by Māori. Minister Horomia confirmed these sentiments in response to questions by Te Ururoa Flavell.

3. The Special Rapporteur had met with politicians, senior officials from twelve government departments, the Human Rights Commission, the Waitangi Tribunal, the Māori Land Court, and leaders of several iwi in NZ.

4. Then Co-leader of the Māori Party, Pita Sharples, reflected on the "woeful compliance with international conventions" in NZ and his Party's "great disillusionment with a Government that discredits the United Nations" (Hansard 21 November 2006: 6682–6687).

5. Domestic options included: (i) diverting Māori from the criminal justice/welfare systems, especially for those under 18; (ii) ensuring implementation of recommendations from previous reports—for example, on child poverty—to address inequalities and disadvantage; (iii) implementing an inquiry and subsequent action plan to address laws, policies and practices that exacerbate over-representation (including seemingly neutral laws/policies); (iv) developing specialist Māori courts for adults (similar to Rangatahi Courts for young people), located on marae and focused on the prevention of criminal offending through the restoration of mana (a strength-based approach).

They would draw upon the strength of Māori kaupapa, and a collective commitment to justice; (v) further consideration of how the use of tikanga Māori (in which whānau or hapū or iwi are tasked with rectifying the imbalance from criminal acts) could develop.

References

Adcock, F. (2012). The UN Special Rapporteur on the rights of indigenous peoples and New Zealand: A study in compliance ritualism. *New Zealand Yearbook of International Law, 10,* 97–120.

Anaya, J. (2011). *Report of the Special Rapporteur on the Situation of Rights of Indigenous Peoples, James Anaya. Addendum: The Situation of Maori in New Zealand.* A/HRC/18/35/Add.4. Geneva: UNHRC.

Andrae, D., McIntosh, T., & Coster, S. (2017). Marginalised: An insider's view of the state, state policies in New Zealand and gang formation. *Critical Criminology, 25*(1), 119–135.

Baldry, E., McCausland, R., Dowse, L., & McEntyre, E. (2015). *A Predictable and Preventable Path: Aboriginal People with Mental and Cognitive Disabilities in the Criminal Justice System.* Sydney: UNSW.

Bull, S. (2001). The land of murder, cannibalism, and all kinds of atrocious crimes? An overview of 'Māori crime' from pre-colonial times to the present day. Unpublished Ph.D. thesis. Victoria University of Wellington, Wellington.

Charlesworth, H. (2010). Swimming to Cambodia: Justice and ritual in human rights after conflict. *Australian Year Book of International Law, 29,* 1–16.

Charlesworth, H., & Larking, E. (2015). Introduction: The regulatory power of the universal periodic review. In H. Charlesworth & E. Larking (Eds.), *Human Rights and the Universal Periodic Review* (pp. 1–21). Cambridge: Cambridge University Press.

Charters, C. (2010). A self-determination approach to justifying indigenous peoples' participation in international law and policy-making. *International Journal on Minority and Group Rights, 17,* 215–240.

Cowan, J. (2015). The universal periodic review as a public audit ritual. In H. Charlesworth & E. Larking (Eds.), *Human Rights and the Universal Periodic Review* (pp. 42–61). Cambridge: Cambridge University Press.

Cunneen, C., & Tauri, J. (2016). *Indigenous Criminology.* Bristol: Policy Press.

Department of Corrections. (2007). *Over-Representation of Māori in the Criminal Justice System*. Wellington: Department of Corrections.

Department of Corrections. (2017). *Prison Facts and Statistics—December 2016*. Wellington: Department of Corrections.

Erueti, A. (2017). The sovereignty of human rights symposium: The politics of international indigenous rights. *University of Toronto Law Journal*. [Online]. https://doi.org/10.3138/UTLJ.67.5. Accessed February 8, 2018.

Iorns Magallanes, C. (1999). International human rights and their impact on domestic law on indigenous peoples' rights in Australia, Canada, and New Zealand. In P. Havemann (Ed.), *Indigenous Peoples' Rights in Australia, Canada, and New Zealand* (pp. 235–277). Auckland: Oxford University Press.

Jackson, M. (1988). *The Māori and the Criminal Justice System: He Whaipaanga Hou—A New Perspective*. Wellington: New Zealand Department of Justice Policy and Research Division.

Jackson, M. (2007). The journey from a Spanish monastery to Whitianga. *Yearbook of New Zealand Jurisprudence, 10*, 59–64.

JustSpeak. (2014). *Unlocking Prisons: How We Can Improve New Zealand's Prison System*. Wellington: JustSpeak.

Lightfoot, S. (2012). Selective endorsement without intent to implement: Indigenous rights and the anglosphere. *The International Journal of Human Rights, 16*(1), 100–122.

McIntosh, T. (2011). Marginalisation: A case study: Confinement. In T. McIntosh & M. Mullholland (Eds.), *Māori and Social Issues* (pp. 263–283). Wellington: Huia Press.

McLachlan, L. (2017, April 11). Waitangi Tribunal finds corrections failing Māori on reoffending rates. *Radio New Zealand*. [Online]. Available http://www.radionz.co.nz/news/national/328603/corrections-'open-to-any-ideas'-over-Māori-reoffending. Accessed February 8, 2018.

Mihaere, R. (2015). A kaupapa Māori analysis of the use of Māori cultural identity in the prison system. Unpublished Ph.D. thesis. Victoria University of Wellington, Wellington.

Mikaere, A. (2007). Seeing human rights through Māori eyes. *Yearbook of New Zealand Jurisprudence, 10*, 53–58.

Morrison, B. (2009). *Identifying and Responding to Bias in the Criminal Justice System*. Wellington: Ministry of Justice.

New Zealand Police. (2017). *Recorded Crime Victims and Offenders Statistics (RCVS and RCOS)*. Wellington: New Zealand Police.

NZ Herald. (2005, March 14). Prime Minister critical of UN committee's process. *NZ Herald.* [Online]. Available http://www.nzherald.co.nz/nz/news/article.cfm?c_id=1&objectid=10115177. Accessed February 8, 2018.

Quince, K. (2007). Māori and the criminal justice system in New Zealand. In J. Tolmie & W. Brooksbanks (Eds.), *The New Zealand Criminal Justice System* (pp. 333–358). Auckland: Lexis Nexis.

Salvation Army. (2017). *Off the Track: State of the Nation Report.* Auckland: Salvation Army Social Policy and Parliamentary Unit.

Stanley, E. (2016). *The Road to Hell: State Violence Against Children in Postwar New Zealand.* Auckland: Auckland University Press.

Stavenhagen, R. (2006). *Report of the Special Rapporteur on the Situation of Human Rights and Fundamental Freedoms of Indigenous People, Rodolfo Stavenhagen. Addendum: Mission to New Zealand.* E/CN.4/2006/78/Add.3. Geneva: UNHRC.

Tauri, J., & Webb, R. (2012). A critical appraisal of responses to Māori offending. *The International Indigenous Policy Journal, 3*(4), 1–16.

Toki, V. (2011). Indigenous rights—Hollow rights? *Waikato Law Review, 19*(2), 29–43.

UN Committee Against Torture [UNCAT]. (2009a). *Convention Against Torture and Other Cruel, Inhuman or Degrading Treatment or Punishment: List of Issues to be Considered During the Examination of the Fifth Periodic Report of New Zealand.* CAT/C/NZL/Q/5. [Online]. Available http://undocs.org/CAT/C/NZL/Q/5. Accessed March 2, 2018.

UN Committee Against Torture [UNCAT]. (2009b). *Convention Against Torture and Other Cruel, Inhuman or Degrading Treatment or Punishment: Written Replies by New Zealand to the List of Issues (CAT/C/NZL/Q/5) to Be Taken Up in Connection with the Consideration of the Fifth Periodic Report of New Zealand.* CAT/C/NZL/Q/5/Add.1. [Online]. Available http://undocs.org/CAT/C/NZL/Q/5/Add.1. Accessed March 2, 2018.

UN Committee Against Torture [UNCAT]. (2009c). *Consideration of Reports Submitted by States Parties Under Article 19 of the Convention, Concluding Observations of the Committee Against Torture, New Zealand.* CAT/C/NZL/CO/5. [Online]. Available http://undocs.org/CAT/C/NZL/CO/5. Accessed March 2, 2018.

UN Committee Against Torture [UNCAT]. (2012). *List of Issues Prepared by the Committee Prior to the Submission of the Sixth Periodic Report of New Zealand (CAT/C/NZL/6)* Adopted by the Committee at Its Forty-Eighth*

Session. CAT/C/NZL/Q/6. [Online]. Available http://undocs.org/CAT/C/NZL/Q/6. Accessed March 2, 2018.

UN Committee Against Torture [UNCAT]. (2014). *Consideration of Reports Submitted by States Parties Under Article 19 of the Convention Pursuant to the Optional Reporting Procedure, New Zealand.* CAT/C/NZL/6. [Online]. Available http://undocs.org/CAT/C/NZL/6. Accessed March 2, 2018.

UN Committee Against Torture [UNCAT]. (2015). *Concluding Observations on the Sixth Periodic Report of New Zealand.* CAT/C/NZL/CO/6. [Online]. Available http://undocs.org/CAT/C/NZL/CO/6. Accessed March 2, 2018.

UN Committee on the Elimination of Racial Discrimination [UNCERD]. (2006). *Reports Submitted by State Parties Under Article 9 of the Convention. Addendum, New Zealand.* CERD/C/NZL/17. [Online]. Available http://undocs.org/CERD/C/NZL/17. Accessed March 2, 2018.

UN Committee on the Elimination of Racial Discrimination [UNCERD]. (2007a). *Answers to Questions Put by the Rapporteur in Connection with the Consideration of the 15th to 17th Periodic Reports of New Zealand (CERD/C/NZL/17).*

UN Committee on the Elimination of Racial Discrimination [UNCERD]. (2007b). *Opening Statement to the Presentation of the 15th–17th Periodic Reports of New Zealand by Ambassador Don MacKay.* United Nations, Geneva, 31 July.

UN Committee on the Elimination of Racial Discrimination [UNCERD]. (2007c). *Report of the Committee on the Elimination of Racial Discrimination.* A/62/18. [Online]. Available http://undocs.org/A/62/18. Accessed March 2, 2018.

UN Committee on the Elimination of Racial Discrimination [UNCERD]. (2012). *Reports Submitted by State Parties Under Article 9 of the Convention. Eighteenth to Twentieth Periodic Reports of States Parties due in 2011: New Zealand.* CERD/C/NZL/18-20. [Online]. Available http://undocs.org/CERD/C/NZL/18-20. Accessed March 2, 2018.

UN Committee on the Elimination of Racial Discrimination [UNCERD]. (2013). *Summary Record of the 2221st Meeting.* CERD/C/SR.2221. [Online]. Available http://undocs.org/CERD/C/SR.2221. Accessed March 2, 2018.

UN Committee on the Elimination of Racial Discrimination [UNCERD]. (2016). *Consideration of Reports Submitted by States Parties Under Article 9 of the Convention, New Zealand.* CERD/C/NZL/21-22. [Online]. Available http://undocs.org/CERD/C/NZL/21-22. Accessed March 2, 2018.

UN Human Rights Committee [UNHRC]. (2015). *Consideration of Reports Submitted by States Parties Under Article 40 of the Covenant Pursuant to the Optional Reporting Procedure, New Zealand.* CCPR/C/NZL/6. [Online]. Available http://undocs.org/CCPR/C/NZL/6. Accessed March 2, 2018.

UN Human Rights Committee [UNHRC]. (2016). *Concluding Observations on the Sixth Periodic Report of New Zealand.* CCPR/C/NZL/CO/6. [Online]. Available http://undocs.org/CCPR/C/NZL/6. Accessed March 2, 2018.

Walker, R. (1990). *Ka Whawhai Tonu Mātou.* Auckland: Penguin Books.

5

Immigration Detention and the Limits of Human Rights

Michael Grewcock

Introduction

It is now 25 years since the Australian government introduced its policy of indefinite mandatory detention for unauthorised non-citizens, mostly asylum seekers seeking entry by boat. In that time, the policy has entrenched patterns of systemic abuse that have been routinely condemned for breaching Australia's obligations under international human rights law and that represent a form of state crime (Grewcock 2009). The multiple harms inflicted on detainees have been replicated at sites on the Australian mainland, on the off-shore Australian territory of Christmas Island, and in the Australian-funded and operated 'regional processing centres' on Manus Island (Papua New Guinea) and Nauru, to where all asylum seekers seeking unauthorised entry into Australia have been forcibly transferred since July 2013.[1]

M. Grewcock (✉)
Faculty of Law, University of New South Wales,
Sydney, NSW, Australia
e-mail: m.grewcock@unsw.edu.au

© The Author(s) 2018   **103**
E. Stanley (ed.), *Human Rights and Incarceration*, Palgrave Studies
in Prisons and Penology, https://doi.org/10.1007/978-3-319-95399-1_5

Neither the passage of time nor the shifting locations of camps have affected the fundamentally abusive character of the detention complex. For example, in 2004, the Human Rights and Equal Opportunities Commission's inquiry into children in immigration detention identified multiple breaches of the *Convention on the Rights of the Child* (CRC) (1989) and other child welfare norms (HREOC 2004). Ten years later, the Commission's follow-up report (AHRC 2014) provided a similar catalogue of abuse. The repeated descriptions of children self-harming, the drawings reflecting their isolation, fear and suicidal ideations, and the muted reports of sexual abuse in the 2014 report prompted denials from the government, sustained personal attacks on the President of the Australian Human Rights Commission, and legislation aimed at silencing critics working within the detention system. When a paediatrician wrote in 2015 that in the Nauru Regional Processing Centre he "saw a six year-old girl who tried to hang herself with a fence tie and had marks around her neck", that he had "never seen a child self-harm of that age before" and that "putting children in detention is child abuse", he had to risk criminal prosecution for speaking out (Grewcock 2015).

This pattern is not limited to children in immigration detention. In 2005, a senior psychiatrist, who had regularly visited the Woomera and Baxter detention centres in South Australia, told an Australian Senate Inquiry that:

> The implementation of immigration detention … has caused severe psychological damage to detainees. I know of no other cohort where such universal mental ill-health has been demonstrated … Better mental health services in detention will not help, because the environment is so toxic that meaningful treatment cannot occur. (Jureidini 2005)

In 2014, the former chief psychiatrist working within the immigration detention network declared that:

> We have here an environment that is inherently toxic … It has characteristics which over time reliably cause harm to people's mental health. We have very clear evidence that that's the case … If we take the definition of torture to be the deliberate harming of people in order to coerce them into a desired outcome, I think it does fulfil that definition. (cited in Marr and Laughland 2014)

The numerous accounts of the impacts on physical and mental health provide some insight into the nature and scale of the harm wrought by a detention regime premised largely on notions of deterrence and the Australian state's capacity to assume near-total control over those who have sought its protection. Within the dominant paradigm of Australian border policing, the alienation of unauthorised refugees through law, institutional practice and ideological 'othering' works to negate their individual and collective agency. Refugees who happen not to have a visa can lawfully be seized, restrained and transferred thousands of miles to face indefinite detention. The normalisation of these practices extends beyond the narrow legal determinations of refugee legitimacy. Even when offshore detainees manage to persuade the authorities that they are 'genuine', the Australian government now refuses to resettle them in Australia, thus condemning them to years of further abandonment and civil death. Moreover, the minority (approximately 400 at the end of 2017) transferred from Manus Island and Nauru to Australia for medical treatment continue to be subjected to multiple levels of detention and oppressive surveillance.

Individual narratives struggle to emerge from within this highly controlled liminal space. When they do, as was the case with Omid Masoumali and his wife 'Pari', they demonstrate the routine indifference and gratuitous cruelty of the Australian authorities. The Iranian couple were detained on Christmas Island in September 2013 and within days were transferred to the detention and processing centre on Nauru. They were determined officially to be refugees in December 2014 and were released into the community on Nauru with no secure immigration status or prospects of resettlement. In April 2016, Omid set himself alight during a visit to the island by UNHCR officials, who reportedly told Pari their "living conditions were ok". Suffering from severe burns and unable to receive adequate medical treatment, Omid was kept on Nauru for 24 hours before being airlifted to a hospital in Brisbane, where shortly afterwards he died. Australia's immigration minister offered his "condolences" but re-iterated refugees detained offshore would "never settle in Australia" (Doherty 2017a).

Meanwhile, Pari, who travelled with Omid to Brisbane, was taken into immigration detention and having been transferred abruptly three times was detained in Melbourne. Deeply traumatised, she was moved

backwards and forwards to hospital by Serco guards for medical treatment. One advocate, who visited Pari regularly, reported in March 2017
that she was:

> [S]uffering extreme infection caused by an untreated abscess, her arms
> too small for regular handcuffs. She is forcibly laced-up with a Serco
> Hannibal Lector leather restraint belt - arms shackled to it. When medi-
> cal staff demanded her arms be freed for drip attachment - the Serco staff
> only allowed one arm to be freed.[2]

The further dislocation and destruction of family networks arising from
Australia's border policing practices is illustrated by the case of Arash
Shirmohamadi, another Iranian refugee detained and subsequently
stranded on Nauru since July 2013. In August 2016, Arash's pregnant
wife was flown from Nauru to Sydney for urgent medical treatment.
Their child was born in March 2017 and remains in Sydney with her
mother on medical advice. Four days after his daughter was born, the
Australian Border Force issued Arash with a custody agreement, the text
of which included:

> I hereby agree to relinquish custody of my minor child.
>   I understand that by signing this agreement the non-custodial parent
> will not automatically be able to seek re-unification with my child and
> that this may mean permanent separation. (cited in Doherty 2017b)

The letter left Arash with a choice: sign and have an opportunity to
re-settle alone in the United States[3] or bring his wife and daughter back
to Nauru to face indefinite abandonment or forced return to Iran. Even
a short-term visit to Australia to meet his daughter was ruled out by the
Immigration Minister (Doherty 2017b).

Contemporary human rights standards (let alone basic norms of
human decency) operate as an obvious benchmark for condemning
such mistreatment and the cascading impacts of immigration detention
on the thousands of refugees who have subjected to it. As numerous
reports by the Australian Human Rights Commission, human rights
NGOs and former detention centre staff have documented, Australia's
detention practices routinely breach, inter alia, the *1951 Refugee*

Convention, the *International Covenant on Civil and Political Rights* (1966), the *Convention Against Torture* (1984), and the *Convention on the Rights of the Child* (1989).[4] Moreover, Australia's systemic breaches of human rights constitute a pattern of state criminality that operates through the tension between the state's 'right' to police it borders and the 'rights' of refugees to move freely in pursuit of protection and long-term security (Grewcock 2009).

It is clear that contemporary conceptions of human rights cannot resolve that fundamental tension. To paraphrase Hannah Arendt's argument that the "rightlessness" of the stateless in 1930s Europe demonstrated the "failure of human rights", universal human rights ultimately derive their existence through the willingness of states to give them juridical and practical meaning (Arendt 1994: 267–302). The conceptualisation of universal rights as contingent upon state sovereignty necessarily means that border controls prevail over claims to a right to free movement and, for refugees, a right to protection. This is illustrated by the escalating border policing regimes mobilised by governments in Australia, the European Union and North America to exclude unauthorised refugees and, in Australia's case, by government denials that its border policing practices breach human rights accompanied by Orwellian arguments that detention is necessary to prevent the rights and safety of refugees being put at risk by people smugglers.[5]

Genealogies and Critiques of Human Rights

This chapter therefore explores the limitations of universal human rights as an ideological framework for condemning and resisting the structural violence arising from immigration detention and related border policing practices. Using the examples of the *1951 Refugee Convention* and the *Convention on the Rights of the Child* (1989), it examines whether concepts of refugee and children's rights provide adequate mechanisms for challenging Australia's criminogenic border policing practices, and legitimising over-arching rights to free movement. In doing so, the chapter engages critically with the work of Samuel Moyn, whose book *The Last Utopia* (Moyn 2010) offers valuable insights into the relationship between human rights and the nation state, and the limitations on universality that necessarily arise from that relationship.

Moyn's iconoclastic genealogy of human rights emphasises their historical contingency and challenges orthodox accounts (for example, Ishay 2004; Lauren 2003) that posit the long-term evolution and normative potential of contemporary human rights frameworks. There are two key features of Moyn's revisionist critique[6] that are relevant to this discussion.

First, Moyn argues that there was no continuity between the Rights of Man espoused by the American and French revolutions and contemporary universalist rights discourses. Rather, the Rights of Man "were deeply bound up with the construction, through revolution if necessary, of state and nation" (Moyn 2010: 20). Fundamentally, rights in this period were "about a whole people incorporating itself in a state" and "[i]f abstract principles were called upon in the era as grounds for creating new states, they were just as important in the justification of the erection of their insurmountable external borders" (Moyn 2010: 26–27). Ultimately, according to Moyn, the Rights of Man fulfilled a "structural role", providing for citizen mobilisations and internal battles within the confines of the state, typically against newly entrenched private property protections, and in circumstances where "social movements in search of new terms of inclusion were often forced to set themselves against rights rather than simply propose new ones" (Moyn 2010: 35).

Moyn's second argument is that the post-World War Two political compact, which was formalised through the United Nations and typically is considered to have provided the genesis of contemporary human rights, was shaped by the commitments of the Western powers to the maintenance of empire in the face of large-scale movements for self-determination and decolonisation. Further, the use of rights by Western states primarily as a rhetorical political device for pursuing the Cold War meant that the principles enunciated in the 1948 Universal Declaration of Human Rights were "doomed to irrelevance". Indeed, Moyn argues that it is important to recognise "what human rights, at the time, were not":

> They were not a response to the Holocaust and not indeed focused on the prevention of catastrophic slaughter. Only rarely did they imply principled dissent from modern state sovereignty … To capture the world's

imagination, they would need profound re-definition in a new ideological climate. (Moyn 2010: 46–48)

For Moyn, that climate did not emerge until the late 1970s when social movements began embracing human rights language (as opposed to the civil rights language of the 1960s) for the first time (Moyn 2010: 121). This underpins Moyn's main claim that human rights took root as a normative political framework for social movements following the "death of other utopian visions" such as national self-determination and communism. In that sense, human rights represented a form of "antipolitics" that have become the core language of a "new politics of humanity' that "trade on the moral transcendence of politics". This new "new utopia" as Moyn describes it, "cannot be a moral one". Instead, its fate may be determined, he speculates, by whether the movements around human rights "should restrict themselves to offering minimal constraints on responsible politics, not a new form of maximal politics of their own" (Moyn 2010: 222–227).

Much more could be said about Moyn's detailed and nuanced thesis, which in my view is weakened by his rather problematic conceptualis-ation of utopia,[7] and his under-estimation of the ways in which collec-tive claims to rights can animate acts of resistance to criminally abusive state practices. Nevertheless, his basic arguments that human rights are *not* deeply embedded in Western liberal tradition, that rights histor-ically have been integral rather than inimical to state sovereignty, and that contemporary human rights, notwithstanding their internationalist underpinnings, must ultimately confront 'politics' in the form of the state, provide useful bearings for analysing the fundamental tensions identified above, and which flow through the *Refugee Convention* and the *Convention on the Rights of the Child* (1989).

The 1951 Refugee Convention

The *1951 Refugee Convention* was one of the emblematic human rights instruments of the post-World War Two period. It was drafted as millions across Europe were being repatriated or re-settled either by military force or through agreements with resettlement states (UNHCR 2000). Refugees displaced by the war had limited agency and little role in determining their migration options, with resettlement occurring almost entirely on terms determined by the Western states. Humanitarian considerations were not necessarily central. Australia, for example, resettled over 170,000 displaced persons, who were selected as 'suitable settlers' between 1946 and 1950 under the so-called Calwell Scheme[8] (Kunz 1988). A further 450,000 refugees migrated under assisted passage schemes between 1947 and 1973 (Australian Bureau of Statistics [ABS] 1974, 1978). These refugees comprised part of the large-scale labour migration encouraged by the Australian government in the post-war period for the purposes of economic development and security. Their compatibility with the 'White Australia Policy' was also important: no non-European refugees were granted entry between 1945 and 1965 (Neumann 2004).

As Moyn argues, the focus of the Allied powers in the late 1940s was to consolidate an international order that was compatible with empire and that human rights principles espoused at the time were, at no point, "primarily understood as breaking fundamentally with the world of states that the United Nations brought together" (Moyn 2010: 44). Notions of universal rights for refugees (especially those former subjects of empire who in large numbers would seek refuge in Western states) were largely absent from the political discourses of the time and not integral to the *Refugee Convention*. Rather, the political context defined the Convention's limits and reaffirmed the dominant role of the nation state within the emerging body of international human rights law.

The Preamble to the *Refugee Convention* located it alongside the 1948 *Universal Declaration of Human Rights* and its affirmation of "the principle that human beings shall enjoy fundamental rights and freedoms without discrimination". At its highest point, the *Universal Declaration* proclaimed a right of free movement within national borders, the right to leave and enter one's own country, the right to seek asylum from persecution and the right to a nationality. However, the *Refugee Convention* was never constructed as a response to large-scale mass displacement as had occurred during World War Two, nor did it accord refugees a generalised right to asylum. Instead, obligations, most notably not to penalise those crossing borders to seek asylum (Article 31) or to *réfoule* (return to a place of danger) (Article 33), were imposed on the Convention's signatory states.

Moreover, the Convention restricted the definition of a refugee to an individual suffering from "well-founded fear of persecution", which initially was limited to events in Europe prior to 1951.[9] While the Convention definition did not distinguish refugees according to their modes of travel—indeed Article 31 acknowledges implicitly that crossing borders without permission is a norm—the Convention was structured around the notion of the individual refugee upon whom was placed the burden of proving persecution and the need for protection to the satisfaction of the receiving state. This enabled border policies within the receiving states to focus on the legitimacy of the refugee, rather than the receiving state's response, and created a hierarchy of legitimacy for forced migrants based on the formal legal distinctions between asylum seeker and refugee. Given the absence of an enforceable right to free movement, it also enabled states like Australia to later institute measures to prevent refugees gaining unauthorised access to Australian jurisdiction for the purposes of seeking protection from persecution and to deny the legitimacy and authenticity of 'boat people' as opposed to those waiting in a notional queue.

Viewed in this light, Australia's detention policies are not an aberration from an historically 'generous' approach to refugees. Rather, they are a mechanism for enforcing an ideological and legal regime for refugees resting on the premise that the receiving state has the primary role in determining who is a legitimate refugee. Since the first arrivals of 'boat people' from Vietnam in 1976, that status increasingly has been accorded to those who have been resettled on terms defined by the Australian state, rather than those who have sought unauthorised entry. Thus, mandatory detention, which was introduced to buttress the 1989 regional plan for the resettlement of refugees from Indo-China by deterring unauthorised boat arrivals, has co-existed with an annual intake of 'legitimate' officially authorised refugees.

Having said that, the mandatory detention policy did represent a turning point in Australian border policing strategy. Ideologically, mandatory detention reinforced the criminalisation of unauthorised refugees arising from their unavoidable use of people-smugglers and an overarching illegality deriving from their non-citizen status and lack of a visa. As a policy norm, mandatory detention also developed its own opaque and internalised institutional dynamics, aided by the decision of the High Court of Australia in 2004 to define mandatory detention as administrative rather than punitive, and enacted in accordance with the Commonwealth government's constitutional powers.[10] The High Court's imprimatur legitimised the police powers bestowed upon immigration officials to forcibly and indefinitely detain unauthorised refugees, regardless of their ages and circumstances, and render them to jurisdictions across Australia and the Pacific. Practices that under criminal law could be characterised as kidnapping, false imprisonment and torture were inscribed in public law as neutral administrative processes.

From its initial ad hoc arrangements, the detention complex evolved into a network of total institutions (Goffman 1968), in which the imperatives of bureaucratic management and control over all aspects of detainees' lives normalised the routine exercise of force, created environments in which individual vulnerabilities were generated, exacerbated and exploited, and where abuse could be ignored, denied, or rationalised as an unfortunate by-product of a necessary deterrence policy.

The mandatory detention policy also facilitated the militarisation of Australian border policing, reflected in July 2015 by the establishment of the quasi-military Australian Border Force[11] and provided a platform for more extensive systems of exclusion, such as the excision of Australia from its own migration zone, the shift to offshore processing, the refusal to resettle those attempting unauthorised entry after July 2013, and naval interdiction and boat turnback policies (Grewcock 2014, 2015). Individually and collectively, each of these aspects of border policing is designed to undermine the *Refugee Convention* and more recent human rights instruments by preventing refugees gaining access to the legal mechanisms Australian governments had put in place since 1976 to determine refugee status and protection visa applications. However, the mandatory detention policy also highlights some of the internal contradictions and limitations of human rights instruments such as *the Convention on the Rights of the Child* (1989) as mechanisms for protecting refugee rights.

The Convention on the Rights of the Child

Within Moyn's schema, the *UN Convention on the Rights of the Child* (1989) is one of the new wave of human rights conventions that aim to transcend conventional state-based politics. The fact it is commonly cited as the most widely ratified human rights convention might reflect its universal normative sentiments but confirmation of this proposition is likely to rest more in its breach than its application. Article 22 of the Convention requires "States Parties" to "take appropriate measures to ensure that a child who is seeking refugee status or who is considered a refugee in accordance with applicable international or domestic law and procedures shall, whether unaccompanied or accompanied by his or her parents or by any other person, receive appropriate protection and humanitarian assistance in the enjoyment of applicable rights set forth in the present Convention and in other international human rights or humanitarian instruments to which the said States are Parties." Nevertheless, the *Convention on the Rights of the Child* (1989) has had, at best, limited impact on the treatment of child refugees subject to mandatory detention and related Australian border policing practices. There are two key principles embedded in the Convention that conflict routinely with these practices. First, is the principle that primary consideration in state policy and decision making be given to the best interests of the child. Second, is the principle that detention only be used as a matter of last resort and for the shortest possible time. Both principles are undermined by the primacy given to border controls and the enduring problems associated with conceptualisations of child agency.

Within the Convention, the best interests principle is shaped to some extent by the priority given to the child remaining within the family unit. Thus, in relation to child protection and custody, separation should only occur in cases of abuse and neglect. Further, parents and guardians are given primary responsibility "for the upbringing and development of the child". In the context of mandatory detention, successive Australian governments and the High Court of Australia have interpreted these obligations as enabling—if not justifying— the detention of children as a means of maintaining the integrity of the family group.[12] The repeated recommendations of the Australian Human Rights Commission in 2004 and 2014 that all children should be removed from immigration detention with their families had little immediate impact on government policy. In 2004, for example, the then immigration minister told journalists: "What it says to people-smugglers is if you bring children, you'll be able to be out into the community very quickly ... We think that is a mistake and we won't be adopting that policy" (cited in ABC Online 2004). Similarly, in 2014, when the government had already begun decanting many of those who had arrived prior to July 2013 into the community on bridging visas, the government argued the recommendations were either redundant, politically motivated and in any event, not applicable on Nauru because it is outside Australian jurisdiction (Grewcock 2015).

The subjugation of child refugees to the exclusionary imperatives of border policing is particularly evident in relation to unaccompanied minors. Under Australian law, the immigration minister, who is responsible for the implementation of the detention policy, is also the guardian for these young people, albeit the tasks are delegated to immigration department staff.

The obvious—and indefensible—conflict of interest inherent in the minister's role and the perverse interpretations of what constitutes the best interests of the child reflect the normalisation of mandatory detention and the capacity of states to ignore so-called international standards. While it is a core principle of the *Convention on the Rights of the Child* (1989), the principle that children be detained as a measure of last resort is consistent with the general prohibition on arbitrary detention in the *International Covenant on Civil and Political Rights* (1966) and was already entrenched as an international human rights norm through three instruments: the *Beijing Rules* (1985), the *Riyadh Guidelines* (1990) and the *Havana Rules* (1990) (see Haydon, this volume). However, despite its routine re-affirmation within the realm of UN-mediated official politics, the last resort principle, which mainly was conceived as a mechanism for limiting imprisonment within the penal justice system, is undermined by leaving its interpretation open to the detaining state. To the extent this is tempered by international human rights standards and monitoring, UNHCR (2012) guidelines specifically rule out the detention of "minors who are asylum seekers".

But the UN Human Rights Committee [UNHRC] found in 2014 that "detention in the course of proceedings for the control of immigration is not per se arbitrary", although it "must be justified as reasonable, necessary and proportionate" (UNHRC 2014: para. 18).

Of course, such criteria are open to highly exclusionary political interpretations, the legitimacy of which has been entrenched over decades in Australia through the sustained alienation and criminalisation of asylum seekers and the 'success' of border policing measures such as mandatory detention and offshore processing in 'stopping the boats'. The Australian government's response that such measures are necessary—the stated levels of accompanying regret range from zero to marginal—for the effective deterrence of unauthorised movement does not prevail over the proliferating human rights based critiques of the detention regime through any moral superiority. Rather, because there is no capacity to enforce international human rights standards, given the 'right' to regulate borders is left intact by international human rights law, successive Australian governments have pushed border controls towards their logical extreme and/or shifted the legal—if not moral responsibilities—to other jurisdictions offshore.

The Limitations of Human Rights

The rights discourse is clearly limited in challenging border controls. Concepts purporting to be the moral and philosophical source of rights, such as 'inherent' and 'universal', are not only historically contingent and malleable in practice, but also are subverted fundamentally by the operation of border controls that are constituted in human rights law as a legitimate expression of sovereign interest. There is no optimum or organic balance between border policing and human rights—the relationship between the two is necessarily contradictory and unstable. The repeated refusals of Australian governments to legislate for greater compliance with international human rights requirements regarding immigration detention illustrate the fundamental contradictions between universal subject based rights and sovereign power, and the subsequent limitations of strategies focused on achieving more human rights-based approaches to border policing.

As discussed above, there are also fundamental legal and philosophical limitations built into the *Refugee Convention*. In particular, there is a profound disconnect between the individual, persecuted refugee idealised in the Convention and the sudden, large-scale movements generated by conflicts outside of the West that characterise contemporary forced migration. The majority of refugees spend years stranded in camps in the developing world, subject to the capricious and negligible resettlement quotas of Western states. Typically excluded by host states and surviving in precarious circumstances, most refugees have little capacity to move freely into developed states to exercise Convention rights to claim protection. Instead, resettlement states like Australia are increasingly resorting to detention and other policing measures designed to punish and deter those seeking unauthorised entry. Such practices seriously limit the capacity of the *Refugee Convention* to underpin a global framework for the long-term protection of the increasingly alienated and criminalised refugee beyond hopes that more comprehensive resettlement mechanisms be put in place.[13]

Given that unauthorised refugee children are defined by the Australian state primarily according to their travel and visa status, such limitations mean that it is difficult to separate the experiences of detained children and the dynamics underpinning their detention from those of refugees as a whole. While the impacts of detention are particularly harsh on children and their mistreatment capable, in some circumstances, of attracting more sympathy than that of their adult counterparts, conceptually children's rights do not offer an inherently different perspective to detention than the wider body of refugee rights. The critical determinants of agency, rights to cross-border movement, and capacities to claim protection are not determined fundamentally by age.

The Normativity and Contradictions of Human Rights

Despite the internal contradictions and limitations of the refugee rights discourse, the language of rights and the normative standards asserted through human rights law have been deployed extensively to condemn

Australia's immigration detention and border policing practices. Indeed, it is arguable that human rights operate as the dominant conceptual foundation for condemning and resisting immigration detention. United Nations monitoring bodies, statutory bodies such as the Australian Human Rights Commission, non-government organisations such as Amnesty International and Human Rights Watch all frame their assessments of detention explicitly within human rights discourse. Moreover, because the *Refugee Convention* is one of the foundational legal expressions of post-World War Two human rights and the United Nations High Commissioner for Refugees one of the most high-profile UN agencies, there is an ideological and institutional infrastructure that posits refugees centrally in the human rights domain.

In addition, formal prohibitions on arbitrary detention are central to human rights law and the wider rights discourse. For example, Article 9 of the *Universal Declaration of Human Rights* (1948) declares that no-one should be subjected to arbitrary arrest, detention or exile. In its report on Australia, the UN Human Rights Committee (2017: para. 36[a]) concluded that the Australian government should "end its offshore transfer arrangements" on Nauru and PNG; "take all measures necessary to protect the rights of refugees and asylum seekers affected by the closure of processing centres, including against non-refoulement, [and] ensure their transfer to Australia or their relocation to other appropriate safe countries"; and consider closing down the Christmas Island detention centre. The Committee also concluded that mandatory immigration detention breaches the prohibition on arbitrary detention in Article 9 of the *International Covenant on Civil and Political Rights* (1966), and expressed concern "about what appears to be the use of detention powers as a general deterrent against unlawful entry rather than in response to an individual risk" (UNHRC 2017: para. 36–37).

Consistent with its approach to date, the Australian government chose to ignore the findings. However, this does not mean that assertions of Australian state authority expressed through border controls necessarily must prevail or that notions of refugee rights are rendered irrelevant. Notwithstanding the limitations of rights discussed above, the language of human rights retains significant normative purchase. As I have discussed at length elsewhere (Grewcock 2009), the Australian state, like other liberal democracies, seeks to construct a degree of legitimacy from its claims to upholding and promoting human rights norms. Of course, these claims are profoundly contradictory, as evidenced in 2017 by Australia's pursuit of a seat on the UN Human Rights Council while simultaneously being condemned by UN human rights bodies for its offshore detention policies. Such cynical government behaviour could be dismissed simply as further evidence of the primarily rhetorical use of rights in political discourse. However, the disjuncture between the Australian government's formal commitments to human rights norms, such as the prohibitions on arbitrary detention, or the government's recent institution of a Royal Commission into Institutional Child Abuse at the same time as widespread allegations of the abuse and sexual assault of children in immigration detention were being disclosed (Grewcock 2016), have driven opposition to Australia's immigration detention policies.

Contrary to the hegemonic support for mandatory detention within Australia's main political parties and state institutions, there have been consistent challenges to the detention policies by a range of activist and civil society organisations, and by detainees. While quite heterogeneous, the networks and organisations opposing immigration detention have routinely expressed their opposition using the language of rights. In some cases, for example in the detailed reports of the Australian Human Rights Commission or non-government organisations such as Amnesty International, this takes a very specific legal form drawn directly from international human rights law. However, within the more fluid, less institutionalised networks of civil society, more visceral notions of rights are expressed. This was exemplified most poignantly by a tweet on Human Rights Day (10 December) 2017 by a refugee marooned on Manus Island:

> As a human being you have the right to express yourself. You have the right to journey wherever you feel safe. You have the right to ask for freedom. You have the right to seek asylum. You have the right to believe the same way you have the right to love.[14]

Rights, Resistance and Free Movement

The various ways in which rights are claimed and formulated highlight an important dynamic that is absent from Moyn's schematic account of human rights—the undifferentiated use of the language of rights to express collective demands and to animate resistance against abusive state practices, even if there are no viable legal mechanisms for acknowledging and enforcing those rights.

Because Moyn focuses on the discrete timeframes associated with different phases and juridical constructions of rights, he downplays the continuities in struggles around rights—and the common claims to rights more broadly defined—that can be identified from the Haitian slave rebellion of the late eighteenth century through to the civil rights campaigns of the mid-late twentieth century. These struggles primarily involved excluded and oppressed groups making demands on the state in circumstances where there were structural tensions between official ideologies of freedom, rhetoric around rights and the limited capacities of lower social classes and subaltern groups to claim them. This does not invalidate the distinctions Moyn makes between the Rights of Man and civil rights but it is arguable these struggles were linked by diffuse desires for equality and a malleable and transferable language of rights.

Consequently, Moyn underestimates the capacity of rights concepts to act as mobilising ideals against the state and in the process become more entrenched within civil society. As Robin Blackburn, writing of the overthrow of slavery in the Americas, argued in response to Moyn:

[There are] many cases of those arguing against slavery and racism appropriating the idea of rights, not infrequently improving it in the process. So, there is a living tradition here that cannot be artificially arrested at some privileged moment that discloses its inner truth … No doubt there is something to [Moyn's] various trackings of the itinerary of the [human rights] concept, but they do not thereby discredit it … The problem for me with Moyn's undoubtedly perceptive rereading is that he seems almost fearful of the increasingly ambitious agenda of rights … The history of abolition shows that a narrow approach to ending slavery usually proves misguided and unfortunate, allowing for the continuance or mutation of oppression and exploitation. (Blackburn 2013: 485–486)

Blackburn's critique of Moyn coincides with a growing body of state crime scholarship (for example, Green and Ward 2000, 2004; Stanley and McCulloch 2013; Lasslett 2014) that explores the ways in which various conceptions of rights are deployed within civil society to identify, condemn and resist organised, deviant and abusive state practices. At the core of this scholarship is an understanding that political struggles for collective rights have the potential to challenge state authority and operate as a conduit for social transformation. The refusal of states to accede to demands that they implement policies consistent with their own stated governing principles not only exposes the structural limitations of rights and the social hierarchies that determine one's ability to access something as basic as right to protection, but also creates a space for looking beyond the current institutional expressions of, and constraints upon, those rights.

The Australian experience of immigration detention demonstrates that refugee rights, including a right not to be detained, can only be shaped from below through campaigns built on solidarity between activists within civil society and refugees themselves. Moreover, the challenge to immigration detention requires more than a focus on the processes of seizure and incarceration. The problem with immigration detention is not just that it is fundamentally abusive; rather, it sits on a continuum of state practices designed to delegitimise, obstruct and criminalise unauthorised movement.

For refugees, individual and collective agency and their capacity to travel remain critical in determining what rights they have. The current refugee crisis occurs in a period characterised, inter alia, by global instability and conflict, and record levels of forced migration. In this context, the claims to migration rights being made by refugees through the very act of flight are rooted in the need for immediate security, the capacity to engage in global travel, contradictory discourses on rights being pursued by major states, UN bodies and NGOs, and minimal prospects for resettlement. The fact that the United States and many European governments are moving towards border policing practices modelled on the Australian approach of excluding those seeking entry suggests that while it may be useful in highlighting the abusive treatment of refugees through practices such as detention, international human rights law is of limited assistance to refugees in achieving what they really require in this situation—protection underpinned by a right to free movement.

However, establishing that right involves confronting border controls as an expression of sovereign power as much as individual practices such as detention. Politically, that is a challenging task given the near hegemonic embrace of border protection within Australian mainstream politics and the unwillingness of the major parties even to allow the refugees currently stranded on Manus Island and Nauru to enter Australia.

Nevertheless, there is a critical mass of opposition to mandatory detention and other border policing policies. There are important links between detainees, many of whom have engaged in repeated protests within the detention centres, and activist networks in Australia. There have been some inspiring acts of solidarity—for example by medical staff refusing to release an infant from a hospital in Brisbane in February 2016 while she was threatened with transfer to Nauru, and there is a visible minority campaigning to "bring them here", or to "let them stay".[15]

While such campaigns necessarily have focused on the plight of those currently detained or targeted by the Australian authorities, the question of whether there should be freedom to cross a border is inevitably posed. For refugees, this is an existential rather than an abstract question, and given the long-term trends in forced migration, it is a question that is not going to go away. Although a right to free movement might appear an unlikely goal, avoiding the question returns us to the current impasse where formal human rights commitments offer a measure for widespread state malpractice but attract minimal sanction or practical way forward for detained refugees. This may reflect the 'utopian' dimensions to human rights identified by Moyn but it also underlines the need for large-scale campaigns mobilised within civil society that can build solidarity, challenge border controls and demand open borders.

Conclusion

The mandatory detention policy sits at the core of Australia's border policing measures to prevent unauthorised refugees seeking entry to claim the protections they are entitled under human rights law. As the case studies of Pari and Arash outlined at the beginning of this chapter illustrate, the abuses associated with this policy extend well beyond acts of incarceration to generalised acts of state violence against the individual and collective bodies and humanity of unauthorised refugees. In this context, rights to not be arbitrarily detained cannot be distinguished from the rights of refugees to exercise agency to travel, to seek protection and resist detention. This is particularly important for refugees themselves. In his extraordinary manifesto on the sustained, peaceful resistance of the refugees stranded on Manus Island, detained Kurdish Iranian journalist Behrouz Boochani wrote in December 2017:

> The refugees were able to re-envision their personhood when suppressed by every form of torture inflicted upon them and when confronted by every application of violence. According to its own logic … the detention regime wanted to manufacture a particular kind of refugee with a particular kind of response. However, the refugees were able to regain their identity, regain their rights, regain their dignity. In fact, what has occurred is essentially a new form of identification, which asserts that we are human beings. (Boochani 2017)

Boochani wrote his manifesto to "communicate our humanitarian message to Australia and beyond", a message defined by:

> Feelings of friendship.
> Feelings of compassion.
> Feelings of companionship.
> Feelings of justice.
> And feelings of love.

At the time of writing, the Australian government has remained steadfast in its border policing policies. However, Boochani's resilience and capacities to resist have been inspirational to those campaigning in

Australia to end immigration detention. While Boochani's prose was a poetic call to human solidarity rather than the formalistic recitation of Australia's human rights record, it demonstrated how a collective sensibility of rights could inspire campaigns for a genuine right to free movement. This is not a right that can be subordinated to politically contingent resettlement processes or mediated through a sovereign state. As with slavery, this is a right that can only achieved through abolition—in this case, of the border controls that justify the incarceration, and all its toxic consequences, of thousands of innocent refugees.

Notes

1. I have analysed these developments extensively elsewhere (see, for example, Grewcock 2009, 2014, 2015, 2016). For an analysis of the situation on Manus Island published shortly before the forced evacuation of the Refugee Processing Centre in November 2017, see Grewcock (2017). See also, Refugee Action Coalition Sydney (2017) public forum marking the twenty fifth anniversary of the detention policy.
2. Private communication with author, 27 March 2017.
3. For a discussion of the resettlement agreement between Australia and the United States, see Grewcock (2017) and Note 5 below.
4. See, for example, Amnesty International (2013), AHRC (2014), and UNHCR (2016).
5. The cynicism and duplicity underpinning Australian government claims to protecting refugee rights were amply demonstrated during the telephone conversation between Australian Prime Minister Malcolm Turnbull and US President Donald Trump on 28 January 2017, regarding the Manus Island 'swap deal'. For the full transcript, *Sydney Morning Herald* (2017).
6. For a discussion of Moyn's contribution to 'critical legal genealogy', see Golder (2017).
7. His use of 'utopia' is problematic in two senses: first, it ignores the distinctions between classical Marxism and utopian socialism (see Engels 1970); and, second, it effectively dismisses all radical social change as impossible. That leaves him essentially nowhere to go politically beyond

a critique of human rights attached to a minimalist program of political reform. In that sense, a politically more useful critique of human rights can be drawn from Mieville's more broadly framed Marxist critique of international law (Mieville 2006).

8. Named for its association with Australia's first Immigration Minister, Arthur Calwell, who promoted the scheme.
9. The temporal and geographic restrictions were lifted in 1967 by the *Protocol Relating to the Status of Refugees*, which Australia did not ratify until 1973.
10. *Al-Kateb v Godwin* [2004] 208 ALR 124.
11. See Divisions 7 and 8 *Migration Act 1958* and *Australian Border Force Act 2015*.
12. *Re Woolley; Ex parte Applicants M276/2003 by their next friend GS* [2004] HCA 49.
13. For a discussion of attempts to establish a new global compact on refugees, see Grewcock (2017).
14. Although this was a public tweet, I have declined to provide the source given the sensitivities of the situation on Manus Island. Copy of tweet in author's possession.
15. See, for example, Refugee Action Coalition Sydney (2018) and Asylum Seeker Resource Centre (2018).

References

ABC Online. (2004). *Vanstone Critical of Human Rights Commission Report.* [Online]. Available http://www.abc.net.au/pm/content/2004/s1107800.htm. Accessed September 1, 2017.

Amnesty International [AI]. (2013). *This Is Breaking People: Human Rights Violations at Australia's Asylum Seeker Processing Centre on Manus Island, Papua New Guinea.* [Online]. Available https://www.amnesty.org/en/documents/ASA12/002/2013/en/. Accessed September 1, 2017.

Arendt, H. (1994). *The Origins of Totalitarianism.* London: Harcourt.

Asylum Seeker Resource Centre [ASRC]. (2017). *Refugees in Australia Need Your Help to #LetThemStay.* [Online]. Available https://www.asrc.org.au/2017/08/29/letthemstay/. Accessed September 1, 2017.

Asylum Seeker Resource Centre. (2018). [Online]. Available https://www.asrc.org.au/. Accessed February 12, 2018.

Australian Bureau of Statistics [ABS]. (1974). *Yearbook Australia, 1974.* Cat. No. 1301.0. Canberra: Australian Bureau of Statistics.

Australian Bureau of Statistics [ABS]. (1978). *Yearbook Australia, 1978.* Cat. No. 1301.0. Canberra: Australian Bureau of Statistics.

Australian Human Rights Commission [AHRC]. (2014). *The Forgotten Children: National Inquiry into Children in Immigration Detention.* [Online]. Available https://www.humanrights.gov.au/our-work/asylum-seekers-and-refugees/publications/forgotten-children-national-inquiry-children. Accessed September 1, 2017.

Blackburn, R. (2013). *The American Crucible: Slavery, Emancipation and Human Rights.* London: Verso.

Boochani, B. (2017, December 9–15). A letter from Manus Island. *The Saturday Paper.* [Online]. Available https://www.thesaturdaypaper.com.au/news/politics/2017/12/09/letter-manus-island/15127380005617. Accessed December 9, 2017.

Doherty, B. (2017a, March 23). Death in detention: "I'd give everything to have him back". *The Guardian.* [Online]. Available https://www.theguardian.com/australia-news/2017/mar/23/death-in-detention-id-give-everything-to-have-him-back. Accessed September 1, 2017.

Doherty, B. (2017b, December 6). Border force tells Nauru refugees to separate from family if they want to settle in US. *The Guardian.* [Online]. Available https://www.theguardian.com/world/2017/dec/06/border-force-tells-nauru-refugees-to-separate-from-family-if-they-want-to-settle-in-us. Accessed December 6, 2017.

Engels, F. (1970 [1880]). *Socialism: Utopian and Scientific.* [Online]. Available https://www.marxists.org/archive/marx/works/1880/soc-utop/. Accessed February 12, 2018.

Goffman, E. (1968). *Asylums: Essays on the Social Situation of Mental Patients and other Inmates.* Harmondsworth: Penguin.

Golder, B. (2017). Contemporary legal genealogies. In J. Desautels-Stein & C. Tomlins (Eds.), *Searching for Contemporary Legal Thought* (pp. 80–98). Cambridge: Cambridge University Press.

Green, P., & Ward, T. (2000). State crime, human rights and the limits of criminology. *Social Justice, 27,* 101–115.

Green, P., & Ward, T. (2004). *State Crime: Governments, Violence and Corruption.* London: Pluto Press.

Grewcock, M. (2009). *Border Crimes: Australia's War on Illicit Migrants.* Sydney: Institute of Criminology Press.

Grewcock, M. (2014). Back to the future: Australian border policing under Labor, 2007–2013. *State Crime, 3*(1), 102–125.

Grewcock, M. (2015). Australian border policing and the production of state harm. In G. Barak (Ed.), *The Routledge International Handbook of the Crimes of the Powerful* (pp. 331–347). Abingdon: Routledge.

Grewcock, M. (2016). Australian border policing, the detention of children and state crime. In L. Weber, E. Fishwick, & M. Marmo (Eds.), *The Routledge International Handbook of Criminology and Human Rights* (pp. 157–168). Abingdon: Routledge.

Grewcock, M. (2017). "Our lives is in danger": Manus Island and the end of asylum. *Race and Class*. [Online]. Available https://doi.org/10.1177/0306396817717860. Accessed February 12, 2018.

Human Rights and Equal Opportunities Commission [HREOC]. (2004). *A Last Resort? Report of the National Inquiry into Children in Immigration Detention*. [Online]. Available https://www.humanrights.gov.au/our-work/asylum-seekers-and-refugees/projects/last-resort-report-national-inquiry-children. Accessed September 1, 2017.

Ishay, M. (2004). *The History of Human Rights: From Ancient Times to the Globalization Era*. Berkeley: University of California Press.

Jureidini, J. (2005). *Submission to Senate Legal and Constitutional References Committee Inquiry into the Administration and Operation of the Migration Act 1958*. Submission 31.

Kunz, E. (1988). *Displaced Persons: Calwell's New Australians*. Sydney: Pergamon Press.

Lasslett, K. (2014). Understanding and responding to state crime: A criminological perspective. In I. Bantekas & E. Mylonaki (Eds.), *Criminological Approaches to International Criminal Law* (pp. 68–92). Cambridge: Cambridge University Press.

Lauren, P. (2003). *The Evolution of International Human Rights: Visions Seen*. Philadelphia: University of Pennsylvania Press.

Marr, D., & Laughland, O. (2014, August 5). Australia's immigration detention regime sets out to make asylum seekers suffer, says chief immigration psychiatrist. *The Guardian*. [Online]. Available http://www.theguardian.com/world/2014/aug/05/-sp-australias-detention-regime-sets-out-to-make-asylum-seekers-suffer-says-chief-immigration-psychiatrist. Accessed September 1, 2017.

Mieville, C. (2006). *Between Equal Rights: A Marxist Theory of International Law*. Chicago: Haymarket Press.

Moyn, S. (2010). *The Last Utopia: Human Rights in History*. Cambridge, MA: Harvard University Press.

Neumann, K. (2004). *Refuge Australia: Australia's Humanitarian Record*. Sydney: UNSW Press.

Refugee Action Coalition Sydney. (2017). *Michael Grewcock: A History of Mandatory Detention in Australia*. [Online]. Available https://www.youtube. com/watch?v=scxC9V42FQI. Accessed February 12, 2018.

Refugee Action Coalition Sydney. (2018). [Online]. Available http://www.refugeeaction.org.au/. Accessed February 12, 2018.

Stanley, E., & McCulloch, J. (Eds.). (2013). *State Crime and Resistance*. London: Routledge.

Sydney Morning Herald. (2017). *Full Transcript: Donald Trump and Malcolm Turnbull Telephone Conversation*. [Online]. Available http://www.smh.com. au/world/full-transcript-donald-trump-and-malcolm-turnbull-telephone-conversation-20170803-gxp13g.html. Accessed February 12, 2018.

UN General Assembly. (1985). *United Nations Standard Minimum Rules for the Administration of Juvenile Justice [Beijing Rules]*. A/RES/40/33. Adopted November 29, 1985.

UN General Assembly. (1990). *United Nations Rules for the Protection of Juveniles Deprived of their Liberty [Havana Rules]*. A/RES/45/113. Adopted December 14, 1990.

UN General Assembly. (1990). *United Nations Guidelines for the Prevention of Juvenile Delinquency [Riyadh Guidelines]*. A/RES/45/112. Adopted December 14, 1990.

UN High Commissioner for Refugees [UNHCR]. (2000). *The State of the World's Refugees: Fifty Years of Humanitarian Action*. Oxford: Oxford University Press.

UN High Commissioner for Refugees [UNHCR]. (2012). *Detention Guidelines: Guidelines on the Applicable Criteria and Standards relating to the Detention of Asylum Seekers and Alternatives to Detention*. [Online]. Available http://www.unhcr.org/publications/legal/505b10ee9/unhcr-detention-guidelines.html. Accessed September 1, 2017.

UN High Commissioner for Refugees [UNHCR]. (2016). *Submission 43 to Senate Legal and Constitutional Affairs Committee Inquiry into the Serious Allegations of Abuse, Self-Harm and Neglect of Asylum Seekers in Relation to the Nauru Regional Processing Centre, and Any Like Allegations in Relation to the Manus Regional Processing Centre*. [Online]. Available http://www.aph.gov. au/Parliamentary_Business/Committees/Senate/Legal_and_Constitutional_ Affairs/NauruandManusRPCs. Accessed September 1, 2017.

UN Human Rights Committee [UNHRC]. (2014). *General Comment No. 35—Article 9 (Liberty and Security of Person)*. CCPR/C/GC/35. [Online]. Available http://undocs.org/CCPR/C/GC/35. Accessed September 1, 2017.

UN Human Rights Committee [UNHRC]. (2017). *Concluding Observations on the Sixth Periodic Report of Australia*. CCPR/C/AUS/CO/6. [Online]. Available http://undocs.org/CCPR/C/AUS/CO/6. Accessed December 1, 2017.

Table of Cases

Al-Kateb v Godwin [2004] 208 ALR 124.

Re Woolley; Ex parte Applicants M276/2003 by their next friend GS [2004] HCA 49.

6

Haunted by the Presence of Death: Prisons, Abolitionism and the Right to Life

David Scott

Introduction

Prisons are haunted by the 'spirit of death'. Irrespective of the physical and material conditions of confinement or levels of security shaping the daily regime, the prison is an institution which deprives human needs and estranges people from their lifeworld (Scott 2016). There is a constant presence of death in prison: *civil death*—death in law; *social death*—death of social relationships; and *corporeal death*—the literal death of the body. All three intertwine to comprise the spirit of death for those who die in prison are often seen as of little social significance; when they do get in the public spotlight they are often blamed for their own suffering and death through constructions of 'negative reputations' about their lack of virtue (Scraton and Chadwick 1987).

D. Scott (✉)
Faculty of Arts and Social Sciences, Open University,
Milton Keynes, UK
e-mail: david.scott@open.ac.uk

© The Author(s) 2018
E. Stanley (ed.), *Human Rights and Incarceration*, Palgrave Studies
in Prisons and Penology, https://doi.org/10.1007/978-3-319-95399-1_6

Prisons are always likely to facilitate an *intensified death consciousness* (JanMohamed 2005). The most crucial elements of a meaningful existence are strong human relationships, active social participation and deep social bonds (Kropotkin 1895; Seale 1998). The daily routines of prison life, however, contain practices that extinguish previous relationships whilst also presenting serious obstacles to the formation of new meaningful interactions. The normal protective factors that facilitate the denial of death are stripped away (Cohen 2001). Imprisonment takes away human intimacy, privacy, mobility and former social status, among other things. These losses present an assault on the very fabric of the self, leading to the unravelling of (possibly) previously secure identities. Propelled down a monotonous road to nowhere and unable to conceive of any new meanings, some prisoners become trapped within thoughts of old mistakes, and their possibilities for a better future appear increasingly distant. Such a loss of hope for the future can prove deadly (Scott and Codd 2010).

Corporeal deaths bring to the forefront concerns regarding the ultimate human rights, the *right to life*, yet the potentially deadly harms of imprisonment are often placed at the margins of political debate or conveniently forgotten or ignored. This chapter explores the ways in which penal abolitionists in England and Wales have contested the spirit of death through the strategies of 'speaking and naming' and 'making something happen'. Each strategy is an attempt to turn a private trouble into a public issue (Mills 1959) and ultimately to generate public condemnation of the brutality and inhumanity of prisons. By shaming the penal apparatus and 'telling truth to power', abolitionists hope to create a conscience regarding the current use of imprisonment. This chapter concludes by arguing that as prisons are places inevitably characterised by the *spirit of death*, all those committed to human rights and social justice should work for prison abolition.

Death and the Violation of Rights

For penal abolitionists, the prison is a violation of fundamental human rights. The *Universal Declaration of Human Rights* [UDHR] (1948) categorically states "No one shall be subject to torture or to cruel, inhuman or degrading treatment or punishment". From a penal abolitionist perspective, both the penal rationale and imprisonment violates these rights. Human rights are significant because they enshrine precisely those human and societal characteristics, values and practices that make society worth protecting. Human rights are envisaged as a means of attempting to limit what a state may do, so it should come as no surprise that the language of rights is deployed against the power to punish through the suspension of the right to liberty. The *European Convention on Human Rights* [ECHR] (1953) (Article 2) and the *International Covenant on Civil and Political Rights* [ICCPR] (Article 6) valorise the 'Right to Life'. Imprisonment denies the value of human life, and leads to direct violations of the right to life. That prisons take life—and are part of a broader apparatus of the state and its power to create death—is therefore a fundamental tenet of the abolitionist position. For abolitionists three different forms of death intersect in the violation of the right to life and formulation of a spirit of death. First, there is civil death, when a human being is denied their basic legal rights. Second, there is social death, when a person is no longer valued as a fellow human being. Third there is corporeal death, the literal death of the body, when a human life comes to an end. Let us now consider each of these spirit of death aspects in turn to illustrate how imprisonment is a violation of fundamental human rights.

Civil Death

Civil death (*civiliter mortuus*) means 'death in law'. It means the loss of citizenship and most legal rights due to the sentence of imprisonment. Whilst it is possibly more accurate to say prisoner legal rights are on a *life-support machine* rather than completely 'dead in law', the courts have done little to protect prisoners from the worst harms generated by prisons. However, courts have offered life support to prisoners in relation to direct infringements of the *right to life*. For example, the European Court of Human Rights [ECtHR] has held that the Prison Service in England and Wales has a positive obligation to protect prisoners' lives from accidents, prisoner or prison officer violence, or neglect. In *Keenan v United Kingdom* [2001][1] the ECtHR held that obligations under Article 2 extended to a duty to prevent suicides when authorities were aware of a "real and immediate risk" to life. This positive obligation to protect corporeal life was further elaborated in *Edwards v United Kingdom* [2002],[2] after the parents of Christopher Edwards, who was murdered by another prisoner in HMP Chelmsford, petitioned the ECtHR. Both Christopher and his attacker suffered from mental health problems and the ECtHR held that, given the failure of the Prison Service to appreciate the vulnerability of Mr. Edwards and the potential dangerousness of the murderer, they had breached Article 2 of the European Convention on Human Rights [ECHR]: the right to life.

Prisoner claims have been marginally successful in recent decades[3] with regards to claims focussed on procedural rights, such as legal advice and access, release terms, discipline, or due process and transparency in the decision making process of penal administrators. But rather than transform the penal landscape and end civil death entirely, most legal victories of prisoners since the 1970s have resulted in the greater judicialisation of penal power. Right of access to the courts has not proved significant in terms of substantive issues such as improving living conditions, health care, education, or working environment and opportunities. When we ask the question 'What *absolute rights* are invested in prisoners?' the answer remains fairly brief. Prisoners in England and Wales have the *absolute right*: to commence legal proceedings at an impartial and independent tribunal; to be allowed uninhibited access to legal advice whether through legal visits or correspondence, and to be guaranteed confidentiality in medical correspondence (Scott 2013).

The legacy of civil death impacts on the protection of procedural rights. Perhaps the most obvious example, here, is the response of the UK government to the ECtHR judgment in *Hirst v United Kingdom* [2004][4] that stated that the denial of the vote to prisoners is a breach of the ECHR. On four different occasions the ECtHR has ruled against the blanket ban on prisoners voting, the most recent being in February 2015. Rather than bring about an alteration in voting rights, the ECtHR ruling has primarily led to political resentment in Britain, with political resistance well illustrated in February 2011 when a cross-party motion to maintain the blanket ban preventing prisoner voting was overwhelmingly supported in the House of Commons. A compromise position was eventually agreed in December 2017, when the Council of Europe accepted the UK government position that prisoners released on temporary licence, primarily for employment reasons (which would be around 100 of the 86,000 prisoner population at any one time), would now be allowed to vote. All other prisoners, however, are to be individually informed of their *forfeiture of their right to vote* as part of their notification of committal to prison. The most significant changes, then, arising from 13 years of debate following the 2004 *Hirst* ruling regard clarification of previous policy and new provision for more information to be given to prisoners about their disenfranchisement.

Where prisoners' claims in the courts fail—still by far the most common outcome—the judiciary often justify their decisions by submitting to the existing authority of the Prison Service and Ministry of Justice. The judiciary has no wish to *be seen* to make penal policy. Sympathetic courts consider that prison authorities hold the public interest, and require the discretion to restrict rights on the grounds of prison security, order, the needs of victims, the prevention of crime or even administrative convenience (Scott 2013). A key principle of civil death—that scrutiny of current restrictions on prisoners are beyond the remit of the courts and rule of law—is regularly upheld.

Social Death

The spirit of death in prison is not just restricted to civil death but also incorporates restrictions on *social relationships* (Patterson 1982). Social death arises when certain people are not accepted as being fully human by wider society and are subsequently denied *human* rights (Esposito and Wood 1982). At its extreme, social death refers to the non-recognition of the prisoner as a fellow human (Patterson 1982; Price 2015). For sociologists like Bauman (1989), social death is predicated upon 'Othering', such that the socially dead person is dehumanised and outcast (Sellin 1976). Social death is a symbolic death, where the former self is consciously extinguished as a worthy moral subject. The prisoner becomes a less eligible subject whose views, opinions and voice can be refused or ignored. As a relational concept, there are three interconnected aspects of social death: the *estrangement* generated through the application of legal punishment; the *denial of human dignity through un-naming*; and the *institutionally-structured violence* of the prison. Let us consider these a little further.

First, *estrangement*. The beginning of social death comes from the initial removal from society and previous social relationships. Prisons create a space of social isolation where prisoners, uprooted from their social milieu and no longer belonging to their former community, are turned into *strangers*. Patterson (1982: 7) called this "natal alienation", referring to the loss of ties and relationships with "both ascending and descending generations". Natal alienation can, however, be expanded to also incorporate the loss of other important social relationships. The prisoner inevitably experiences abandonment as they are no longer part of their previous world and they often have no voice, or no one will listen to them. De-socialised and depersonalised, the enforced stranger is estranged and Othered. Perceived as an 'enemy within' who is hostile to the norms and values of law-abiding culture, the prisoner is considered a threat to the moral community (Cacho 2012).

Considered as *"ineligible for personhood"* (ibid.: 6, emphasis in original) and undeserving of help, the estranged "Other" can be pathologised and subjected to permanent suspicion: they are deemed to be "ethically irreproachable" (ibid.: 4) and not to be trusted, welcomed or recognised as a rights bearing individual. Further, once the stigma of punishment has been applied it is very difficult to remove. Whatever the length of incarceration (and whether the prisoner is sentenced or on remand), imprisonment has long term effects.

Second, *the denial of dignity through un-naming*. Prisons debase human dignity and foster an environment where prisoners are treated without honour or respect. Dehumanisation means: to treat a person as a 'thing'; to place them beyond identification, empathy and compassion; and, to deny their moral autonomy, common humanity or even their suffering (Scott 2008). Dividing practices that categorise people as either deserving or undeserving, worthy or unworthy, eligible or less eligible for care and support are, for example, often deeply engrained in prison officer occupational cultures (ibid.).

One aspect of social death is the manner in which the names and identities of the prisoners are removed. How prison officers and prisoners address each other illustrates the way social relationships are structured and hierarchies of power reproduced in the prison. Previous research (Scott 2011) found that the legitimate terms for prisoners when referring to staff were 'Boss', 'Officer', 'Mr', 'Mrs' and 'Sir'. 'Disciplinarian' prison officers legitimately referred to prisoners by: nick names (Smithy, Jonesy); second names (Smith, Jones); first names; prisoner number; and, abusive terms ('dicks', 'dickheads', 'cunts', 'bollocks', 'wanker'). These forms of address become a means of institutionalising lesser eligibility and informally maintaining a psychic divide.

These negative constructions are further evident when examining the language used to describe self-harm and self-inflicted deaths in prison (Scott and Codd 2010). Official discourse has often privileged explanations where the person who died is understood as being personally culpable for their own death (Topp 1979; HMCIP 1999). Their individual character is identified as pathological: they were 'weak' or 'high risk inadequates' who would have committed 'suicide' whether they were in prison or not. Their death is directly linked to vulnerabilities and risk factors that existed prior to imprisonment (such as unemployment, substance misuse, mental health problems, child abuse, and social isolation) or through the nature of their offence (such that they are spouse killers), or their sentence length (Wool and Pont 2006). In other words, the Prison Service "believes that the continuing high levels of apparent self-inflicted deaths are a product of the high proportion of prisoners with key risk factors" (HM Government 2005: 10).

This understanding is founded through the institutionalisation of negative reputations and dividing practices that categorise prisoners as deserving or non-deserving of care and attention (Scraton and Chadwick 1987; Malloch 2000; Cohen 2001). Negative categorisations justify hostility, neglect and moral indifference, and lead to blaming prisoners for their own dreadful predicament (Coles and Ward 1994). Those who harm themselves or attempt to take their own lives are labelled as "pathetic" manipulators whose harming act is part of a "general display of attention-seeking behaviour" (Topp 1979: 26).

For Liebling (1992: 233) both the staff and prisoner argot is a "language of contempt", referring to self-harmers as "slashers" and "cutters". When they die it is interpreted as a manipulative gesture gone wrong.

The third aspect of social death is *institutionally-structured violence*. Rather than a perverse or pathological aberration, this violence is an inevitable and thoroughly legal feature of prison life. Institutionally-structured violence is constructed through the operation of the daily rules, norms and procedures and it impacts upon how interactions are formed and performed. It is the determining context of the *social relationships* that pertain in prison. It occurs when: autonomy and choices are severely curtailed; human wellbeing, potential and development are undermined; feelings of safety and sense of security are weak; and human needs are systematically denied through the restrictive and inequitable distribution of resources.

Restrictions on prisoner contact and relationships within the prison are structurally organised and, whilst physical violence is relational and dependent upon a number of contingencies, *institutionally-structured violence* is embedded within and socially produced by the situational contexts of daily prison regimes (Sykes 1958). Prison architecture determines the location of events and the distribution of bodies and, in so doing, also highly regulates relationships and subsequently physical violence. The general lack of privacy and intimacy, insufficient living space and personal possessions, the indignity of eating and sleeping in what is in effect a lavatory, living and breathing in the unpleasant smells of body odour, urine and excrement, and the humiliation of defecating in the presence of others are all institutionally-structured situational contexts.

In one way or another, the sense of loss and wasting affects all prisoners (Medlicott 2001). Existence is only the here and now. The heavy weight of the mundane realities of prison life appear endless, distorting the real flow of time. As such, time consciousness results in an incredibly painful awareness of the passing of wasted time that can never be recaptured or spent differently. This can lead to prisoners trying to make escape attempts through the consumption of drugs and other illicit substances, or worse, being consumed by death consciousness (JanMohamed 2005).

Corporeal Death

In 2016, 354 people died in prisons in England and Wales. On average, nearly one person dies every day. Of these, 120 people took their own lives, which is more than one self-inflicted death every three days. In the last six years alone, over 500 prisoners have killed themselves. Nearly half of the current prison population, around 40,000 people, have thoughts about suicide (suicidal ideation). It is estimated that 46% of female prisoners and 21% of male prisoners have attempted suicide at some point compared to six per cent of the population overall. Over half of female prisoners (55%) and 40% of male prisoners have experienced suicidal ideation during their lifetime, compared to 4% of women and 14% of men in the wider community (Scott and Codd 2010; Prison Reform Trust 2016). Ministry of Justice data shows that 48,108 *Assessment, Care in Custody and Teamwork* [ACCT] documents were opened in 2016[5] and, in that year, incidents of self-harm reached a record high of 40,161, with 2740 prisoners requiring hospital treatment (Travis 2017). In 2017 these figures deteriorated still further. There were 49,287 ACCT documents opened in 2017[6] and government data shows 42,837 recorded incidents of self-harm in prisons in England and Wales from September 2016 to September 2017 (Ministry of Justice 2018: 1), which is equivalent to a prisoner being recorded as self-harming every 12 minutes. Further, there were 3007 prisoners hospitalised for serious incidents of self-harm from September 2016 to September 2017, which is eight hospitalisations for self-harm a day, or one every three hours (Ministry of Justice 2018).

Prisons have historically proved extremely adept at extinguishing human relationships. By its very nature the prison orients people towards loss, trauma and endings, and away from the fulfilment of human needs and hope for the future. Corporeal death is therefore closely intertwined with *civil death* and *social death*. As JanMohamed (2005: 23) puts it, "death is first felt and then acted out by the body". The prisoner's body becomes "totally saturated with death" (ibid.). Through monotonous deprivations the prisoner is forced to exist in a perilous state of an increasing consciousness of death that can lead them to acting out thoughts of death (Holland 2000; JanMohamed 2005). Further, pre-existing civil and social death makes the corporeal death of prisoners appear much less socially and politically significant because they have ceased to count (symbolically) long before they took their own life. *The presence of the spirit of death is then perhaps the very essence of penal confinement.*

Contesting the Spirit of Death

Given the record high number of self-inflicted deaths in English and Welsh prisons, activists and organisations are increasingly contesting prisons on the grounds of *the spirit of death*. Although there exists a diversity of abolitionist social movements[7] one uniting theme is the recognition that corporeal death should be understood within the context of both civil and social death.

Abolitionists and reformers have deployed two different strategies in recent times. The first—*speaking and naming*—is reactive and emphasises the importance of following political channels as a way of trying to contest the spirit of death. The second—*making something happen*—is a creative strategy that focuses on direct action protests to challenge the invisibility of prisoner deaths and to get people to acknowledge and talk about the problem.

Speaking and Naming

One of the key characteristics of both civil and social death is that the prisoner no longer counts, both in law and in politics. The immediate humanitarian and ethical responsibility that falls upon us is the necessity to challenge this invisibility of the estranged Other (the prisoner). This means *speaking out* and *speaking with* families and decision makers alike and *naming* the prison for what it is: a place of violence, suffering and death.

Speaking is by necessity relational. When we speak we not only take a position but also begin a relationship through dialogue, for all who participate in a discussion "share an interactive space of reciprocal expo-sure" (Cavarero 2005: 190). Speaking with prisoners establishes a new social relationship and transcends social death. When individuals speak they thus engage in a political process, which not only starts a conver-sation but which may ultimately lead to a new way of conceiving the world being fostered. Speaking generates a new democratic public space (Cavarero 2005), what Bauman (1999) refers to as an *agora* (a Greek term meaning a place for a political assembly). But to create an *agora* it is essential we *speak alongside* and *with* others. Each human voice is unique, but voice also arises out of a given social and material context and often, though not necessarily always, the strongest voices will be those that are part of a chorus. Speaking not only provides solidarity with sufferers but also allows new social alliances, bonds and meanings to be built. But alongside the act of saying it is also important what is said. When speaking the spirit of death must be *named* if it is to be revealed and overcome.

The importance of *speaking* and *naming* is well illustrated in the high profile case of Sarah Reed. Sarah died in HMP Holloway, north London, on 11 January 2016. She was found dead with a ligature round her neck. She had been on remand for psychiatric observation following an alleged offence at a mental hospital where she had been sectioned. Sarah, aged 32, had been the high profile victim of physical violence by PC James Kiddie only a couple of years earlier. PC Kiddie had thrown Sarah to the floor by her hair and savagely punched her in the face after being detained on suspicion of shoplifting. The assault by PC Kiddie was caught on CCTV coverage and attracted national media attention (Taylor 2017). Sarah was a black woman who had expe-rienced mental health problems since the death of her baby daughter in 2003 (Jasper 2017). Shortly before she took her own life Sarah had asked her mother, Marilyn Reed, to: "Please help me to get out of here; I shouldn't be in here; I'm not being treated ... I need my medication". The inquest jury concluded that Sarah had taken her own life "when the balance of her mind was disturbed" (INQUEST 2017). Rather than blaming Sarah for her own death the inquest noted the prison had failed to give her appropriate care, monitoring and medication for her health problems and "were not convinced that she intended to take her life" (ibid.). Rather than an individual suffering from serious mental health problems, Sarah had been treated as a disorderly prisoner who needed to be disciplined and controlled. She spent her "last days either chanting, screaming, banging and spitting, or in a trance like state" (ibid.; see also Taylor 2017). Isolated, she had been denied showers whilst there was no attempt to clean her cell. Her cell was placed behind a screen and she was denied visits, telephone calls and had virtually no positive interactions with staff. Although Sarah was checked hourly under the ACCT, her psychotic illness remained untreated. The prison service had failed in their duty of care. Because Sarah was a victim of police brutality, the campaign around her tragic death captured the national headlines.

In this case, the abolitionist inspired organisation INQUEST followed the pattern of speaking out, speaking with and naming the prison for what it is: an institution haunted by the spirit of death (INQUEST 2017). Through their campaign work—that includes direct support to the bereaved, press releases, media interviews, political lobbying, meetings with the Justice Secretary, and submissions to the House of Parliament Joint Committee on Human Rights—INQUEST, continually highlight the inappropriateness of prisons as places of safety. They campaign for greater investment in mental health services, a national diversion scheme, and changes in how police respond to people with mental health problems. They have highlighted how Sarah's case is one among many. In 2016, 22 women died in prisons in England and Wales, with ten having self-inflicted deaths [SIDs]. The rate of SIDs in female prisons stood at 2.6 per 1000 prisoners compared to a rate of 1.3 per 1000 prisoners for all prisoners. Deborah Coles, Director of INQUEST, has powerfully stated:

> The legacy of Sarah's death and the inhumane and degrading treatment she was subjected to must result in an end to the use of prison for women. The state's responsibility for these deaths goes beyond the prison walls and extends to the failure to implement the Corston review,[8] tackle sentencing policy and invest in alternatives to custody and specialist mental health services for women. (INQUEST 2017)

For INQUEST there is a clear need to turn this private trouble into a public issue (Mills 1959). INQUEST and those representing the family of Sarah Reed have also made explicit calls for state accountability and the implementation of recommendations (Jasper 2017). *Speaking out* about deaths in prison then directly involves *speaking with* government and telling 'truth to power'. It also involves reversing the *un-naming* of social death.

An important grassroots campaign, led by Sarah's mother Marilyn Reed, has also raised questions regarding the differential treatment of Black, Asian and Minority Ethnic women and the stigma attached to mental health problems. The 'Sarah Reed Campaign for Justice' led a candlelit vigil outside Holloway prison on the day Sarah Reed was buried, and have engaged media interviews, speeches and peaceful protests outside HMP Holloway before it closed in July 2016. Most significantly of all it involved the 'Say her name' campaign that symbolically called for the name of Sarah Reed to be heard and recognised as a member of the human family (Sarah Reed Campaign for Justice 2016; Lamour 2016). At the start of the inquest into her death the coroner read out the following statement from Marilyn Reed: "Sarah was adored and loved by the whole of her family. She was very much treasured. Her death has been devastating for us" (cited in Taylor 2017). The circumstances surrounding her death were subject to extensive media coverage and the July 2017 inquest became a rallying point for demands for an independent inquiry into deaths in custody (Khan 2017). Four months after Sarah Reed died in Holloway prison, women from pressure group *Sisters Uncut* held a protest at the prison to commemorate the 77 women who had died in British jails over the past decade. They accused the prison system of being institutionally sexist. In June 2017 the same group occupied and 'reclaimed' the empty prison. Speaking and naming—keeping the story in public consciousness as a warning about the harms and violence of imprisonment—is an *act of collective remembering* and the first step towards acknowledgement. It can also help generate a bad conscious about the very use of imprisonment—that is, that knowledge of the deadly harms generated by imprisonment should make us all feel uncomfortable about sending people to prison in the first instance.

Making Something Happen

The high profile self-inflicted deaths of two transgender prisoners in male prisons[9]—Vikki Thompson,[10] a 21 year old from West Yorkshire who had taken her own life in HMP Armley, Leeds in November 2015 and Joanne Latham, a 38 year old who died just a few weeks later in HMP Woodhill, Milton Keynes in November 2015—also resulted in direct actions against imprisonment. On the 27th August 2016, three anarchist abolitionist inspired groups 'Action for Trans Health', 'No Prisons Manchester', and the 'Incarcerated Workers Organising Committee' protested at their deaths and the dehumanising treatment of transgender prisoners at the annual Manchester Gay Pride March. Photographs and a video of the protest were shared by members of the transgender community across the country, leading to a big influx of the transgender community into the prison abolitionist movement. A film was made of the 'No Pride' demonstration, which received a significant number of views on YouTube and elsewhere.[11]

Through direct actions, abolitionist groups consistently showed how to both *say and to name* the prison for what it is: a place of violence, suffering and death. Making a concerted effort to highlight the facts generated considerable media interest and also led to direct action campaigns. But it can also work the other way round—where activism can be the first step in the conversation and an attempt to create a dialogue with the media, criminal process practitioners and politicians. Tales of corporeal death remind us of the need to challenge the ever present violence in prisons. And, sometimes, activists need to *make something happen* to break the silence of social death in the first place (Mathiesen 2004).

It is important that we consider how the injuries of imprisonment are represented: What is the nature of suffering in prison? Who are the people at the receiving end of suffering? How can people in the wider community identify with those suffering in prison? And, what are our ethical responsibilities to alleviate that suffering? These questions are all culturally mediated and shaped by hegemonic representations of the prison (Alexander 2012). The hegemonic narratives of prison life deny rather than acknowledge the suffering of prisoners—the trauma of the prisoner experiences is culturally erased through talk of prisons as 'holiday camps' or that prison sentences are 'easy'. Sometimes there appears to be nobody listening. The strategy of *making something happen* is about disrupting such assumptions and sending a message that an alternative way of thinking and *knowing* about human suffering in prison should be established.

Nowhere has this been more apparent in the wake of the self-inflicted death of Stephen Connell, who died at HMP Hindley[12] in February 2016. He was found with numerous cuts on his body and his family were immediately worried that Stephen had been neglected by the Prison Service. His family wanted to know why Stephen was not being appropriately monitored by the self-harm and suicide awareness policy [ACCT] among other failings in terms of his 'care'. Nine months after his death, serious concerns about the prison were raised again when HM Chief Inspector of Prisons (2016: 19) described the prison as perhaps the worst prison of its category in the country,[13] pointing out that cell bells often went unanswered while prisoners had limited access to listeners[14] and the "poor" day to day care for prisoners who were struggling to cope.

The Chief Inspector recorded 75 incidents of self-harm between April-October 2016, and noted that 161 ACCT reports were opened in six months prior to the HMCIP inspection at HMP Hindley (HMCIP 2016). They revealed that there had been a systematic failure to implement recommendations from the Prison and Probation Ombudsman [PPO] following the death of Jake Hardy in the prison in 2012. They noted that 66% of prisoners were locked in their cells for 18 hours every day and that high numbers of prisons felt unsafe, with many prisoners deliberately isolating themselves through fear. HMP Hindley presented considerable dangers to all who entered its walls. Failing to provide duty of care, it is a place steeped in institutionally-structured violence.

On 30 December 2016, a noise demonstration outside HMP Hindley was held in response to the death of Stephen Connell, the failure of the prison to implement PPO recommendations, and the publication of the damning HMCIP Report. A noise demonstration is a way of sending a message to prisoners that their experiences are not being ignored. Whilst prisoners cannot see the demonstration outside the gates, they can hear the pots, pans, whistles and musical instruments, as well as speeches amplified through loud speakers. The noise demo is a way of generating media attention to raise awareness of the plight of prisoners. More significantly, it directly shows solidarity with prisoners and breaches social death.[15]

A noise demonstration is really about *making something happen*—generating a story, building solidarity among activists, highlighting a controversial aspect of prison life and starting a conversation that would not otherwise occur. It provides an important challenge to the current hegemonic understandings of the violence of incarceration and the presence of the spirit of death. Whilst its effectiveness on policy is limited, direct action is a form of democratic participation that facilitates a voice that is otherwise silenced.

A Matter of Life and Death

The emptiness and time weariness of the prison reveals a constant presence of death and consciousness of loss, endings and abandonment. The prison is soaked in violence—it is an institution structured in such a way as to deliberately deprive human need. It is designed to inflict pain. Prisons destroy social bonds and relationships, they undermine meaning, and generate so much human suffering that it is impossible for prisoners or staff to meet the needs of the people that they encounter on a daily basis. It should come as no surprise that corporeal deaths have always occurred in large numbers in prisons. Prison and death go hand in glove. The prisoner becomes a potentially death-bound-subject. Civil death, social death and corporeal death are deeply ingrained in the daily operational practices of penal confinement. They are its essence. The death of the (former) self is coupled together with a loss of honour, dignity and social status. When a person dies in prison, the focus turns to their individual weakness, inadequacy or culpability rather than on a tragic loss of life.

Prisoners are however also active in contesting the pains of prison, and challenging death. Collective and organised prisoner rebellion specifically directed at changing prison regimes either through violent or non-violent protest have been part of prison life since its inception, and there are strong connections between prisoner resistance and efforts to bring about progressive reforms that can undermine the spirit of death. Prisoner rebellions continue to occur relatively frequently across the penal estate, although the extent and nature of such direct action are often hidden through media silencing (Berger and Losier 2018). Prisoners also continue to perform key roles as campaigners, lobbyists and claimants, impacting on state bodies such as Parliament, the Prison Ombudsman and the Law Courts in their attempts to improve procedural protections or living conditions. Some, such as John Hirst and Mark Leech, were highly successful prisoner-campaigners, winning a number of cases in both the domestic and European courts. Prisoner struggles for legal rights have also been supported by ex-prisoners working in organisations such as the Prisoners' Advice Service [PAS]. PAS is an independent charity providing free legal advice and support to all adult prisoners in England and Wales. It also runs the 'Prisoners' Legal Rights Group', a forum for knowledge transfer, whose membership includes, among others, prisoners and ex-prisoners (Scott 2009).

These vital prisoner actions disturb common sense understandings. They dovetail with those engaged in direct action demonstrations who engage in speeches, photos, flyers, placards, press releases, banners, media interviews and casual conversations with bystanders to send a message that something is wrong. Even if the act is small, they *make something happen*. They highlight civil death, social death and corporeal death and are a step in developing a new democratic space—a modern day *agora* or public space where people can learn about and engage in dialogue about contemporary prison life. Those who make some noise now—such as by speaking, naming or playing instruments at public gatherings outside prisons—are helping to create a new public space that sheds light upon the spirit of death haunting the prison. Their direct activism and lobbying raises the profile of deaths in prison and creates rational, informed dialogue.

Hearing the voice of families, ex-prisoners, current prisoners, researchers and sometimes the voice of those who have worked in prisons, can provide powerful testimony of the damage prison creates both for prisoners and the wider community. Prison authorities and officers should also speak out and name the prison for what it is by talking openly about the harmful consequences they see on a daily basis. To facilitate a new *agora* we need to listen to the voice of experience, and to hear the suffering and hardship that prison generates for all. Ultimately this means naming the prison for what it is: an institution of violence, suffering and death.

Through highlighting our common humanity, dignity and human rights—especially the *right to life*—there is an opportunity to offer a more life affirming message about how we deal with individual and collective problems, troubles and wrongdoing. Abolitionists must then say NO to the prison, NO to the spirit of death, but YES to policies and practices which build social bonds, meet human needs and facilitate human potential.

Notes

1. *Keenan v United Kingdom* [2001] 33 EHRR 38.
2. *Edwards v United Kingdom* [2002] 35 EHRR 19.
3. The key case which opened the way to legally challenge the civil death of prisoners in the courts was *Golder v United Kingdom* [1975] 1 EHRR 542.
4. *Hirst v United Kingdom* [no. 2] (2004) EHRR (and 6 October 2005).
5. ACCT is an individualised care plan for prisoners at risk of suicide or self-harm. The ACCT is designed to provide flexible care and support for at-risk prisoners. At any one time between 1500 and 2000 prisoners in England and Wales are subject to ACCT care plans. See FOIA Request, 2 February 2017.
6. See FOIA Request, 16 January 2018.
7. Abolitionist social movements have a long history in the UK. INQUEST has had a presence since 1981. Other abolitionist groups include: those inspired by Anarchism, such as 'Empty Cages Collective' and 'Incarcerated Workers Organising Committee'; broad based socialist inspired groups like 'Manchester No Prisons' and 'Pies Not Prisons'; and more practitioner and policy orientated groups like 'Reclaim Justice Network' and 'Reclaim Holloway'. Further abolitionist interventions inspired by feminism, such as those by 'Sisters

Uncut', have engaged in activism around deaths in prison along-side other campaigns. Following several transgender deaths in prison, 'Action for Trans Health' have also engaged in abolitionist activism.

8. In 2007, the Corston review explored the criminal justice processing and imprisonment of women with vulnerabilities. See Malloch, this volume.

9. The placement of transgender prisoners based on their perceived biological sex has meant that they have been imprisoned in institutions that do not match their gender identity. One key concern is the use of segregation for transgender prisoners, which denies them equal access to facilities, healthcare, recreation and socialising with peers. Poor provision has meant that transgender prisoners have been routinely denied access to gender appropriate clothing, make-up, hormone treatment and gender surgeries necessary for their health and wellbeing. It is also known that the withdrawal of such items and treatments have serious negative health outcomes, including increased risks of suicidal ideation and self-harm.

10. Following the deaths of Vikki Thompson and Joanne Latham the transgender policy of the prison service was reviewed (completed in December 2016). The most recent prison service policy on transgender prisoners is *PSI 17 The Care and Management of Transgender Offenders*, effective 1 January 2017 (NOMS 2016).

11. See Action for Trans Health (2016) for details. This initiative also mirrored actions elsewhere, for example by No Pride in Prisons (now People Against Prisons Aotearoa) in New Zealand. Following the death of Jenny Swift, a 42 year old transgender prisoner, on 30 December 2016, a noise demonstration was organised by the same groups alongside the *Queer Agenda Sheffield* outside HMP Doncaster. The protest coincided with the Trans Prisoner Day of Action and Solidarity, an annual international event protesting against the treatment of transgender and non-binary prisoners. In a press release the organisers stated that current policies on transgender prisoners cause "extreme psychological distress and loss of dignity, as well as putting them at risk of violence by other prisoners" (Manchester No Prisons 2016). This demonstration received local media attention (Duffy 2017) and also mobilised a large number of transgender activists to engage with the abolitionist movement.

12. There have been three self-inflicted deaths at HMP Hindley since 2012: Jake Hardy in 2012, Stephen Connell in 2015 and Anthony Hill in 2017.
13. In early 2018 the focus shifted to HMP Liverpool, which was described by politicians, the media and the HMCIP as the worst prison in the country.
14. Listeners are prisoners who are trained by the Samaritans to listen and offer support to prisoners who are experiencing difficulties coping or thoughts of self-harm. The scheme was developed at HMP Swansea in the early 1990s and the listener will often be asked to share a cell with those prisoners that they are helping so they are available for immediate support.
15. At this demonstration the police deployed a large number of officers and police helicopter in response to a small demonstration of around 30 protestors. This seemed excessive at the time and, to avoid conflict, the demo ended earlier than planned. On 22 March 2017 it was revealed that HMP Hindley is the proposed site of a new mega prison in Greater Manchester.

References

Action for Trans Health. (2016). *No Pride in Prisons*. [Online]. Available https://www.youtube.com/watch?v=JbX3hk20Ctw. Accessed February 20, 2018.

Alexander, J. C. (2012). *Trauma: A Social Theory*. Cambridge: Polity Press.

Bauman, Z. (1989). *Modernity and the Holocaust*. Cambridge: Polity Press.

Bauman, Z. (1999). *In Search of Politics*. Cambridge: Polity Press.

Berger, D., & Losier, T. (2018). *Rethinking the American Prison Movement*. London: Routledge.

Cacho, L. M. (2012). *Social Death*. New York: New York University Press.

Cavarero, A. (2005). *For More Than One Voice*. Stanford: Stanford University Press.

Cohen, S. (2001). *States of Denial*. Cambridge: Polity Press.

Coles, D., & Ward, T. (1994). Failure stories: Prison suicides and how not to prevent them. In A. Ward & T. Ward (Eds.), *Deaths in Custody: International Perspectives* (pp. 127–142). London: Whiting and Birch.

Duffy, T. (2017, January 23). Protest over Jenny Swift's death in Doncaster prison. *Liverpool Echo*. [Online]. Available http://www.liverpoolecho.co.uk/

news/liverpool-news/protest-over-jenny-swifts-death-12492583. Accessed February 20, 2018.

Esposito, B., & Wood, L. (1982). *Prison Slavery.* Washington: Committee to Abolish Prison Slavery.

FOIA Request. (2017). *SIDS of Prisoners, 2 February 2017 (David Scott).* [Online]. Available https://www.whatdotheyknow.com/request/sids_of_prisoners_on_acct#incoming-930900. Accessed February 20, 2018.

FOIA Request. (2017). *Self Harm and SIDS in Prisons in England and Wales, 16 January 2018 (David Scott).* [Online]. Available https://www.whatdotheyknow.com/request/self_harm_and_sids_in_prisons_in#incoming-1097148. Accessed February 20, 2018.

HM Chief Inspector of Prisons [HMCIP]. (1999). *Suicide is Everyone's Concern.* London: HMCIP.

HM Chief Inspector of Prisons [HMCIP]. (2016). *Report on an Unannounced Inspection of HMP Hindley by HM Chief Inspector of Prisons, 4–15 July 2016.* London: HMIP.

HM Government. (2005). *Government Response to the Third Report from the Joint Committee on Human Rights: Deaths in Custody.* HL 69/HC 416. London: HMSO.

Holland, S. P. (2000). *Raising the Dead: Readings of Death and (Black) Subjectivity.* Durham: Duke University Press.

INQUEST. (2017). *Jury Concludes Unnecessary Delays and Failures in Care Contributed to Death of Sarah Reed at Holloway Prison.* [Online]. Available https://www.inquest.org.uk/sarah-reed-inquest-conclusions. Accessed February 20, 2018.

JanMohamed, A. R. (2005). *The Death-Bound-Subject.* Durham: Duke University Press.

Jasper, L. (2017, July 24). Those who failed Sarah Reed must be held to account. *The Guardian.* [Online]. Available https://www.theguardian.com/commentisfree/2017/jul/24/sarah-reed-death-avoidable-mental-illness-holloway-prison?CMP=share_btn_tw. Accessed February 20, 2018.

Khan, O. (2017, July 2). The independent report into deaths in custody must be delayed no longer. *The Guardian.* [Online]. Available https://www.theguardian.com/uk-news/2017/jul/02/the-independent-report-into-police-custody-deaths-must-not-be-delayed-any-longer. Accessed February 20, 2018.

Kropotkin, P. (1895). *In Russian and French Prisons.* London: Black Rose Books.

Lamour, P. (2016, February 23). Sarah Reed's death demands a paradigm shift in how black women are treated. *The Guardian*. [Online]. Available https:// www.theguardian.com/commentisfree/2016/feb/23/sarah-reed-death-custo-dy-paradigm-shift-black-women-blaksox-campaign. Accessed February 20, 2018.

Liebling, A. (1992). *Suicides in Prison*. London: Routledge.

Malloch, M. (2000). *Women, Drugs and Custody*. Winchester: Waterside Press.

Manchester No Prison. (2016). *Press Statement*. Manchester: Manchester No Prison.

Mathiesen, T. (2004). *Silently Silenced*. Winchester: Waterside Press.

Medlicott, D. (2001). *Surviving the Prison Place: Narratives of Suicidal Prisoners*. Aldershot: Ashgate.

Mills, C. W. (1959). *The Sociological Imagination*. Oxford: Oxford University Press.

Ministry of Justice. (2018). *Safety in Custody Statistics, England and Wales 2017*. London: Ministry of Justice.

National Offender Management Service [NOMS]. (2016). *PSI 17: The Care and Management of Transgender Offenders*. PSI 17/2016. [Online]. Available https://www.justice.gov.uk/offenders/psis/prison-service-instructions-2016. Accessed March 2, 2018.

Patterson, O. (1982). *Slavery and Social Death*. London: Harvard University Press.

Price, J. M. (2015). *Prison and Social Death*. London: Rutgers University Press.

Prison Reform Trust. (2016). *The Bromley Briefing*. London: Prison Reform Trust.

Sarah Reed Campaign for Justice. (2016). *Launch of Sarah Reed Justice Campaign*. [Online]. Available https://www.youtube.com/watch?v=I7x2n-WYKBhU. Accessed February 20, 2018.

Scott, D. (2008). Creating ghosts in the penal machine: Prison officer occupational morality and the techniques of denial. In J. Bennett, B. Crewe, & A. Wahidin (Eds.), *Understanding Prison Staff* (pp. 168–186). London: Routledge.

Scott, D. (2009). Resistance as reform. *Criminal Justice Matters, 77,* 20–21.

Scott, D. (2011). That's not my name. *Criminal Justice Matters, 84,* 8–9.

Scott, D. (2013). The politics of prisoner legal rights. *Howard Journal of Criminal Justice, 52*(3), 233–250.

Scott, D. (2016). *Emancipatory Politics and Praxis*. London: EG Press.

Scott, D., & Codd, H. (2010). *Controversial Issues in Prisons*. Buckingham: Open University Press.

Scraton, P. & Chadwick, K. (1987). "Speaking ill of the dead": Institutionalized responses to deaths in custody. In P. Scraton (Ed.), *Law, Order and the Authoritarian State: Readings in Critical Criminology* (pp. 212–236). Milton Keynes: Open University Press.

Seale, C. (1998). *Constructing Death*. Cambridge: Cambridge University Press.

Sellin, J. T. (1976). *Slavery and the Penal System*. Oxford: Elsevier.

Sykes, G. (1958). *The Society of Captives*. Princeton, NJ: Princeton University Press.

Taylor, D. (2017, July 20). Care failings contributed to death of woman in prison, inquest finds. *The Guardian*. [Online]. Available https://www.theguardian.com/society/2017/jul/20/care-failings-contributed-to-death-of-woman-sarah-reed-in-prison-inquest-finds. Accessed February 20, 2018.

Topp, D. O. (1979). Suicide in prison. *British Journal of Psychiatry, 134,* 24–27.

Travis, A. (2017, April 27). Prison statistics reveal big rise in self-harm and assaults on staff. *The Guardian*. [Online]. Available https://www.theguardian.com/society/2017/apr/27/prison-statistics-reveal-big-rise-in-assaults-on-staff-and-self-harm. Accessed February 20, 2018.

Wool, R., & Pont, J. (2006). *Prison Health*. London: Quay Books.

Table of Cases

Edwards v United Kingdom [2002] 35 EHRR 19.
Golder v United Kingdom [1975] 1 EHRR 542.
Hirst v United Kingdom [no. 2] (2004) EHRR (and 06/10/2005).
Keenan v United Kingdom [2001] 33 EHRR 38.

7

Human Rights for 'Hard Cases': Alternatives to Imprisonment for Serious Offending by Children and Youth

Nessa Lynch

Introduction

Across contemporary western jurisdictions, it is almost ubiquitous to have specialised systems for sentencing young offenders, including separate places of detention (Muncie and Goldson 2006). Nonetheless, in even the most outwardly progressive of human rights cultures, a young offender convicted of a serious violent offence is liable to a sentence of imprisonment administered through the adult correctional system (CRIN 2015). New Zealand's presumptive regime for murder sentencing means, for instance, that a child who was 13 at the time of the offence is serving a sentence of 18 years imprisonment (*R v Nelson* [2012]), and a young person who was 16 at the time of the offence is serving a sentence of life imprisonment with a minimum period of imprisonment of 17 years (*R v Slade & Hamilton* [2005]).

N. Lynch (✉)
Victoria University of Wellington, Wellington, New Zealand
e-mail: nessa.lynch@vuw.ac.nz

© The Author(s) 2018
E. Stanley (ed.), *Human Rights and Incarceration*, Palgrave Studies
in Prisons and Penology, https://doi.org/10.1007/978-3-319-95399-1_7

In New Zealand, there are approximately 90 under-18-year olds currently serving sentences of imprisonment in adult correctional facilities (Department of Corrections 2017a). This situation is mirrored in comparable jurisdictions (O'Brien and Fitz-Gibbon 2016).

Patently, such juxtaposition of youth, vulnerability and high-tariff sentences of imprisonment in adult prison raise concerns for the rights and interests of the young offender. But, top-end offences such as homicide are the most serious harms and wrongs in the criminal law, and the interests and rights of victims and the public must also be considered. Young offenders who commit such offences receive relatively little attention in the human rights literature, posing as they do conceptual challenges to norms of youth justice, such as the paramountcy of best interests. The human rights framework itself gives little concrete guidance on such matters, except broad expressions of principle.

It is not proposed here to contest the harmful effects of the sentence of imprisonment, nor to dispute that decarceration and prison abolition are worthy long-term goals. The principal argument made is that in a vacuum of analysis by scholars or guidance from human rights bodies, and in the absence of concrete alternatives for protection and accountability, young offenders will continue to be subject to adult punitive sentences. New Zealand is used as a case study to sketch what a human rights compliant model of age-appropriate accountability for such youth might look like, using the offence of homicide as an example. Such instances of serious offending are 'hard cases', with public discourse focussed on rights as a zero-sum game.

The 'Hard Cases'

A range of terms such as child, youth, young person, juvenile offender or young offender may be used to denote youth in conflict with the law. Article 1 of the United Nations *Convention on the Rights of the Child* (CRC) uses the term "child" to refer to all those aged less than 18 years, unless the age of majority is reached earlier, but as detailed below a number of jurisdictions (e.g. Scotland, New Zealand) have ages of penal majority which are less than 18.

The dominant approach across western common law jurisdictions (such as England and Wales, Republic of Ireland, Scotland, most Australian states) is to remove the young person to the adult court when homicide is alleged. With some exceptions, notably Canada and Western Australia, this means that the young person is removed from the youth court. The consequence of removal from the protections and specialised procedures of the youth justice system is that, upon conviction, the young offender is subject to the adult sentencing regime. As Table 7.1 demonstrates for homicide, particularly murder, this generally involves a sentence of life imprisonment.

Table 7.1 Sentencing powers for youth convicted of homicide across a selection of jurisdictions

Jurisdiction	Murder	Manslaughter[a]	Statutory exceptions for youth
New Zealand	Presumption of life unless manifestly unjust	Discretionary	Life without parole prohibited
England and Wales	Mandatory life imprisonment	Discretionary	Shorter minimum murder non-parole periods
Republic of Ireland	Mandatory life imprisonment	Discretionary	
Scotland	Mandatory life imprisonment	Discretionary	
Canada	Mandatory life imprisonment	Min 4 years if firearm was used	10 years 1st degree murder 7 years 2nd degree murder[b]
ACT	Life is a discretionary maximum	Discretionary 20-year max[c]	Age should be relevant in exercise of discretion
New South Wales	Life is a discretionary Maximum	25-year max	Age should be relevant in exercise of discretion

(continued)

Table 7.1 (continued)

Jurisdiction	Murder	Manslaughter[a]	Statutory exceptions for youth
Queensland	Mandatory life imprisonment	Max penalty—life imprisonment	Life imprisonment is not mandatory for murder[d]
South Australia	Mandatory life imprisonment	Max penalty—life imprisonment	Offender must be treated as an adult for murder
Tasmania	Life is a discretionary maximum	Discretionary	Age should be relevant in exercise of discretion
Victoria	Life is a discretionary maximum	Discretionary 20-year max	Age should be relevant in exercise of discretion
Western Australia	Presumptive sentence of life imprisonment[e]	Discretionary 20-year max	Life is a discretionary maximum for murder
Northern Territory	Mandatory life imprisonment	Discretionary	

[a]Culpable homicide in Scotland
[b]However, the Attorney-General can request that the Youth Court give a full adult sentence of life if the offender was over 14 at the time of offending
[c]28-year maximum in aggravating circumstances
[d]There is a high threshold for giving a life sentence to youth offenders. It must have been a "particularly heinous offence"
[e]Life sentence may not be given where it would be clearly unjust and the offender is unlikely to pose a threat

The consequence of removal to the adult system are sentences which are exponentially more punitive than those available through the youth justice system, and which in some cases involve detention exceeding the amount of time which the child or young person has been alive. Table 7.2 illustrates a sample of New Zealand children and young persons convicted of murder between 2002 and 2015. Apart from one fixed sentence, all received a life sentence, with minimum non-parole periods ranging from 10 to 17 years (see further, Lynch 2018).

Table 7.2 Children and young persons convicted of murder in New Zealand 2002–2015 ordered by sentence length (N = 18)[a]

Date	Sex	Age[b]	s104[c]	Sentence[d]	MPI (years)[e]
2012	M	13	n/a	18 years (fixed)	x
2002	M	15	n/a	Life	10
2003	F	14	n/a	Life*	10
2004	M	16	Displaced	Life	10
2004	M	16	n/a	Life	10
2007	M	16	n/a	Life	10
2008	M	16	n/a	Life*	11
2010	M	15	n/a	Life	11
2011	M	14	Displaced	Life	11
2010	M	14	Displaced	Life*	11.5
2010	F	16	Displaced	Life*	11.5
2009	M	15	Displaced	Life*	12.5
2007	M	15	Displaced	Life	14
2013	F	14	Displaced	Life	14
2014	M	15	Displaced	Life	14
2014	M	15	Displaced	Life*	14.5
2010	M	16	Displaced	Life*	15.5
2004	M	16	Applied	Life	17

[a]There were 21 relevant convictions during this period, but sentencing notes could not be located for three of these cases
[b]Age at time of offence
[c]Indicates that presumption of 17-year minimum period of imprisonment applies because of presence of specified statutory aggravating factors, and whether it was displaced or applied
[d]For lead offence only, * indicates concurrent sentence applied
[e]Minimum period of imprisonment

The Harmful Effects of Imprisonment

At June 30, 2017, there were 49 sixteen-year-olds serving a sentence in an adult prison (45 male, 4 female).[1] Of those aged 17, and considered to be adults under the current New Zealand legislation, 42 males (33 sentenced, 9 remand) and four females (remand) were held in adult prisons.[2]

The harmful effects of custody, are uncontested here. The use of the adult sentences of imprisonment for youth is contrary to international standards for youth justice (Goldson and Kilkelly 2013). It is traumatic and punitive (Tomasevski 1986; Halsey 2017; Ashkar and Kenny 2008). It is criminogenic, with young offenders who enter prison as a teenager almost destined to return for further offending (Department of Corrections 2007). The sentence of imprisonment is used disproportionately against Māori (Jackson 1988; Waitangi Tribunal 2017), with over half of prisoners identifying as Māori (Department of Corrections 2017b). Young offenders may also be in physical danger from adult prisoners (Defence for Children International 2003; McDonald 2006). While those under 18 are to be kept separate from adults, the Chief Executive may authorise mixing. While young males can be held in Youth Units, young females are always held in the general section of the women's prisons (Department of Corrections 2017c; Goldingay 2012).

Hurdles to Abolition of the Use of Imprisonment

There is surprisingly little scholarship on the appropriate sentencing of children and young persons who commit very serious offences, particularly homicide. The treatment of the two English boys found guilty of the murder of James Bulger has received considerable academic treatment, but centred largely on the socio-political context and the media and public reaction (James and Jenks 1996; Haydon and Scraton 2000) than an attempt to propose a principled approach to dealing with the harm and wrong encompassed in the murder. An edited collection by Cavadino (1996) placed the Bulger trial in context comparing the punitiveness of the English approach to more tolerant Continental European approaches. Similarly, David Green's (2012) comparative study of the Bulger murder and a similar incident in Scandinavia highlights the societal poles of punitiveness and tolerance.

While considerable progress has been made in the diversion and de-carceration of young offenders for minor or moderate offending, there has been little progress with abolition or even reduction of the use of imprisonment for young offenders who commit top-end violent offences such as murder. Three principal hurdles have resonance across jurisdictions: (i) the limits of guidance in human rights instruments; (ii) punitiveness; and (iii) societal expectations.

The Human Rights Framework for Serious Offending by Children and Young People

First, international human rights standards do not provide enough guidance on principled responses to serious violent offending by children and young persons, particularly in balancing the public's right to safety and victims' rights or interests. This vacuum leaves space for punitiveness to flourish.

International human rights standards are increasingly influential on domestic youth justice practice (Muncie 2005; Muncie and Goldson 2006). The most widely applicable is the *UN Convention on the Rights of the Child* (CRC) (1989) and its associated standards. The United Nations also has several specialist Rules that provide standards for the operation of the youth justice system (*Beijing Rules* 1985) and for young persons in custody (*Havana Rules* 1990) (see Haydon, this volume). Regional instruments such as the Council of Europe's *Child Friendly Justice Guidelines* 2010) have also been developed. There is by now considerable academic and practice literature on the application of such standards in national youth justice systems (Goldson and Muncie 2012; Hollingsworth 2007). Unsurprisingly, the vast majority of this literature focuses on the child or young person who is in conflict with the law; the child or young person as suspect, defendant or offender (see, e.g., Kilkelly 2008). There is, rightly, much discussion of how such children and young persons may often be more appropriately categorised as victims themselves, as a result of parental or state abuse and neglect, mental and physical health problems, lack of education, and poverty (Goldson and Kilkelly 2013; Haydon, this volume).

The United Nations Committee on the Rights of the Child (UNCRC) (2007) have elaborated on the fundamental strands of a principled youth justice system:

> ***Best interests must be a primary consideration (Article 3)*** - This requires a child-centred approach, where the best interests of the child or young person are a primary consideration. Without losing "attention to effective public safety", this means "that the traditional objectives of criminal justice, such as repression/retribution, must give way to rehabilitation

and restorative justice objectives in dealing with child offenders" (CRC 2007: para. 10). This does not preclude consideration of the interests of other parties. As Alston (1994: 13) comments, this formulation seems "to impose a burden of proof on those seeking to achieve such a non-child-centred result to demonstrate that, under the circumstances, other feasible and acceptable alternatives do not exist".

Non-discrimination (Article 2) - This requires a focus on ensuring that particular groups of children and young persons such as female youth, homeless youth, disabled youth, ethnic minorities and indigenous youth are not discriminated against.

Participation (Article 12) - The basis is that the child or young person is considered to be an individual with their own rights and interests, capable of having a role in any decisions affecting them. The child or young person must be assisted to participate effectively in proceedings and to have their views taken into account commensurate with their age and abilities.

Reintegration (Article 40.1) - Rehabilitation implies that responsibility rests solely with an individual who can be removed from society for treatment and once restored, released. Reintegration has a different starting point. It rejects the assumption that the difficulties which children and young persons face are necessarily individual and considers the social environment of the child or young person.

As to the use of detention, Article 37(b) of the CRC states that custody "shall be used only as a measure of last resort and for the shortest appropriate period of time" (Goldson 2002). The sentence of imprisonment in an adult prison is clearly contrary to the CRC. Article 37(c) and (d) of the CRC requires that young persons in custody are treated humanely, are separated from adult prisoners in custodial settings and have appropriate access to family and legal advisors. As the UNCRC has observed (2007: para. 85):

> Every child deprived of liberty shall be separated from adults. A child deprived of his/her liberty shall not be placed in an adult prison or other facility for adults. There is abundant evidence that the placement of children in adult prisons or jails compromises their basic safety, well-being, and their future ability to remain free of crime and to reintegrate. The permitted exception to the separation of children from adults stated in

Article 37 (c) of CRC, "unless it is considered in the child's best interests not to do so", should be interpreted narrowly; the child's best interests does not mean for the convenience of the States parties. States parties should establish separate facilities for children deprived of their liberty, which include distinct, child-centred staff, personnel, policies and practices.

In relation to responding to children who have committed serious crimes, human rights bodies have set out broad principles, but are shorter on detail. The Committee on the Rights of the Child (2007: para. 71) sets out:

> In cases of severe offences by children, measures proportionate to the circumstances of the offender and to the gravity of the offence may be considered, including considerations of the need of public safety and sanctions. In the case of children, such considerations must always be outweighed by the need to safeguard the well-being and the best interests of the child and to promote his/her reintegration.

The *Beijing Rules* give more guidance, providing that custodial interventions should not be imposed "unless the juvenile is adjudicated of a serious act involving violence against another person or of persistence in committing other serious offences and unless there is no other appropriate response" (Rule 17.1(c) & Rule 18.1).

In contrast to the extensive guidance given on conditions for disposition of minor offending, such as the diversion of young persons from judicial processes (Rule 11; UNICEF 2003, 2006, 2010), there is little discussion of appropriate outcomes for children and young persons who commit top-end violent offences.

Punitive Responses to Top-End Violent Offending

Second, across jurisdictions, sentencing for top-end violent offences for *all* offenders has become more punitive and less discretionary (Tonry 2009). The tide of punitiveness has not left young offenders behind. Punitive sentences such as life imprisonment, whole-of-life terms or long periods of imprisonment without parole are enshrined in legislation without specific exceptions for children and youth (CRIN 2015). It is also apparent that in some aspects, young offenders are treated in a *more* punitive manner than in the past. In a New Zealand context, Graham (2011) discusses the 1954 murder case which inspired the film 'Heavenly Creatures', where the 16-year-old female co-offenders served around five years imprisonment before discretionary release by the Minister of Justice, with an emphasis on rehabilitation. In a similar 2009 killing, the two young female offenders were each sentenced to life, with a minimum period of 10 years for the 14-year-old (*Te Wini v R* [2013]) and 14 years for the 17-year-old (*Churchward v R* [2011]). Further, public safety, rather than rehabilitation is now the paramount consideration for release by the Parole Board (*Parole Act 2002*; Allen 1981).

Reforms to sentencing and juvenile transfer laws and more punitive treatments are "grounded in concerns about public protection and the belief there is no good reason to exercise leniency with young offenders" (Steinberg and Scott 2003: 1009). Public opinion on the rights and responsibilities of children and youth remain "a confusing accumulation of inconsistencies" (Cuncannon 1997: 282). As Fionda (2001: 77) details:

> The notion of children as objects of concern, as lacking competence to think their actions through and as capable of outgrowing their troublesome and immature behaviour has, to some extent, been sidelined in the quest for a politically expedient and therefore highly retributive response to youth crime.

The law views all children or young persons as vulnerable, deserving of protection and largely incompetent to make decisions until he or she comes in conflict with the criminal law (Hollingsworth 2007). Then the child or young person appears to undergo a legal transformation into an individual capable of making rational and informed choices (Baird and Samuels 1996). Children and young persons may be considered "most competent when they are most delinquent" (Cuncannon 1997: 291).

Guggenheim (2005) argues that the changing image of children and youth from vulnerable to competent and autonomous has worsened the lot of the young offender as society increasingly views such children as sophisticated and culpable.

Societal Expectations

Third, there may also be a gulf between societal expectations for responses to offences like murder and rape, and the short-term outcomes available in youth justice systems. International studies of public opinion find general support for the rehabilitation of young offenders (Nagin et al. 2006; Piquero and Steinberg 2010; Roberts and Hough 2005). A recent study of New Zealand public opinion found that those surveyed supported rehabilitative and preventive measures for young offenders, with victims of crime having less punitive attitudes than non-victims (Barretto et al. 2016). However, public opinion on the appropriate response to very serious violent offending by young persons is less clear. Roberts (2004: 508) notes:

> It seems clear that the public become more opposed to discounted sentencing for juveniles as the age of the offender or the seriousness of the offense increases. Indeed, for the most serious crimes, people probably see no justification for according any mitigation to the offender. The seriousness of murder appears to swamp any sympathy for the offender that is elicited by the presence of mitigating factors such as age.

Roberts (2004: 508) also posits that "most people believe that for murder the penalty for juveniles should be the same as the penalty for adults", but acknowledges that specific research, particularly surveys which provide detail on the circumstances of the offender, is needed. Such a study by Applegate and Davis (2006) used vignettes to elicit public views of the sentencing of young offenders for murder, and found that the respondents were less punitive than expected in most cases, and in favour of shorter terms of imprisonment.

Taken together, these three factors have meant that young offenders convicted of homicide continue to be dealt with through adult trial and under sentencing principles focussed on retribution and deterrence rather than reintegration.

Principled Alternatives to the Sentence of Imprisonment—A Case Study

The abolition of the use of custody for youth is an admirable and worthy long-term goal. But it is the contention here that unless concrete alternatives are proposed, in the short to medium term, the punitive status quo will remain. Other more punitive voices will provide the blueprint for legislation and policy.

The proposals below establish a pragmatic policy blueprint for alternatives to long sentences of adult imprisonment for young offenders convicted of homicide. The New Zealand system is used as a case study, but these proposals have comparative relevance. These proposals are relatively simple and achievable in the short to medium term, they reflect the public's legitimate interest in safety and accountability for serious crime, and they advance a rights-based approach to all children and young people in conflict with the law.

A Single Jurisdiction for Youth

In New Zealand, the age of criminal responsibility is 10 years (*Crimes Act 1961*: s.21). The term "child" refers specifically to a 10–13-year-old, and a 14–16-year-old is a "young person" (*Oranga Tamariki Act 1989*: s.2). The protections of the youth justice system currently end at 17 years. An Act of Parliament which would raise this age to 18 for most offences (but not homicide or top-end violent offending) has been passed and will be brought into force by mid-2019 (*Oranga Tamariki Legislation Act 2017*: s.2).

The present approach in New Zealand, as in other comparable jurisdictions is juxtapositionary. The youth justice system is regarded as tolerant and evidence based (Lynch 2013), with principles emphasising community and family based dispositions. Because of a legislative emphasis on diversion and de-carceration, custody is used as a last resort, and only a small minority of cases result in these orders (Lynch 2016a). A "young person" may be prosecuted for all types of offending, but generally in the specialised youth court. Here, young people may receive a "supervision with residence" (custodial) order, and are subsequently detained in "youth justice residences".

In what James and Jenks (1996) term a "conceptual eviction", when the child or young person is alleged to have committed a very serious offence such as homicide, there is a removal to the adult court and adult sentencing systems. These jurisdictional exceptions mean that the young defendant is exposed to the full adversarial criminal trial, without the benefit of protective aspects such as closed court hearings, judges and lawyers who are trained in communicating with children, and the specialist legislative principles which generally underpin youth justice systems. The effect on young defendants is stark, including trauma from the process itself and a lack of effective participation (Royal College of Psychiatrists 2006). Upon transfer, the young person is subject to the *Sentencing Act 2002* with its emphasis on retribution, deterrence and mandatory sentencing.

A single jurisdiction for youth—meaning that the child or young person would be dealt with by the existing specialised youth court whatever their alleged offence—would mean that the child or young person would be dealt with in a more age appropriate manner, with the specialised trained personnel and procedures envisaged in international human rights standards (CRC 1989: Article 40.1).

A significant hurdle, to the establishment of a single jurisdiction for youth, is the narrow scope of powers currently available in the youth jurisdiction. In New Zealand, detention of a maximum six months is allowed, with an attendant period of supervision (*Oranga Tamariki Act 1989*: s.283). Comparable jurisdictions prescribe similarly constrained periods of detention. For example, in New South Wales, the maximum period is two years (*Children (Criminal Proceedings) Act 1987*: s.33(g)). This means that where public safety requires a longer period of detention or supervision, the child or young person must be transferred to the adult system for sentences. While the New Zealand youth justice system has largely remained a bastion of tolerance in an increasingly punitive penal environment (Pratt and Clark 2005; Lynch 2013), the narrow scope of orders available to the Youth Court widen the exclusionary approach where top-end offending is concerned.

As an example of a somewhat counter-intuitive effect, the maximum custodial order available to the New Zealand Youth Court was originally three months, but this was doubled through legislative reform in 2010 (Lynch 2010). Prima facie, this appears punitive in intent. On closer examination, the effect of the change was a reduction in overall punitiveness and sentences of imprisonment for youth. A report on the first year of the reforms showed a dramatic reduction in the number of transfers to the adult court (Lynch 2016a). The decline is likely to be due to the availability of expanded supervision with residence orders within the youth jurisdiction, with the implication that judges appear to have increased confidence that public safety and rehabilitative programmes can be achieved without transferring the young person to the adult system (ibid.). While on principle, the expansion of Youth Court orders was opposed by many, including the author, the overall effect was that young offenders who would have served time in adult prisons were dealt with in a more age-appropriate and tolerant manner. Scholars and human rights advocates must be open to the idea of broader powers within the youth justice system to respond appropriately to top-end offences. This is permissible within the human rights framework, where the interests of others such as victims and the public must also be considered.

A Requirement that Young Offenders Serve Sentences of Imprisonment in Youth Justice Custody Rather Than an Adult Prison

It is not contended that youth justice custody is a perfect solution. Studies highlight that custody also poses a significant risk of harm for young offenders (Kilkelly et al. 2002). Nonetheless, where it is necessary that a young offender be detained, there must be a strict requirement that he or she is kept in a specialised youth justice residence. No young person should be detained with adult prisoners.

This power is already available in New Zealand, with the legislative ability for those aged 14–16 years to serve a sentence of imprisonment in the custody of the Ministry for Vulnerable Children (Department of Corrections 2017a). Thus there is no legal reason why young persons should not be held in age-appropriate facilities.

Removal of Mandatory or Presumptive Sentencing Provisions for Youth

As noted above, a conviction for top-end violent offending is currently a conduit to a lengthy sentence of adult imprisonment, with mandatory or presumptive sentencing regimes having a considerable effect. Such removal or restriction of judicial discretion reduces opportunities for proportionate and appropriate outcomes for young offenders (Feld 2012; Lynch 2018).

Murder sentencing is tightly prescribed in New Zealand and is an example of how such laws have punitive effect on youth. There are three potential judicial decision points once a young offender has been convicted of murder.

1. To impose the presumptive sentence of life imprisonment unless "manifestly unjust" to do so (*Sentencing Act 2002*: s.102).
2. To fix the minimum period which the offender must serve before he or she is eligible to apply for parole (MPI). Where life imprisonment is imposed, it will be a minimum term of ten years. The judge is required to fix the MPI necessary for accountability, denunciation, public protection and deterrence (*Sentencing Act 2002*: s.103).
3. To impose the presumptive 17 year MPI in cases where one or more of a list of 10 aggravating factors is present (e.g. particular vulnerability of the victim), unless it would be "manifestly unjust" to do so (*Sentencing Act 2002*: s.104).

The New Zealand Parliament has chosen not to enact a specific rule for youth even though, for the majority of other offences, such youth would be dealt with in a very different system.[3] The idea of the "manifestly unjust" standard was to give the judiciary 'wriggle room' to rebut the presumptive sentence where the circumstances of the offence and/or the offender warrant it. However, the term is not defined in the legislation. In one decision, sentencing a 14 year old girl for murder (*R v O'Brien* [2003]: para. 19), it was said:

> "Unjust" can only mean that in the context of a particular murder and a particular offender, the normal sentence of life imprisonment runs counter to both a Judge's perception of a lawfully just result and also offends against the community's innate sense of justice. "Manifestly" means that the injustice must be patently clear or obvious.

Unfortunately, as Table 7.2 demonstrates, since the presumptive provision was enacted in 2002, only one child (a 13-year-old) has received a fixed sentence instead of the presumptive sentence of life. This suggests that despite the small amount of judicial discretion permitted, judges find themselves bound by the presumptive provision. The particular (temporal) characteristics of youth such as vulnerability and lesser capacity mean that the presumptive sentence of life imprisonment is disproportionate and particularly punitive (Feld 2012). Such a presumption should be entirely removed for youth, so that judges may craft a more proportionate sentence. As Table 7.1 shows, such presumptive and mandatory sentences are also in operation in comparable jurisdictions. Fitz-Gibbon's (2016) study of judicial and legal professionals also suggests that discretion would temper the punitive effect of these sentences.

As an example, in the sentencing of manslaughter in New Zealand, there is no presumptive or mandatory sentence, and judges have carved out some measure of tolerance for youth. In a recent case where a 13 year old child was found guilty of manslaughter (*P v R* [2016]), the Court of Appeal disagreed with the High Court that a minimum term of imprisonment was required and approved of the expert assessor's comment that denunciation and deterrence has little relevance in the case of a young child. P's deficiencies in capacity (particularly his youth and his brain injury) meant that the rational choice theories underpinning these principles were of limited effect. While not at odds with the importance of protecting the public, the Court of Appeal (para. 54) concluded that public safety would be more likely to be ensured through P's successful rehabilitation and reintegration:

> P is a young person who is developing, and whose rehabilitative needs are therefore changing. We view imposition of an MPI as inconsistent with the flexibility required best to facilitate P's rehabilitation.

In this, there is a recognition that P as the 13-year-old who carried out a manslaughter may be a very different individual two to three years later (Lynch 2016b). The Court also recommended that P serve his three year, three month sentence in a youth justice residence rather than a prison. Thus, specific legislative exceptions to mandatory or presumptive sentences may promote age-appropriate accountability.

A Legislative Cap

While judicial discretion may be a potential disruptor of punitive penal policy, set legislative maxima on periods of detention for youth may be a more lasting method of reducing sentences of imprisonment. As Table 7.1 demonstrates, it is already the practice in a number of jurisdictions to have a cap on sentences for youth.

In New Zealand, this is already the case for some types of indefinite sentence. Preventive detention is not permitted to be imposed on those aged less than 18 (*Sentencing Act 2002*, s.87(2)(b)). In 2010, a sentence of life without parole was introduced as part of a 'three strikes' sentencing regime, with a presumption that this sentence will be imposed where a second or third strike offender is convicted of murder (*Sentencing Act 2002*: s.86E). This has the penal populist objectives of allegedly increasing public confidence in the criminal justice system, implementing 'truth-in-sentencing' and improving public safety (Ministry of Justice 2009). Nonetheless, those aged less than 18 were specifically exempted from the sentence. These examples demonstrate that the idea of tempering the worst excesses of punitive sentencing for youth through legislation is not completely foreign to the New Zealand system.

A Reverse Onus for Risk

As discussed above, international human rights standards hold that custody should be a last resort where public safety is at risk. However, there is thin guidance on how this principle will translate into sentencing legislation. The power to authorise detention of young offenders should be constrained by legislative maxima (see above), and that the onus should be on the state, to justify the continued detention. As the Child Rights International Network (CRIN) establishes:

> ... the only justification for the detention of a child should be that the child has been assessed as posing a serious risk to public safety. Courts should only be able to authorise a short maximum period of detention after which the presumption of release from detention would place the onus on the state to prove that considerations of public safety justify another short period of detention. (CRIN 2015: 5)

This model is somewhat analogous to detention in the mental health context (e.g. under the *Mental Health (Compulsory Assessment and Treatment) Act 1992*) where those who pose a risk to themselves or others may be detained for short periods until the risk diminishes (Bell and Brookbanks 2005). This would require a recognition, somewhat like psychiatric or psychological conditions requiring compulsory treatment, that the criminogenic and risk factors present for young offenders may often be temporal. The most temporal of these is of course youth itself.[4]

Principled and Appropriate Parole Process

Even if the reforms above were implemented, there still remains the treatment of young offenders currently in prison. Parole processes for these young offenders, particularly those serving life imprisonment, is a pressing issue. For example, the United States Supreme Court has declared that the mandatory sentence of life without parole is unconstitutional when imposed on offenders who were juveniles at the time of committing the crime. This has left states with the requirement to reform laws, and to consider the situation of those 'juvenile lifers' currently in prison (Feld 2012; Levick and Schwartz 2012).

Young persons who go into prison at a young age are incredibly disadvantaged and many have been failed by the state through the care system (Stanley 2017). This filters out in the sentencing decisions of young offenders sentenced for murder in New Zealand, particularly young female offenders:

> Your childhood was marred by violence and drugs. Your parents constantly separated and reconciled. By the age of 10 you had attended 10 different schools. Your parents separated for the last time when you were 12. You moved to Australia with your father where it is alleged [suppressed]. You then went back and lived with your mother for a short time. Your mother was unable to care for you. You then lived on the streets and you associated with gang members. You came to the attention of the Child, Youth and Family Services. You have used drugs for a number of years. One of the supervisors who has had your care describes you as at high risk with complex needs and displaying challenging behaviour. You have a lack of trust in others. It is acknowledged that you are difficult to manage. (*R v Bennett* [2010])

> She appears to have moved between the care of a number of family members in her short life and had, consequentially, a highly disrupted upbringing ... also suffered serious physical and sexual abuse whilst growing up allegedly at the hands of persons who should have offered her care and protection. Two men are to be brought to trial in relation to these incidents but that, of course, cannot undo the damage that has been done. (*R v Te Wini* [2012])

Such young offenders may be at a considerable disadvantage compared to adult offenders in applying for parole. As Levick and Schwartz (2012: 393–394) explain in the American context:

In addition to being denied access to useful programming, many juvenile lifers entered prison at a tumultuous developmental time in their lives. They were ill-equipped for life in prison, where they had to adjust to a primitive, Darwinian battle to survive … There is little support for "positive identity formation," but there is extensive peer support for additional criminality. There are lost opportunities for learning … These factors place juvenile lifers far behind the starting line for a race that measures their performance every day that they are in prison. This is the most practical, and trenchant, of problems …

Since so little of their lives is spent outside the prison, they have few points of reference to a stable crime-free life. They are entirely dependent on the state to provide the courses, education and opportunities to prove that they are 'safe' to release.

An Entitlement to Automatic Name Suppression

International human rights standards emphasise the importance of the reintegration of the young offender. Notoriety has a particular impact on children and youth convicted of serious offending. In a New Zealand case, a 12 year old convicted of manslaughter for his part in a group killing, appears regularly in the media with the label 'New Zealand's youngest convicted killer' while it is likely that few members of the public could name his older co-offenders (Wright Monod 2017). This inevitably goes against best interests and hampers reintegration.

Recent court decisions on name suppression for a child convicted of manslaughter has provided guidance on the assessment of the public interest in cases of serious offending by young offenders. The High Court decision (*R v DP and RP* [2015]) treated the child as an adult because he had left the youth jurisdiction, and held that the public had a legitimate interest in knowing his identity. Conversely, the Court of Appeal's (*DP v R* [2015]) reasoning suggested that the public interest lay more in the promotion of effective rehabilitation and reintegration of the young offender. Due to the fact that the child would still be a teenager when he was released, there was considerable public interest in his successful desistance from further offending. As was noted at [para. 31]:

Those prospects are likely to be severely compromised by name publication and associated publicity on his release. DP and the public generally will be reminded of serious offending which occurred at a time when he was open to suggestive and compulsive behaviour and in a state of developmental immaturity. Publicity will not allow him to move forward as he attempts to adjust to life in the community.

There is a strong case for automatic name suppression for children and young persons convicted in the adult jurisdiction, with the Crown able to argue for publication where there is a strong public interest (Lynch 2016c). This could take a similar form to s.201 of the *Criminal Procedure Act 2011* which provides that the identity of a person accused or convicted of sexual offences will be automatically suppressed, unless the court orders otherwise.

Concluding Remarks

This chapter has contended that the (often older) young offenders who are convicted of serious violent offending such as murder have become 'casualties' in the advocacy 'wars'. Youth justice scholarship, non-governmental organisations and the guidance provided by human rights frameworks have tended to concentrate on the younger offenders who have committed minor to moderate offending. These images of petty crime, successful diversion, community responses, and desistance from crime are more palatable to the public and hence to government. The small minority of young offenders who commit serious and exceptional offences such as murder and rape are conveniently written off as exceptions. There is perhaps a reluctance to acknowledge that some children and young persons commit extremely serious offences, in a belief that this will undermine a more politically palatable message that most youth crime is less serious. There is also an unwillingness to examine how victim's rights and interests sit in the international standards for youth justice, particularly where the victim of the offence is also a child or young person. These questions cannot readily be resolved here, but it is contended that this unwillingness by both scholars and practitioners to engage publicly with these questions has also contributed to the gap where outdated attitudes to young offenders remain.

It is contended here that the broad expressions of principle contained in human rights frameworks must, like in other youth justice practices, be translated into concrete models for national youth justice systems. As this case study of the New Zealand response to youth who commit top-end violent offences argues, unless principle translates into readily adoptable and achievable policy, the punitive status quo will persist.

Notes

1. Under 17s are remanded to youth justice residences.
2. Letter concerning Official Information Act request to the Department of Corrections, July 24, 2017.
3. Somewhat counterintuitively, 10–14-year-old children may only be sentenced to custody for homicide. In all other situations, a child will be diverted, or a community based response put in place. See generally Lynch (2016).
4. It is acknowledged that this model could mean that some young offenders would be detained for longer due to their static risk factors.

References

Allen, F. A. (1981). *The Decline of the Rehabilitative Ideal: Penal Policy and Social Purpose*. New Haven, CT: Yale University Press.

Alston, P. (1994). The best interests principle: Towards a reconciliation of culture and human rights. *International Journal of Law, Policy and the Family, 8*(1), 1–25.

Applegate, B. K., & Davis, R. K. (2006). Public views on sentencing juvenile murderers: The impact of offender, offense, and perceived maturity? *Youth Violence and Juvenile Justice, 4*(1), 55–74.

Ashkar, P. J., & Kenny, D. T. (2008). Views from the inside: Young offenders' subjective experiences of incarceration. *International Journal of Offender Therapy and Comparative Criminology, 52*(5), 584–597.

Baird, M. I., & Samuels, M. B. (1996). Youth, family and the law: Defining rights and establishing recognition. *Journal of Law & Policy, 5,* 177–189.

Barretto, C., Miers, S., & Lambie, I. (2016). The views of the public on youth offenders and the New Zealand criminal justice system. *International Journal of Offender Therapy and Comparative Criminology.* [Online]. https://doi.org/10.1177/0306624X16644500. Accessed February 9, 2018.

Bell, S. A., & Brookbanks, W. J. (2005). *Mental Health Law in New Zealand.* Wellington: Brookers.

Cavadino, P. (Ed.). (1996). *Children Who Kill: An Examination of the Treatment of Juveniles Who Kill in Different European Countries.* Winchester: Waterside Press.

Child Rights International Network [CRIN]. (2015). *Inhuman Sentencing: Life Imprisonment of Children Around the World—Research Report.* [Online]. Available https://www.crin.org/sites/default/files/life_imprisonment_children_global_0.pdf. Accessed February 7, 2018.

Council of Europe. (2010). *Guidelines of the Committee of Ministers of the Council of Europe on Child Friendly Justice: Adopted by the Committee of Ministers of the Council of Europe on 17 November 2010.* Strasbourg: Council of Europe Publishing.

Cuncannan, J. (1997). Only when they're bad: The rights and responsibilities of our children. *Washington University Journal of Urban & Contemporary Law, 51,* 273–301.

Defence for Children International. (2003). *Kids Behind Bars: A Study on Children in Conflict with the Law: Towards Investing in Prevention, Stopping Incarceration and Meeting International Standards.* [Online]. Available http://www.kidsbehindbars.org/english/docs/RapportKBBtotaal.pdf. Accessed February 7, 2018.

Department of Corrections. (2007). *About Time: Turning People Away from a Life of Crime and Reducing Re-offending.* Wellington: New Zealand Department of Corrections.

Department of Corrections. (2017a). Official information request.

Department of Corrections. (2017b). *Prison Facts and Statistics—September 2017.* [Online]. Available http://www.corrections.govt.nz/resources/research_and_statistics/quarterly_prison_statistics/prison_stats_september_2017.html. Accessed February 7, 2018.

Department of Corrections. (2017c). *Prison Operations Manual.* [Online]. Available http://www.corrections.govt.nz/__data/assets/pdf_file/0008/627065/Prisoner-Guide-to-POM-050717.pdf. Accessed February 7, 2018.

Feld, B. C. (2012). Adolescent criminal responsibility, proportionality, and sentencing policy: Roper, Graham, Miller/Jackson, and the youth discount. *Law & Inequality, 31,* 263–330.

Fionda, J. (Ed.). (2001). *Legal Concepts of Childhood.* Oxford: Hart Publishing.

Fitz-Gibbon, K. (2016). Minimum sentencing for murder in England and Wales: A critical examination 10 years after the Criminal Justice Act 2003. *Punishment & Society, 18*(1), 47–67.

Goldingay, S. (2012). "Without fists": Age mixing and its influence on safety and criminal contamination in women's prisons. *Youth Studies Australia, 31,* 17–25.

Goldson, B. (2002). New punitiveness: The politics of child incarceration. In J. Muncie, G. Hughes, & E. McLaughlin (Eds.), *Youth Justice: Critical Readings* (pp. 386–400). London: Sage.

Goldson, B., & Kilkelly, U. (2013). International human rights standards and child imprisonment: Potentialities and limitations. *The International Journal of Children's Rights, 21*(2), 345–371.

Goldson, B., & Muncie, J. (2012). Towards a global 'child friendly' juvenile justice? *International Journal of Law, Crime and Justice, 40*(1), 47–64.

Graham, P. (2011). *So Brilliantly Clever: Parker, Hulme & the Murder that Shocked the World.* Wellington: Awa Press.

Green, D. A. (2012). *When Children Kill Children: Penal Populism and Political Culture.* Oxford: Oxford University Press.

Guggenheim, M. (2005). How children's lawyers serve state interests. *Nevada Law Journal, 6*(3), 805–835.

Halsey, M. (2017). Child victims as adult offenders: Foregrounding the criminogenic effects of (unresolved) trauma and loss. *British Journal of Criminology, 58*(1), 17–36.

Haydon, D., & Scraton, P. (2000). "Condemn a little more, understand a little less": The political context and rights' implications of the domestic and European rulings in the Venables-Thompson case. *Journal of Law and Society, 27*(3), 416–448.

Hollingsworth, K. (2007). Responsibility and rights: Children and their parents in the youth justice system. *International Journal of Law, Policy and the Family, 21*(2), 190–219.

Jackson, M. (1988). *The Māori and the Criminal Justice System: He Whaipaanga Hou—A New Perspective.* Wellington: New Zealand Department of Justice Policy and Research Division.

James, A., & Jenks, C. (1996). Public perceptions of childhood criminality. *British Journal of Sociology, 47*(2), 315–331.

Kilkelly, U. (2008). Youth justice and children's rights: Measuring compliance with international standards. *Youth Justice, 8*(3), 187–192.

Kilkelly, U., Moore, L., & Convery, U. (2002). *In Our Care: Promoting the Rights of Children in Custody*. Belfast: Northern Ireland Human Rights Commission.

Levick, M. L., & Schwartz, R. G. (2012). Practical implications of Miller v. Jackson: Obtaining relief in court and before the parole board. *Law & Inequality, 31*(2), 369–409.

Lynch, N. (2010). Changes to youth justice. *New Zealand Law Journal,* 129–130.

Lynch, N. (2013). "Contrasts in tolerance" in a single jurisdiction: The case of New Zealand. *International Criminal Justice Review, 23*(3), 217–232.

Lynch, N. (2016a). *Youth Justice in New Zealand* (2nd ed.). Wellington: Thomson Reuters.

Lynch, N. (2016b). Case note: The sentencing of the vulnerable: P v R. Te Wharenga. *The New Zealand Criminal Law Review, 61,* 103–109.

Lynch, N. (2016c). Permanent name suppression for a child convicted of homicide. *New Zealand Law Journal,* 13.

Lynch, N. (2018). 'Manifest injustice?' The judiciary as moderator of penal excess in the sentencing of youth for murder. *Howard Journal of Crime and Justice, 57*(1), 57–76.

McDonald, L. (2006). *Investigation of the Circumstances Surrounding the Death at Auckland Public Hospital of Prisoner Liam John Ashley of Auckland Central Remand Prison on 25 August 2006, Report to: Chief Executive Department of Corrections*. Wellington: New Zealand Department of Corrections.

Ministry of Justice. (2009). *Sentencing and Parole Reform Bill—Initial briefing* (SP/ADV/1). Law and Order Select Committee. Tabled April 29, 2009.

Muncie, J. (2005). The globalization of crime control—The case of youth and juvenile justice: Neo-liberalism, policy convergence and international conventions. *Theoretical Criminology, 9*(1), 35–64.

Muncie, J., & Goldson, B. (Eds.). (2006). *Comparative Youth Justice*. London: Sage.

Nagin, D. S., Piquero, A. R., Scott, E. S., & Steinberg, L. (2006). Public preferences for rehabilitation versus incarceration of juvenile offenders: Evidence from a contingent valuation survey. *Criminology & Public Policy, 5*(4), 627–651.

O'Brien, W., & Fitz-Gibbon, K. (2016). "Cemented in their cells": A human rights analysis of Blessington, Elliott and the life imprisonment of children in New South Wales. *Australian Journal of Human Rights, 22*(1), 111–133.

Piquero, A. R., & Steinberg, L. (2010). Public preferences for rehabilitation versus incarceration of juvenile offenders. *Journal of Criminal Justice, 38*(1), 1–6.

Pratt, J., & Clark, M. (2005). Penal populism in New Zealand. *Punishment & Society, 7*(3), 303–322.

Roberts, J. V. (2004). Public opinion and youth justice. *Crime and Justice: A Review of Research, 31,* 495–542.

Roberts, J., & Hough, M. (2005). Sentencing young offenders: Public opinion in England and Wales. *Criminal Justice, 5*(3), 211–232.

Royal College of Psychiatrists. (2006). *Child Defendants* (Occasional Paper 56). [Online]. Available http://www.rcpsych.ac.uk/usefulresources/publications/collegereports//op/op56.aspx. Accessed February 7, 2018.

Stanley, E. (2017). From care to custody: Trajectories of children in post-war New Zealand. *Youth Justice, 17*(1), 57–72.

Steinberg, L., & Scott, E. S. (2003). Less guilty by reason of adolescence: Developmental immaturity, diminished responsibility, and the juvenile death penalty. *American Psychologist, 58*(12), 1009–1018.

Tomasevski, K. (Ed.). (1986). *Children in Adult Prisons: An International Perspective.* New York: St. Martin's Press.

Tonry, M. (2009). The mostly unintended effects of mandatory penalties: Two centuries of consistent findings. *Crime and Justice: A Review of Research, 38*(1), 65–114.

UN Committee on the Rights of the Child [UNCRC]. (2007). *General Comment No. 10 (2007): Children's Rights in Juvenile Justice* (CRC/C/GC/10). [Online]. Available http://undocs.org/CRC/C/GC/10. Accessed February 7, 2018.

UN General Assembly. (1985). *United Nations Standard Minimum Rules for the Administration of Juvenile Justice [Beijing Rules]* (A/RES/40/33). Adopted November 29, 1985.

UN General Assembly. (1989). *Convention on the Rights of the Child* (A/RES/44/25). Adopted November 20, 1989.

UN General Assembly. (1990). *United Nations Rules for the Protection of Juveniles Deprived of their Liberty [Havana Rules]* (A/RES/45/113). Adopted December 14, 1990.

UNICEF. (2003). *Juvenile Justice Systems: Good Practices in Latin America.* Panama: UNICEF Regional Office for the Americas and the Caribbean.

UNICEF. (2006). *Juvenile Justice in South Asia: Improving Protection for Children in Conflict with the Law*. Kathmandu: UNICEF Regional Office for South Asia.

UNICEF. (2010). *Good Practices and Promising Initiatives in Juvenile Justice in the CEE/CIS Region*. Geneva: UNICEF Regional Office for CEE/CIS.

Waitangi Tribunal. (2017). *Tū Mai te Rangi! Report on the Crown and Disproportionate Reoffending Rates* (WAI 2540). [Online]. Available http://maorilawreview.co.nz/2017/04/tu-mai-te-rangi-the-crown-and-dispropor-tionate-maori-reoffending-rates/. Accessed February 7, 2018.

Wright Monod, S. (2017). Portraying those we condemn with care: Extending the ethics of representation. *Critical Criminology, 25*(3), 343–356.

Table of Cases

R v Nelson [2012] NZHC 3570.
DP v R [2015] NZCA 476.
P v R [2016] NZCA 128.
R v DP & RP [2015] NZHC 1765.
Te Wini v R [2013] NZCA 201.
Churchward v R [2011] NZCA 531.
R v O'Brien [2003] HC New Plymouth T6/02.
R v Slade and Hamilton [2005] NZCA 19.
R v Bennett [2010] HC AK CRI-2009-292-002198.
R v Te Wini [2012] HC ROT CRI-2008-270-000361.

8

Entrenching Women's Imprisonment: An Anti-carceral Critique of Rights Based Advocacy and Reform

Bree Carlton and Emma K. Russell

Introduction

Carceral abolitionists have identified how prison reform projects can provide precursors, rationales and justifications for expansion (Spade 2011; Carlton 2016). These risks arise when advocates fail to mount a structural critique of the prison and challenge its inherent violence. Historically, efforts to improve systems of imprisonment have been incorporated into a "carceral humanism" (Kilgore 2014; Brown and Schept 2016), which attempts to rebrand or repackage carceral control as the caring provision of social services (Heiner and Tyson 2017). Through the mobilisation of a combination of institutional discourses,

B. Carlton (✉)
Senior Lecturer in Criminology, School of Humanities and Social Sciences, Deakin University, Melbourne, Australia
e-mail: bree.carlton@deakin.edu.au

E. K. Russell
Department of Social Inquiry, La Trobe University, Melbourne, VIC, Australia
e-mail: E.Russell@latrobe.edu.au

© The Author(s) 2018
E. Stanley (ed.), *Human Rights and Incarceration*, Palgrave Studies in Prisons and Penology, https://doi.org/10.1007/978-3-319-95399-1_8

181

presumed benevolence and unchallenged carceral logics, reforms can entrench and expand imprisonment (Schept 2015; Musto 2016). Women—especially poor, Indigenous and women of colour—have often borne the brunt of such 'caring' reform efforts in the penal sphere, resulting in heightened surveillance, gendered discipline and more frequent administrative punishment (Hannah-Moffat 2001; Davis 2003).

The relationships between human rights, imprisonment, reform and abolition are multi-faceted and complex. Abolitionists are quick to mobilise in support of struggles for prisoner rights—the right to health, education, and freedom from torture and degrading treatment *are* key examples of anti-carceral campaign demands. However, we are also deeply critical of liberal rights frameworks that advocate formal recognition in the absence of a structural critique of power and oppression. In the penal sphere, such liberal rights campaigns have contributed to the proliferation of 'gender-responsive' and 'culturally sensitive' correctional policies that legitimise imprisonment whilst doing little to unravel the webs of criminalisation that continue to entrap those most marginalised by their race, gender, disability and class status (Russell and Carlton 2013). As such, careful consideration of the historical role played by reformist and rights-based lobbying in the formalisation of women's imprisonment is an important task.

In this chapter, we draw from an historical case study from the Australian state of Victoria: the Fairlea Research Group's (FRG) 1982 anti-discrimination campaign, *Prisoner and Female: The Double Negative* (Hancock 1982). This campaign argued for a women-specific prison policy as an antidote to women's experiences of discrimination in the system. FRG utilised the newly developed *Equal Opportunity Act 1977* (VIC), which passed in Victorian Parliament in 1979, making it unlawful to discriminate on the basis of sex or marital status. FRG therefore sought to take expedient advantage of a developing rights consciousness in a local context to challenge women's imprisonment practices. We use this campaign to analyse the extent to which rights-based lobbying can create meaningful change within prison systems and influence social change more broadly. We also consider the potential for this advocacy to legitimise and sustain carceral systems.

The FRG's anti-discrimination intervention in the early 1980s prompted government recognition that imprisoned women had specific needs and experiences that required protections and policies. In some ways, the programs and prison construction that ensued over the following decade resulted in improved conditions in Fairlea Women's Prison (the primary prison for women in Victoria until 1996). However, these changes mostly presented a progressive veneer, as behind closed doors the discriminatory violence of women's incarceration continued (see Carlton and Russell 2018). Instead, we suggest that the FRG's anti-discrimination campaign contributed inadvertently to the consolidation and legitimation of a women's correctional system, which was a precursor to more prison beds and rapidly growing women's prisoner numbers in Victoria since the late 1980s.

While acknowledging the dangers and limitations of liberal rights-based and reformist approaches, we also argue that the *Double Negative* report laid critical foundations for a subsequent wave of anti-carceral feminist (Carlton 2016; Thuma 2014, 2015) activism from the late 1980s and the early 1990s. These activists occupied a radical standpoint, but used anti-discrimination legal tools and the information they generated to create pressure for accountability, promote decarceration, and build a grassroots coalition movement that challenged the structural conditions of women's criminalisation and imprisonment. FRG's research generated vital toolkits that were picked up in their campaigns that deployed reform not in isolation, but as part of an arsenal of resistance strategies designed to disrupt dominant public discourses and dismantle the institutional secrecy and borders fortifying the women's prison.

Viewed retrospectively, the FRG's *Double Negative* campaign resonates with the emergent rights consciousness associated with the development of key international conventions such as the *International Covenant on Civil and Political Rights* (1966) and the *Convention for the Elimination of All Forms of Discrimination Against Women* (1979). The FRG foregrounded an anti-discrimination framework and elucidated how the prison system failed to ensure women's equal access to treatment and conditions. Whilst they did not explicitly utilise the language of human rights, the FRG focused on systemic change through policy reform that would, it was hoped, ameliorate women's discriminatory experiences in prison. However, their approach had unintended consequences. By lobbying for a specific policy for women and mapping out an administrative strategy to achieve this, the FRG's efforts ultimately contributed to *legitimising* and *professionalising* the women's prison system. The *Double Negative* campaign reflects critical lessons about the necessities, risks and benefits of rights-reflecting reformist efforts in prisons. As a case study, it reminds us that the inclusion of women's 'rights' in the prison system will not alter its fundamental violence.

The Research Context

This research adopts an abolitionist standpoint (Davis 2003). It draws from activist archives generated through decades of feminist critiques, lobbying, strategising, organising and action undertaken at the coalface of campaigns for change in the women's prison system in Victoria between 1982 and 2005.[1] A consistent and repeated strategy across much of the activist work around women's prisons over this period of time has been the use of the state's evolving Equal Opportunity law to make the case that women are subject to discriminatory treatment in prison (Hancock 1982; Equal Opportunity Commission Victoria 1993; Cerveri et al. 2005; Centre for the Human Rights of Imprisoned People [CHRIP] 2010). The FRG's *Double Negative* campaign in 1982 represented the first iteration of this approach to campaigning for imprisoned women's rights in Victoria.

The methodological approach we deploy in this project is outlined in detail elsewhere (Carlton and Russell 2018). In brief, we draw on documentary research, various archival texts, and semi-structured interviews and focus groups to interrogate official claims that penal reform initiatives constitute markers of progress. We do this by mapping the mobilisation of activist critiques alongside official reform discourses and women's accounts of carceral violence—the forms of physical, sexual and psychological violence and harm experienced within and through systems of imprisonment and correctional control.

Since the early 1980s, the history of women's imprisonment in Victoria has been underpinned by three key elements that appear out of step: (i) the cyclical repackaging and rolling out of official penal reform policies and discourses of penal progress; (ii) 'inside-out' resistance (Faith 2000), including systemic advocacy campaigns and direct action to challenge, cease and dismantle ongoing violent and discriminatory practices in women's prisons[2]; and, most importantly, (iii) a steady trajectory of prison expansion. Essentially our research has sought to understand why Victorian women's prisons have been looked upon as 'progressive' and 'best practice' examples in correctional innovation compared to other Australian states and territories. In particular we have sought to make meaning of the intersections between the repeated emergence of liberal reformist agendas in women's imprisonment and the sustained proliferation of systemic advocacy campaigns and anti-carceral feminist activism, which we have closely documented elsewhere (Carlton 2016; Carlton and Russell 2015, 2018).

A critical contemporary impetus for this project was the introduction of the *Victorian Charter of Human Rights and Responsibilities* (2006), an act of parliament that included protections for prisoners' human rights. Almost simultaneously, Corrections Victoria released the *Better Pathways Strategy* (Department of Justice Victoria 2005, 2007) for imprisoned women, which comprised a "Gender Responsive Justice" (Bloom et al. 2003) reform framework that aimed to prevent women's re-imprisonment and respond to women's experiences of victimisation and ill mental health within the prison system. However, as we have previously demonstrated (Russell and Carlton 2013), the *Better Pathways* policy discourse, while undoubtedly informed by activist critiques, merely reproduced gendered and racialised logics that could only work to compound discriminatory criminalisation and expand imprisonment. In fact, the release of *Better Pathways* was quickly followed by unprecedented expansion in women's prison numbers and renewed discrimination claims highlighted by imprisoned women and advocates (Cerveri et al. 2005; CHRIP 2010). This history closely reflects Gender Responsive Justice developments in Canada, the United States, the United Kingdom and New Zealand (Hannah-Moffat 2000; Braz 2006; Shaylor 2009).

To the best of our knowledge only one woman involved in the early work of the FRG later adopted an abolitionist position. Rather, the work of FRG more closely reflected a liberal rights approach, focusing on improving the existing system and pressuring the government to introduce correctional policies that recognised women's experiences and rehabilitative needs. In this way, the FRG was distinct from the later anti-carceral feminist coalitions that emerged during the late 1980s and 1990s, spearheaded by activist groups such as Women Against Prison and the People's Justice Alliance. Although these groups were informed by and indebted to the work of FRG, they stood in contrast to the latter by advancing an abolitionist social movement grounded in critiques, strategies and actions designed to struggle against and subvert structures of oppression that reproduce violence and injustice. These structures are understood to comprise a continuum spanning civil society and the state, forming the basis of criminal justice institutions (Carlton 2016; George and McCulloch 1988; Harris 2011). The longer-term aim of anti-carceral feminist movements was to dismantle and abolish women's prisons *not* solely reform them.

Anti-carceral feminist campaigns peaked in the late 1980s and early 1990s with a series of biannual mass demonstrations called the Fairlea 'Wring Outs' (which involved thousands of activists and community members surrounding Fairlea Women's Prison holding hands and making noise in order to connect with women inside) and the 1993 'Save Fairlea' vigil, a 24-hour camp outside the prison that lasted for five months (Carlton 2016). These campaigns combined reformist lobbying with grassroots organising and coalitional direct action. During this time anti-carceral feminist activists engaged in covert research, public awareness-raising and education, and legal rights-based challenges to the conditions of women's imprisonment (Carlton and Russell 2018). They were directly informed by the FRG's *Double Negative* campaign, which was initiated at a time when the abolition of a women's prison was not considered beyond the realm of possibility. It is critical to note there has been continued and sustained abolitionist systemic advocacy campaign work surrounding women's prisons to the present day. However, anti-carceral feminist camapigns and social movements were mobilised cohesively in the 1980s and 1990s.

Histories of Liberal Reform Efforts in the Women's Prison

In 1976, members of the Victorian parliament discussed the abolition of the women's prison system due to the record-low number of women imprisoned at Fairlea, which was then the only prison for women in the state (Victorian Women's Prison Council 1975–1977: 2). Sandy Cook, co-founder of FRG and fierce advocate for women prisoners, recalled that when she commenced her position as an educator at Fairlea around that time, there were only 24 women incarcerated (Hancock 1982: 3): "The day I arrived they [prison officers] said, 'you won't be here for too long, because we're going to be closing the women's prison'".[3] This discourse was circulating at a time when women were largely neglected in the Victorian prison system (as they had been throughout its history) and invisible to outsiders: there were no distinct policies to guide practice at Fairlea Women's Prison and a limited public awareness and knowledge about women's experiences of criminalisation and imprisonment. FRG systematically challenged this invisibility and neglect. But the idea of abolishing women's prisons, even if fleeting, became a lost opportunity.

FRG was founded in the late 1970s by former-prison education worker Chris Burnup, academic Linda Hancock, and Sandy Cook. It soon grew to include formerly-imprisoned women and other activists. In 1979, the FRG began a six-month project investigating and documenting the concerns of women imprisoned at Fairlea and the discriminatory conditions inside the prison. This culminated with a formal submission to the Equal Opportunity Board and the publication of the ground-breaking report, *Prisoner and Female: The Double Negative* in 1982, which is discussed in detail below. Although the FRG's challenge to the prison system was unprecedented in its research and argumentation, the group's emergence must also be contextualised in relation to traditions in liberal and philanthropic reformism associated with women's imprisonment. Women's labour both inside and outside Victorian prisons has played a fundamental role in defining and driving penal reform agendas. Since the early 1950s, there has been a tradition of women's groups pressuring for women's prison reform, including bet-ter conditions and improved rehabilitative efforts. The establishment of Fairlea Women's Prison itself in 1956 was, at least in part, a product of these efforts (see Russell 1998).

Not afraid to stand in opposition to the government, the FRG made considerable contributions to feminist legal and social research, lobby-ing and prison advocacy. These contributions were informed and driven by a combination of influences including liberal reformist ideals as well as feminist and social justice politics. FRG member Chris Burnup reflected that the small numbers of women in Victorian prisons com-bined with the complete lack of public policy and awareness of their experiences reduced public visibility for incarcerated women who expe-rienced "Dickensian"-style brutal conditions.[4] Sandy Cook suggested that women were viewed as "mad" or "bad" and not "real prisoners".[5] The FRG's concerns were fuelled by administrative practices witnessed while working with and advocating for women in Fairlea Women's Prison, such as the use of behavioural modification drugs and forced sterilisations, lack of access to quality medical care and rehabilitative programs, and the pains associated with separation from children.[6] For Sandy Cook, her involvement with FRG was driven by a hope to expose what she characterised as the "conspiracy of silence" in relation to the discriminatory and brutal conditions inflicted upon women in prison.[7]

Around the time of FRG's formation and research, there was a grow-ing sense of unrest in Fairlea Women's Prison with reports of hunger strikes, riots and fires.[8] By the time that the *Double Negative* report was published, imprisoned women's concerns about their treatment and conditions had escalated. On 6 February 1982, four women were apprehended after escaping the prison and in the evening on the same day a fire was deliberately lit in the remand section of Fairlea. The fire resulted in the deaths of three women and the complete destruction of a significant section of the prison. Following these events, Fairlea's capacity was reduced to space for 30 women. As a result, women were moved to Pentridge men's prison, into B Annexe and the Jika Jika High-Security Unit, which vastly compounded their experiences of carceral violence and discrimination (see Carlton and Russell 2018). In *Double Negative*, the FRG raised concerns regarding the punitive isolation and classification of women deemed by staff as "unmanageable" or concerned about their rights:

> Poor management is evidenced by negative methods of control and the lengths to which prisoners must go to draw attention to their grievances (e.g., it took seven days without food to break a strike by prisoners in 1981). (Hancock 1982: 62)

Women imprisoned at Fairlea and Pentridge were actively engaged in struggles for their rights and improved conditions throughout the 1980s and 1990s, often in collaboration with 'outside' activists. These efforts frequently focused on the friendly façade that Fairlea Women's Prison presented (in spite of the administrative violence within) as well as the punitive excesses associated with the segregation of women to men's prisons (Carlton and Russell 2018). It was after the release of *Double Negative* that this practice became commonplace for women in the Victorian system marked as unruly and troublesome.

The *Double Negative* Report

The release of FRG's *Double Negative* report in 1982 marked an important political moment in Victorian women's imprisonment history. It represented the first comprehensive research profile of women in prison in a context defined by their invisibilisation and neglect. At this time, the implications of Victoria's new equal opportunity law for women's experiences of discrimination in a range of contexts were beginning to be explored.[9] Internationally, feminist movements connected across various locales were forcing women's rights onto political agendas and the *Convention on the Elimination of Discrimination Against Women* (1979) was adopted in the United Nations General Assembly. In a scholarly context, feminists were beginning to mount strident challenges within criminology and the social sciences more broadly. This led to the emergence of methodological and theoretical approaches that exposed the gendered dimensions of institutional regulation and control—including criminalisation, sentencing and imprisonment (Carlen 1983, 1988;

Heidensohn 1985; Cook and Davies 1999)—and how these were linked to social and epistemological structures of oppression. Outside the academy and in a local context, the FRG's efforts to document women's prison experiences was a radical approach at a time when there was otherwise a virtual absence of this knowledge.

The published *Double Negative* report—hand-typed across 71 pages including appendices—included the FRG's submission to the Victorian Equal Opportunity Board, which evidenced women's discrimination in the prison system. The submission used a section within the *Equal Opportunities Act 1977* (VIC) to construct Victoria's first legal case highlighting areas of prison conditions and the provision of services and programs that disadvantaged imprisoned women in ways distinct to men (Hancock 1982: 27). The submission was restricted to particular areas where a case of discrimination could be made, including accommodation, poor access to medical facilities, education, industries, visits, and recreation (Hancock 1982). In addition to the equal opportunity submission, the *Double Negative* report contained important supplementary sections, including a press release, direct accounts from women imprisoned at Fairlea, and future recommendations. It argued for recognition of the harmful effects of imprisoning women in a system designed for men, who form the majority of the overall prisoner population.

Drawing on both official and unofficial sources of evidence, the FRG used "publicly available documents [correctional reports and statistics] to compare what the women were getting compared to the men".[10] The collection of evidence involved covert research conducted inside Fairlea prison: speaking to prison staff, those holding positions in office and most importantly, imprisoned women. As Linda Hancock relayed:

> Once I was in there it was fine and I told them what I was doing I said look we want to improve things for you here … This was qualitative research we had to have women expressing themselves in their own words … we had the numbers from the stat[istic]s but they only tell one part of the story. But the other part is experiential and it's giving voice to those who are disadvantaged and unable structurally to do it themselves, so that's how we saw it.[11]

The inclusion of women's voices in a public report about their imprisonment was a significant intervention into the silence and secrecy that continues to characterise the Victorian prison system. Imprisoned women identified numerous rights issues and violations, including cruel and inhumane treatment, lack of personal security and meaningful work and education. One woman reflected her experience of the isolation cellblock used for punishment as "cold, miserable and lonely" (Hancock 1982: 49). There was a cell labelled "the cage". As the *Double Negative* report described:

> It is an isolated cell, open to the air, which is closed off from other cells in the cellblock. As there are no special facilities for psychiatric prisoners, "the cage" is used for psychiatric patients and increasingly in drug related psychiatric cases. (ibid.)

Imprisoned women further characterised their infantilising treatment by prison staff:

> The general attitude is that one should suffer for one's crimes so that one does not offend again. The women are treated very much like bad children. The entire emphasis is that one has done wrong, which, in such an alien and unsympathetic environment, begins to manifest itself in the personal belief that one is never going to be able to [do] anything right. (ibid.: 61)

Women imprisoned at Fairlea saw the programs provided there as grossly inadequate. As one woman argued, "present 'industries' 'are a joke', limited to housekeeping tasks. They don't recognise women's need to support themselves (and often their children) on release" (ibid.: 53).

The *Double Negative* report advocated for opportunities for imprisoned women to be actively involved in the administrative and managerial decisions that affect the running of the prison, including the necessary establishment of clearer lines of communication between various levels of prison staff and prisoners (Hancock 1982: 63). It also called for the provision of information on women's rights in relation to security classification procedures specifically (ibid.: 63). Whilst the *Double Negative* report refers to discrimination in place of the language of rights, the campaign's focus more broadly reflects a growing awareness of women's rights, applied here to the context of incarceration. FRG's research painstakingly documented the discriminatory effects of imprisonment—tied in their view to the absence of woman specific correctional policy and programming—in a prison system designed for the male majority.

Beyond Double Negative: The Risks of Engaging and Advocating in Prison

Advocating for the rights of imprisoned peoples is a sensitive and difficult process, given that it revolves around closed institutional spaces determined by unequal power relations and poor transparency. Members of FRG reflected on their experiences of advocating 'from the inside', when working as an education programs coordinator, for example. Punishments could be arbitrarily meted out to imprisoned women for having pursued their basic rights, such as access to education. Sandy Cook characterised this as "heartbreaking":

> What they'd [prison officers] do if they [imprisoned women] came to education, sometimes the officers would say that [the women] wouldn't get paid their money. That money was to either buy deodorant or toiletries or a treat for their children on Saturdays. And I'd say, "can we work out some way around this for this particular woman?", and I'd come into work the next day and that woman would be scrubbing the floors in front of my office on her hands and knees.[12]

Sandy also recalled one woman begging her: "Sandy, we know you mean well but please stop trying to help us", because retribution would follow. In this regard, FRG's work carried significant risks for imprisoned women. These risks were associated with the punitive and unaccountable nature of the prison regime and they had to be carefully managed in order to reduce the harms associated with informal retributive action by prison staff.

Through the promotion of *Double Negative*, FRG recognised that the campaign to improve women's prison conditions had achieved short-term gains. Inside Fairlea, this included refurbishments and developments to include single room accommodation options, easier access for children and families, the introduction of a social worker and the broader provision of educational programs. At the beginning of their report, FRG (Hancock 1982: 2) noted: "the changes at Fairlea have shown that change is possible. However, the situation is temporary. In the absence of a policy on minimum standards, Fairlea may be only a showpiece for a small number of model prisoners." Overshadowing this recognition that some important changes had been made, FRG (ibid.) was deeply concerned about the absence of policies for women prisoners: "There is no policy for women prisoners in Victoria and, further, there is no satisfactory policy making mechanism."

Above all, the *Double Negative's* recommendations are premised on internal changes to the women's prison system and additional resourcing for community consultation, policy development, increased system transparency and formalised administration. FRG provided a highly prescriptive approach to policy formation and system professionalisation, critiquing the lack of a systematic approach to Fairlea's operation, but they also imbued prisons with the potential for *humanising* effects. As they argued:

> A prison or correctional institution of any type cannot be operated successfully over a long period of time unless careful and detailed attention is given to the development of a sound organizational structure, based upon recognized principles of modern management, sound administration, and the explicit goals of the agency. Prisons are not just places of punishment, but are also places for training and humane assistance. Creative leadership and innovative programs will lead to a re-examination of the organization and kinds of personnel needed. (Hancock 1982: 61)

By advocating that time and resources be dedicated towards the 'success' of a 'modern' prison system, the *Double Negative* campaign inadvertently contributed to the formalisation and legitimation of a women's correctional system in Victoria. The activities of FRG were, in some ways, driven by an idealistic faith in liberal reform: that genuine change could occur within the prison system for women. FRG concerns were largely centred upon recognising and responding to the deficiencies of a male-centred system, rather than dismantling the system itself. In the 1980s, this came down to advocating for improved treatment and conditions for women in prison, relative to men. FRG made arguments for women-specific facilities, programs, policies and procedures to guide practices in women's prisons. Ultimately, FRG attempted to create pressure for reform from within the system (by those working there) and at higher levels of government (through lobbying ministers, for example) in order for a women's correctional policy to be developed and implemented (Hancock 1982). Whilst the attempt to gather and disseminate 'insider' testimonies of Fairlea prison was quite radical at the time, FRG's goals primarily focused upon using anti-discrimination legal frameworks to evidence the inequitable access to conditions, treatment and programs experienced by women.

Following the release of the *Double Negative* report, Linda Hancock recalled the importance of networking within government and lobbying individuals to raise questions about the position of women in prison in parliament.[13] FRG put forward a legal case that was accepted by the Equal Opportunity Board. However, the submission never received a hearing at the Equal Opportunity Commission and nor did the Board push for change beyond an internal process of conciliation with the Office of Corrections (OoC) that was eventually abandoned and left unresolved. In response to FRG's advocacy, Minister Toner made public the state government's commitment to end "the double disadvantage that women prisoners experience" and focus on *alternatives* to women's imprisonment (Toner 1982). In spite of the acknowledgement by Minister Toner that there was a need for reform, it was a decade before a gender-specific policy was introduced.[14]

Legacies and Opportunities

By harnessing the newly implemented equal opportunity legal framework in Victoria, FRG sought to secure official recognition of women's experiences of imprisonment and trigger a commensurate reform response. As Linda Hancock argued:

That was a major thing we aimed at. That at least when we walked away, they had to have a policy on women in prison and respect special needs … For a government at that time not to have a gendered policy for incarceration … was quite incredible to us. Because at the same time you had Germaine Greer and Betty Friedman and all the others making sure that people knew that women were very different in terms of needs and policy, yet here was a very retrograde and backward policy area.[15]

In addition to triggering public discussions and government action on women's penal reform, *Double Negative* spotlighted the issue of gender discrimination within the prison system in Victoria. It also provided a public statement that challenged OoC impunity and the institutional and social context in which women were silenced, rendered invisible and abandoned.[16]

The *Double Negative* report provided a detailed blueprint for developing professionalised systems of correctional administration and bureaucracy centred around women. In the years following its publication, the OoC adopted new policies, programs and practices purporting to respond to the unique needs of women in prison. For example, in 1991, the recommendations put forward by FRG in *Double Negative* were closely reflected in the launch of Victoria's first women's specific correctional framework, the *Agenda for Change* (Women Prisoners and Offenders Advisory Committee 1991). This framework was and continues to be publicly represented by correctional officials as a watershed moment of change in the women's prison system in Victoria.[17] However, imprisoned women's accounts and the 'activist archive' suggest that the discriminatory conditions well documented in the *Double Negative* continued—and in many ways worsened—throughout the 1980s and 1990s. For example, in the late 1980s anti-carceral feminist campaigns galvanised around cruel and degrading strip-searching practices and the deadly risks of segregating women within men's prisons (George and McCulloch 1988; Equal Opportunity Commissioner 1991). The campaigns spotlighted the failures associated with the *Agenda For Change* and in particular its lack of implementation. One campaign archive compiled by Women Against Prison activist Amanda George in the 1990s contains a lever arch folder titled "Agenda for

Change", which includes substantive records of policy notes, memos and copious correspondence with corrections personnel documenting and challenging implementation failures and policy rhetoric. In one such example, Amanda George wrote by hand to the OoC Women's Policy Advisory Committee, arguing: "the policy as usual looks good, and of course policy is an important start. I just hate the double speak of 'Intensive management = punishment; strip-searches with dignity'".[18] Her point highlights some of the insidious effects of penal policy, including glossing over or repackaging carceral violence in 'gentler' language to legitimise it (Braz 2006; Shaylor 2009). The task for her and others is to confront the "shield of words", adopted by criminal justice agencies, that soften and reconstruct the practices of containment (Christie 1981: 13).

FRG's pressure for penal change through the 1982 *Double Negative* campaign created significant pressure for government to publicly recognise that women were disadvantaged within the prison system. However, the inadvertent longer-term consequences of the development of gender-specific penal policy in Victoria include the legitimisation and formalisation of the women's correctional system, which provided part of the groundwork for its subsequent expansion. As FRG member Sandy Cook acknowledged, the more that they lobbied and campaigned around the need for appropriate policies and responses to women in prison, the more the system seemed to grow in size. As she stated:

> I think part of the problem is [that] the policy response, by and large, adopts the language of a reformist agenda. But what it puts in place is something quite different, under the guise of the newly implemented … language of progression.[19]

Historical analyses of reformist and liberal rights campaigns in the criminal justice sphere suggest that they are often replete with unintended consequences (Gottschalk 2006; Bumiller 2008; Murakawa 2014). Whilst significant victories for imprisoned women's rights were achieved in the years following the *Double Negative* campaign, such as the OoC ceasing the discriminatory practice of segregating women to men's prisons for punishment, parallel developments complicated any successes. In 1996, the Victorian women's prison system was subject to wholesale privatisation, bringing with it increasingly restricted access to information and frequent rights breaches (George 2002; McCulloch and George 2009). Although privatisation only lasted four years due to its catastrophic failures, since that period there has been steadily increasing women's prison numbers, buttressed by consistently high rates of re-incarceration and a widening net of interventions and control associated with front and back-end support service structures (Carlton and Segrave 2013).

A report by Victorian Ombudsman Deborah Glass in November 2017 arising from a snap inspection of the main women's prison, the Dame Phyllis Frost Centre (DPFC), highlights in striking detail the continuum of discriminatory treatment experienced by women in the Victorian prison system. In a context of dramatic expansion and overcrowding [with prisoner numbers at DPFC growing by 65% in the past five years (Victorian Ombudsman 2017: 4)], the Ombudsman's inspection was intended to assess the prison's compliance with the *Optional Protocol to the Convention Against Torture and other Cruel, Inhuman and Degrading Treatment or Punishment* (OPCAT), which Australia (and the state of Victoria) eventually ratified in late 2017. In spite of four decades of anti-discrimination campaign work and the formal introduction of human rights 'protections' (i.e. the *Victorian Charter of Human Rights and Responsibilities* [2006]), the Ombudsman's report echoes the *Double Negative* (and other reports arising out of systemic advocacy campaigns in the decades since) in numerous ways. The Ombudsman contemporaneously documents women in prison's inequitable access to health care and meaningful programs in prison; the absence of transparency and accountability in relation to internal disciplinary processes and separation orders; and the withholding of family and visits as punishment among many other issues. The Ombudsman (2017) further expressed concerns regarding the high recorded incidence of self-harm among women particularly in the management unit, and the use of force and restraints used on women in DPFC (including pregnant women leaving the prison for medical visits) compared to other prisons in Victoria. She also highlighted the damaging nature of routine strip-searching before and after contact visits and recommended that this traumatising practice be abolished to avoid potential breaches of the Human Rights Charter and OPCAT (Victorian Ombudsman 2017: 5). Corrections Victoria accepted all of the Ombudsman's recommendations except the abolition of routine strip-searches: "it does not consider that its current practice with respect to observation and supervision of women changing into overalls before contact visits amounts to strip-searching ... [also] it is of the view that its practices are compliant with the Charter" (ibid.: 14). This response from the penal authorities alerts us to the possibility that harsh and degrading treatment in women's prisons may be legitimised by the very legislative frameworks designed to prevent them.

In retrospect, FRG members described their concerns as extending beyond correctional policy to encompass the need for alternatives to women's imprisonment, because they believed that injustice and violence had defined the lives of women imprisoned at Fairlea. They aimed to promote public awareness about imprisoned women's experiences of social and economic disadvantage and to create pressure for the government to reduce prison numbers. As Sandy Cook explained:

> There were so many women in prison who we didn't believe should be in prison ... [we wanted] to try and get as many women as possible out. And then for those that were in [prison, we wanted] to try and change what was happening in that really archaic institution, so at least there would be education, good health ... so that those women that were there would be given really worthwhile opportunities ... so the numbers would be cut right back.[20]

The *Double Negative* recommendations prescribed the use of community based sanctions and alternatives to imprisonment in order to reduce women's prison numbers. Thus, FRG advocated reducing women's prison numbers, particularly among those who were in contact with the system for non-serious offences, through the use of non-custodial initiatives such as community service, halfway houses, and attendance centres (Hancock 1982: 66). However, the over-arching aim driving FRG's *Double Negative* campaign was reformist *not* abolitionist— they aimed principally to ameliorate women's discrimination *within* the prison system, rather than dismantle it altogether. And whilst new women-specific correctional frameworks were adopted on paper, official discourses of progress and reform belied the reality of women's continuing discriminatory treatment in prison.

The *Double Negative* campaign succeeded in documenting women's prison experiences at a time when they were virtually invisible. Moreover, FRG's efforts to advocate within and around the prison system by building a legal case charging discrimination against women provided an important foundation for subsequent anti-carceral feminist campaigns to build upon. From the mid-1980s onwards, activist coalitions picked up and continued this important work but with a broader and more radical perspective—arguing that *no* women should be in prison (Women and Imprisonment Group 1996). Anti-carceral feminists fiercely challenged official secrecy and impunity through government lobbying, grassroots organising and direct action (Carlton and Russell 2015; Carlton 2016). Moreover, they collected evidence to mount subsequent anti-discrimination campaigns, but pursued these rights-based avenues in conjunction with abolitionist strategies and aims. Later anti-carceral feminist activists such as Amanda George and Jude McCulloch characterised the *Double Negative* campaign as a critical starting point for their advocacy and activism.[21] FRG member Sandy Cook was more modest, characterising the contributions of FRG and particularly its emphasis on reformism as a "drop in the ocean" compared to later campaigns.[22]

Conclusion

In a sense, FRG's *Double Negative* campaign provided a critical precursor for the transition into a formalised women's correctional system, which would instil a cycle of reform and expansion. Moreover, imprisoned women's experiences of violence and discrimination continued and intensified throughout the 1980s and 1990s, regardless of official discourses of 'progress' and 'change' for women in prison. Despite these trajectories, FRG's efforts were not futile. The use of anti-discrimination legislation and rights-based advocacy became a foundational feature of subsequent anti-carceral feminist campaigns challenging women's imprisonment. Through research, fierce advocacy and government lobbying, FRG laid a critical foundation for an emergent anti-carceral feminist movement that extended the focus beyond the administration of the women's prison system to challenge the structural conditions underpinning women's criminalisation and imprisonment, including gender, racial and economic inequalities.

FRG's contribution was grounded upon an anti-discrimination framework consistent with a legal rights strategy focused upon equitable access to treatment and rights in prison. The *Double Negative* campaign contributed, perhaps only temporarily, to the improvement of conditions in Fairlea Women's Prison. But it also represented the first of a series of claims for the rights of imprisoned women to be free from discrimination and it developed a critical knowledge base about women's prison experiences in a local context. Thus, perhaps the FRG's greatest achievements were enabling a discourse of imprisoned women's rights and shifting their entrenched invisibility.

Examining the nexus between liberal rights campaigns and system consolidation illuminates many of the risks and possibilities associated with the former in the context of imprisonment. The limitations of the *Double Negative* campaign—which focused foremost on advancing women's rights *within* the prison system largely without recognition that the system itself is violent—are further highlighted by subsequent anti-carceral feminist campaigns in the late 1990s that pursued imprisoned women's rights through anti-discrimination frameworks as part of an arsenal of radical strategies and tactics, including grassroots coalition-building, mass demonstrations, blockades and direct actions that aimed to disrupt and dismantle what they saw as a continuum of violence from the community to the women's prison. This approach reflects the recognition that a rights compliant prison is still a prison—eliminating discrimination within the system will not mitigate the institution's inherent violence. Further understanding how such work evolved and grew from the early reformist efforts of FRG through to the heady era of anti-carceral feminist activism will yield vital knowledge for advocates and campaigners seeking to navigate rights-based strategies to challenge and transform institutional injustice.

Notes

1. The period 1982–2005 encompasses the FRG's *Double Negative* campaign through to the introduction of the most recent iteration of gender responsive correctional policy, the *Better Pathways Strategy*, which is discussed below.
2. Systemic advocacy can be defined as "action taken to influence or produce systemic change to ensure fair treatment and social fairness" (Flat Out 2014: 5).
3. Interview with Sandy Cook conducted by Bree Carlton, 11 May 2015, Melbourne.
4. Focus group with Chris Burnup, Linda Hancock and Sandy Cook conducted by Bree Carlton and Emma Russell, 11 December 2013, Kew.
5. Interview as above at 3.
6. Focus group as above at 4.
7. Ibid.
8. For example, 'Fairlea blaze sorts rebels from the rest'. *The Age*, 9 January 1980, p. 4.
9. In 1979, the Equal Opportunity Board determined its first sex discrimination complaint, finding in favour of the applicant, Deborah Lawrie, who had been excluded from employment as a pilot. See: *Ansett Transport Industries (Operations) Pty Ltd v Wardley* (1984). EOC 92003 at 75,260.
10. Ibid.
11. Ibid.
12. As above at 3.
13. As above at 4.
14. In 1984 Toner made a public presentation at the Australian Institute of Criminology Conference about reform in the women's correctional system. In this speech, she made no reference to the work of FRG or the *Double Negative* Report.
15. As above at 4.
16. As above at 4; Jude McCulloch, interviewed by Bree Carlton, 12 August 2016, Melbourne.
17. John Griffin, Interview conducted by Bree Carlton, 30 April 2015, Melbourne; Sue Wynne-Hughes, Interview conducted by Bree Carlton, 22 November 2016, Red Hill, Victoria.
18. George, unpublished correspondence.

19. As above at 3.
20. As above at 4.
21. McCulloch as above at 14; Interview with Amanda George conducted by Bree Carlton and Emma Russell, 6 May 2014, Flemington.
22. As above at 4.

References

Bloom, B., Owen, B., & Covington, S. (2003). *Gender Responsive Strategies: Research, Practice, and Guiding Principles for Women Offenders*. Washington, DC: National Institute of Corrections [NIC].

Braz, R. (2006). Kinder, gentler, gender responsive cages: Prison expansion is not prison reform. *Women, Girls, & Criminal Justice, 7*(6), 87–91.

Brown, M., & Schept, J. (2016). New abolition, criminology and a critical carceral studies. *Punishment & Society, 19*(4), 440–462.

Bumiller, K. (2008). *In an Abusive State: How Neoliberalism Appropriated the Feminist Movement against Sexual Violence*. Durham, NC: Duke University Press.

Carlen, P. (1983). *Women's Imprisonment: A Study in Social Control*. London: Routledge & Kegan Paul.

Carlen, P. (1988). *Women, Crime and Poverty*. Milton Keyes: Open University Press.

Carlton, B. (2016). Penal reform, anti-carceral feminist campaigns and the politics of change in women's prisons, Victoria, Australia. *Punishment & Society*. [Online]. https://doi.org/10.1177/1462474516680205. Accessed February 7, 2018.

Carlton, B., & Russell, E. K. (2015). "A gender for change": Cycles of women's penal reform and reconfigurations of anti-prison resistance in Victoria, Australia. *Champ pénal/Penal Field, 12*, 1–24.

Carlton, B., & Russell, E. (2018, January 10). 'We will be written out of history': Feminist challenges to carceral violence and the activist archive. *Oñati Socio-Legal Series, 8*(2), 267–287. Available at SSRN: https://ssrn.com/abstract=3099424.

Carlton, B., & Seagrave, M. (2013). *Women Exiting Prison: Critical Essays on Gender, Post-release Support and Survival*. Oxford: Routledge.

Centre for the Human Rights of Imprisoned People [CHRIP]. (2010). *Culturally and Linguistically Diverse (CALD) Women in Victorian Prison: Update on Developments Since the 2005 Request for Systemic Review of Discrimination Against Women in Victorian Prisons*. Melbourne: CHRIP.

Cerveri, P., Colvin, K., Dias, M., George, A., Hanna, J., Jubb, G., et al. (2005). *Request for a Systematic Review of Discrimination Against Women in Victorian Prisons*. Melbourne: Victorian Council of Social Service.

Christie, N. (1981). *Limits to Pain*. Oxford: Oxford University Press.

Cook, S., & Davies, S. (1999). *Harsh Punishment: International Experiences of Women's Imprisonment*. Boston: Northeastern University Press.

Davis, A. Y. (2003). *Are Prisons Obsolete?* New York: Seven Stories Press.

Department of Justice Victoria. (2005). *Better Pathways: An Integrated Response to Women's Offending and Re-offending*. Melbourne: Victorian Government Department of Justice.

Department of Justice Victoria. (2007). *Better Pathways in Practice: The Women's Correctional Services Framework*. Melbourne: Victorian Government Department of Justice.

Equal Opportunity Commissioner. (1991, May 11). Inquiry into Sex Discrimination at Barwon Prison. *The Age*, p. 10.

Equal Opportunity Commission Victoria [EOCV]. (1993). *Inquiry into Allegations of Discrimination at Barwon Prison*. Melbourne: EOCV.

Faith, K. (2000). Reflections on inside/out organizing. *Social Justice, 27*, 158–167.

Flat Out. (2014). *Strategic Plan: 2014–2016*. [Online]. Available http://www.flatout.org.au. Accessed January 9, 2018.

George, A. (2002). Tales of a private women's prison: Writ in women's lives. *Hecate, 28*(1), 145–153.

George, A., & McCulloch, J. (1988). *Women & Imprisonment in Victoria: A Report*. Melbourne: Fitzroy Legal Service.

Gottschalk, M. (2006). *The Prison and the Gallows: The Politics of Mass Incarceration in America*. Cambridge: Cambridge University Press.

Hancock, L. (1982). *Prisoner and Female: The Double Negative*. Melbourne: Victorian Council of Social Services.

Hannah-Moffat, K. (2000). Prisons that empower: Neo-liberal governance in Canadian women's prisons. *British Journal of Criminology, 40*(1), 510–531.

Hannah-Moffat, K. (2001). *Punishment in Disguise: Penal Governance and the Federal Imprisonment of Women in Canada*. Toronto: University of Toronto Press.

Harris, A. P. (2011). Heteropatriarchy kills: Challenging gender violence in a prison nation. *Washington University Journal of Law & Policy, 37*, 13–65.

Heidensohn, F. (1985). *Women and Crime*. London: Macmillan.

Heiner, B., & Tyson, S. (2017). Feminism and the carceral state: Gender-responsive justice, community accountability, and the epistemology of anti-violence. *Feminist Philosophy Quarterly, 3*(1): Article 3. [Online]. https://doi.org/10.5206/fpq/2016.3.3. Accessed February 7, 2018.

Kilgore, J. (2014). *Repackaging Mass Incarceration.* [Online]. Available http://www.counterpunch.org. Accessed November 30, 2017.

McCulloch, J., & George, A. (2009). Naked power: Strip searching in women's prisons. In J. McCulloch & P. Scranton (Eds.), *The Violence of Incarceration* (pp. 107–123). New York: Routledge.

Murakawa, N. (2014). *The First Civil Right: How Liberals Built Prison America.* Oxford: Oxford University Press.

Musto, J. L. (2016). *Control and Protect: Collaboration, Carceral Protection, and Domestic Sex Trafficking in the United States.* Oakland: University of California Press.

Russell, E. (1998). *Fairlea: The History of a Women's Prison in Australia, 1956–1996.* Melbourne: Australian Scholarly Publishing.

Russell, E., & Carlton, B. (2013). Pathways, race and gender responsive reform: Through an abolitionist lens. *Theoretical Criminology, 17*(4), 474–492.

Schept, J. (2015). *Progressive Punishment: Job Loss, Jail Growth, and the Neoliberal Logic of Carceral Expansion.* New York: New York University Press.

Shaylor, C. (2009). Neither kind nor gentle: The perils of "gender responsive justice". In J. McCulloch & P. Scraton (Eds.), *The Violence of Incarceration* (pp. 145–163). New York: Routledge.

Spade, D. (2011). *Normal Life: Administrative Violence, Critical Trans Politics, and the Limits of Law.* Brooklyn: South End Press.

Thuma, E. (2014). Against the "prison/psychiatric state": Anti-violence feminisms and the politics of confinement in the 1970s. *Feminist Formations, 26*(2), 26–51.

Thuma, E. (2015). Lessons in self-defense: Gender violence, racial criminalization, and anticarceral feminism. *WSQ: Women's Studies Quarterly, 43*(3/4), 52–71.

Toner, P. (1982). *Speech Launching Prisoner and Female: The Double Negative.* Melbourne: Department of Community Welfare Services.

UN General Assembly. (1966). *International Covenant on Civil and Political Rights.* [Online]. Available http://www.refworld.org/docid/3ae6b3aa0.html. Accessed November 30, 2017.

UN General Assembly. (1979). *Convention on the Elimination of All Forms of Discrimination Against Women*. A/RES/34/180. [Online]. Available http:// undocs.org/A/RES/34/180. Accessed November 30, 2017.

UN General Assembly. (2003). *Optional Protocol to the Convention Against Torture and Other Cruel, Inhuman and Degrading Treatment or Punishment*. A/RES/57/199. [Online]. Available http://undocs.org/A/RES/57/199. Accessed November 30, 2017.

Victorian Ombudsman. (2017). *Implementing OPCAT in Victoria: Report and Inspection of the Dame Phyllis Frost Centre*. Melbourne: Victorian Government Printer.

Victorian Woman's Prison Council [VWPC]. (1977). *Biannual Report: 1975–1977*. Melbourne: Victorian Woman's Prison Council.

Women and Imprisonment Group. (1996). *Wring Out Fairlea Demands*. Melbourne: Fitzroy Legal Service.

Women Prisoners and Offenders Advisory Committee. (1991). *Women Prisoners and Offenders: The Agenda for Change*. Melbourne: Victorian Office of Corrections.

9

From Conflict to 'Peace': The Persistent Impact of Human Rights Violations in Northern Ireland's Prisons

Phil Scraton

Introduction

During the twentieth century's last three decades Northern Ireland endured a civil war euphemistically understated as 'the Troubles'. Within a population of approximately 1.7 million, 3636 people were killed as a direct consequence of the Conflict (McKittrick et al. 1999: 1477). The number of lives ended prematurely as a consequence of physical injury, mental anguish and suicide is inestimable. In their comprehensive study of poverty and social exclusion, Hillyard et al. (2005: 6) record that half of their interviewees knew someone who had been killed. Some 88,000 households experienced the loss of a close relative and 50,000 households had a resident injured. Approximately 28,000 people

P. Scraton (✉)
School of Law, Queen's University, Belfast, Northern Ireland, UK
e-mail: p.scraton@qub.ac.uk

© The Author(s) 2018   **207**
E. Stanley (ed.), *Human Rights and Incarceration*, Palgrave Studies
in Prisons and Penology, https://doi.org/10.1007/978-3-319-95399-1_9

were forced from employment and 54,000 households relocated in a form of ethnic cleansing.

Within Northern Ireland the incarceration of politically-affiliated prisoners, regularly involving abusive interrogations, became the defining context of imprisonment. They were interned without trial or were convicted in special courts convened without juries. In 2000, as a key element of political transition from conflict initiated by the negotiated *1998 Good Friday/Belfast Agreement*, the majority of politically-affiliated prisoners were released on licence regardless of time served. Their release left prisons over-staffed and many prison guards without experience of interacting with 'ordinary' prisoners. Years earlier, at the height of civil war and with devolved powers to the Northern Ireland Assembly rescinded, a "clear and enforceable Charter of Rights" had been identified by the Standing Advisory Commission on Human Rights (1977: para. 6.15) as crucial to conflict resolution. Following the release of politically-affiliated prisoners, however, the rights of ordinary prisoners were overlooked within a discourse determined by the political imperatives of conflict transformation.

Acknowledging the legacy of the Conflict, this chapter addresses the institutional neglect of prisoners' rights post-2000. It notes that a decade of stagnation ensued throughout which the Northern Ireland Prison Service [NIPS] failed to initiate necessary rights reforms required to address serious deficiencies in conditions, policies and practices. Throughout the 2000s, despite political devolution to the Northern Ireland Assembly, policing and justice matters remained under UK Government Direct Rule. In 2010 policing and justice powers were finally devolved and the newly formed Department of Justice commissioned an independent review of prisons. This chapter considers its findings and, focusing on the rights of prisoners, interrogates the adequacy of the subsequent political response. Further, it reveals NIPS' resistance to successive damning Inspectorate reports and the reluctance of official bodies to engage with egregious human rights abuses across the penal estate. Finally, it details the consequences for prisoners held in conditions condemned by successive Inspectorate reports, questioning the effectiveness of human rights interventions and exploring the radical potential offered by abolitionism.

From 'Conflict' to 'Peace'

Colonisation, central to the relationship between Britain and Ireland, has generated persistent political and academic controversy. Subjected to British Rule from the twelfth century, Ireland remained a site of struggle for independence culminating in the *1916 Proclamation of the Republic*. It declared "the right of the people to the ownership of Ireland, and to the unfettered control of Irish destinies, to be sovereign and indefeasible". Four years later, following determined armed struggle, the Irish Free State was reconstituted as a British Commonwealth Dominion. The *Government of Ireland Act 1920* cemented partition and six of the nine northern counties of what was the province of Ulster were renamed Northern Ireland, remaining within the United Kingdom. Ireland became a sovereign state in 1937, securing full independence as the Republic of Ireland in 1949. In the wake of partition, Ulster endured relentless conflict as nationalists and republicans, experiencing institutionalised political discrimination and economic marginalisation, continued their campaign for Ireland's reunification. They considered "the use of a [British] legal system to support the Unionist state as wholly unjustifiable" (Boyle et al. 1975: 7).

In the six counties, from the moment of partition through to the late 1960s, the uneasy peace was disrupted regularly as the minority Catholic/Nationalist/Republican [CNR] population in the North remained ruled by 'special' powers administered by political representatives of the Protestant/Unionist/Loyalist [PUL] majority (see Boyle et al. 1975). Emergency legislation was woven into the fabric of Northern Ireland's governance. Renewed annually, the *Civil Authorities (Special Powers) Act (NI) 1922* became permanent 11 years later. The sectarian Royal Ulster Constabulary [RUC], a police force accommodating the notorious part-time reservist B Specials recruited exclusively from PUL communities, enforced the Act. 'Special powers' included discretionary prohibition of public meetings, named organisations and 'seditious literature', and the imposition of curfews and internment without trial. Marginalised socially, economically and politically, CNR communities also endured the discretionary imposition of special powers.

Institutionalised denial of civil and political rights amounted to a form of apartheid. Internment without trial, targeting Republican activists, was used repeatedly (see O'Dowd et al. 1980).

Organised civil rights marches culminated in the deployment of the British Army in 1969. At the behest of the Unionist government, the RUC, the British Army and the UK security services policed the border with the Irish Republic and its communities. Initially a broad strategy underpinned the development of "a series of institutions to guarantee equality of treatment and freedom from discrimination for the Catholic community" (Hillyard 1987: 282). The Unionist government, however, initiated a hard-line response to the civil rights movement including further repressive legislation. Internment without trial was re-introduced, affirming the British State's "clear and unequivocal" commitment to "suppressing political opposition" (ibid.: 284).

Within six months 2300 people were arrested and interned without trial in compounds at Long Kesh, a former military base. Their detention and interrogation constituted egregious breaches of the European Convention on Human Rights. Internment was justified as combatting civil unrest while maintaining the political *status quo*. In 1972 the Conservative UK Government suspended the semi-autonomous Northern Ireland parliament and imposed direct rule. With the "full force of the British Army" deployed across the six counties, a "new system of arrest and detention" was introduced (Boyle et al. 1975: 32). Abandonment of due process was complete when trial without jury followed. Rolston and Tomlinson (1986) record an exponential expansion in long-term male imprisonment and a shift in the prison population from 'ordinary' to politically affiliated prisoners. It had lasting consequences for penal policy, prison management and prisoners' rights.

Initially, politically affiliated prisoners were granted 'special category status'. From the mid-1970s they were incarcerated in H-Blocks within HMP Maze/Long Kesh, a high security prison constructed by the British Army and staffed by the NIPS. In 1979 the British Government withdrew special category status, adopting a policy of criminalisation and reconstituting the politics and conditions of incarceration in Northern Ireland. British soldiers patrolled the streets, emergency powers were normalised, CNR communities were infiltrated and trials held without juries. Those convicted of Conflict-related offences were designated 'ordinary criminals'. Demanding political status, Republican prisoners refused prison clothes, wore blankets and mounted a 'no-wash' protest. Successive hunger strikes in 1980 and 1981, and the Conservative Government's refusal to negotiate prisoners' demands, led to the deaths of ten Republican prisoners (see McKeown 2001).

Throughout the Conflict the NIPS was administered by the Northern Ireland Office [NIO] under UK Government direct rule. Politically affiliated prisoners constituted up to two-thirds of Northern Ireland's prison population (see McEvoy 2001) and their containment dominated the politics, policies and operational practices of incarceration. For 'ordinary prisoners' the early Victorian Crumlin Road Gaol (HMP Belfast), remained Northern Ireland's main male prison. It closed in 1996 following the expansion of the high security Maghaberry Prison. Women prisoners, previously held in Armagh Gaol—built in the late eighteenth and early nineteenth centuries, were moved to Mourne House, a self-contained, high security women's unit within Maghaberry (see Moore and Scraton 2014). A second male prison was built at Magilligan on the north coast of Northern Ireland—remote, relatively inaccessible and poorly served by public transport. It continues to hold sentenced low and medium risk prisoners, many sharing cells without in-cell sanitation and forced to slop out. Hydebank Wood Young Offenders' Centre (YOC) was opened in 1979 as a low security prison close to Belfast.[1]

In 1998 the UK and Irish Governments signed the "complex" and "imaginative" *Belfast/Good Friday Agreement* (Harvey 2003: 1002). In 2000 prisoners affiliated to republican and loyalist paramilitary organisations that had declared ceasefire were released on licence regardless of time served (McEvoy 2001). The reduction in the 'high risk' maximum security prison population brought the closure of HMP Maze/Long Kesh. Emerging from three decades of civil war the politics of imprisonment in Northern Ireland faced considerable challenges. The few remaining politically affiliated prisoners were transferred to HMP Maghaberry to be 'integrated' into the general prison population. Soon after, the Chief Inspector of Prisons assessed Maghaberry as "the most complex and diverse prison establishment in the UK" (HMIP 2003).

A significant reduction in the long-term prison population led to an excess of mid-career prison governors and guards on permanent contracts expected to adapt from regimes predicated on minimal contact to active engagement with prisoners.

The Agreement also established an independent commission on policing, including wide-ranging community consultation and focusing on professionalism, impartiality and, significantly, human rights compliance (ICP 1999). In 2001 the RUC was renamed the Police Service of Northern Ireland [PSNI]. Consistent with police reform, the release on licence of the majority of political prisoners and the withdrawal of British Government Direct Rule provided the foundations for a reformed prison system prioritising prisoners' rights. Yet no parallel initiative on imprisonment was forthcoming and Northern Ireland's prisons entered a decade of stagnation.

Claiming political prisoner status, the relatively few remaining politically affiliated prisoners protested vehemently against the policy of integration into the "mainstream" prison population (Northern Ireland Affairs Committee 2004: 6). Growing unrest triggered a policy review that recommended a return to their separation (Steele 2004). Opposed by the Prison Officers' Association and the Chief Inspector of Prisons, separation was introduced, on condition that "control of the wings" would "not be ceded to prisoners" (Northern Ireland Affairs Committee 2007: 31). Separation did not extend to politically affiliated women prisoners (see Scraton and Moore 2005).

Also significant within the Agreement was the establishment of 'independent' commissions to progress and monitor the transition from conflict to peace. They included Commissions for Equality, for Human Rights, for Children and Young People, and for Victims and Survivors. Given the severity and legacy of the Conflict—lives lost, forced displacement of families, special powers, military occupation, paramilitary policing, suspension of jury trials and political imprisonment—it was anticipated that the Commissions would map the contested road to peace. The Human Rights Commission [HRC] and, to an extent, the Children's Commissioner were given responsibilities to monitor prisons and other places of confinement.

'Normalising' Prisons: Affirming Rights?

Soon after the release of politically affiliated prisoners the HRC prioritised "the human rights of prisoners" (Scraton and Moore 2005: 7). While acknowledging that prisons are "literally" sites of exclusion, the then UK Chief Inspector of Prisons affirmed that those most marginalised "need the protection of human rights" (Owers 2004: 108). The HRC focused initially on children and women in custody (see Kilkelly et al. 2002) and those detained under mental health legislation (Davidson et al. 2003). Following the death of a 19 year old young woman, in Mourne House women's unit, its Commissioners visited the unit. They were "deeply concerned at aspects of the treatment of women they witnessed" (Scraton and Moore 2005: 3).

Consequently, the HRC used its statutory powers to initiate independent research into the treatment of women and girls in custody, specifically the regime's compliance with international human rights law and standards. Focusing on potentially egregious breaches of the European Convention on Human Rights (right to life; freedom from torture and inhuman and degrading treatment; right to a private and family life; freedom from discrimination) the in-depth research recorded women prisoners' profound concerns, detailing the systemic denial of their rights. These included: exceptionally high security levels; inhibitions on movement; restrictions on privacy; high ratio of male staff; guards' lack of empathy; excessive lockdown and strip-searching; use of the punishment block and isolation; inhibited access to recreational facilities, education classes, telephones and mail (Scraton and Moore 2005). The Prison Service Director General dismissed the research findings.

In 2004, following the transfer of women prisoners to a unit within Hydebank Wood male young offenders' centre, the research continued. While the research was in progress a woman took her own life, there were two further serious suicide attempts, a judicial review of the treatment of a child held on 23 hour lock-up in the punishment block and a hunger strike by a Republican woman prisoner. The HRC called for an independent, public inquiry into the deterioration of the regime, its administration, management and operation. There was no response from the UK Government. In July 2007, the HRC published the Hydebank Wood research findings (Scraton and Moore 2007). They concluded that its previous recommendations for a gender-responsive strategy within a discrete women's therapeutic facility had not been addressed and "urgent progress regarding self-harm, substance use, mental ill-health, therapeutic provision, counselling, occupational therapy and constructive work and educational opportunities" was necessary (ibid.: 127).

Derived in part on the research, a broader submission was made to the Northern Ireland Affairs Committee (2007) focusing on conditions in all four jails. It condemned the prison estate as unfit for purpose, demonstrating that its operation consistently breached international human rights standards. Neither management teams nor guards had received appropriate training responsive to the identifiable needs of a complex prison population. Operational policies and landing practices were determined by historical priorities inherited from holding politically affiliated prisoners. The operational ethos was reactive rather than proactive—evident in successive death in custody findings. Mental healthcare was "seriously deficient in the very jurisdiction that most required therapeutic intervention". Self-harm and suicide were attributable to "locking up the most vulnerable", with those "most in need of treatment enduring the most punitive responses" (ibid.: 193–194). Limited association time and insufficient work opportunities resulted in prisoners' locked in their cells—a form of solitary confinement—for at least two-thirds, often more, of their sentence. Contact with families, especially with children, was inhibited severely by regime restrictions and unaffordable telephone costs.

For women and girls no discrete operational strategy existed. There was no commitment to separate site provision and no discrete, gender-specific policies and practices. Inadequate mental healthcare was exacerbated by random and regular invasive strip-searches and overuse of punishment cells—particularly damaging for those in distress. Women's 'best interests' were disregarded exposing deficiencies in child protection procedures, gender-specific provision, healthcare, counselling, education and advocacy. The "seriousness of evidence gathered" showed that incarcerated children, aged 15–17, held within the Hydebank Wood campus, were "at risk of harm and possibly death". Those "most vulnerable" and requiring therapeutic help were "often managed in punishment cells" (Northern Ireland Affairs Committee 2007: 196).

It was evident that there had been no consideration given to adapting regimes, conditions and policies responsive to the identified needs and human rights of 'ordinary' prisoners. In this 'new era' Maghaberry's independent inspection report recorded the prison's extraordinary diverse and complex population, particularly noting the institutional failure to accommodate the particular needs of the relatively few women prisoners held in Mourne House (HMCIP 2003). Following the eventual transfer of women to Hydebank Wood Young Offenders' Institution inspectors condemned the regime for women as inadequate (HMIP and CJINI 2005). Their assessment was endorsed by the Commissioner for Human Rights for the Council of Europe, who reported that within a predominantly male institution women prisoners could not "receive appropriate treatment" and conditions were "likely to aggravate their fragile condition" (Gil-Robles 2005: para. 126). The UN Committee Against Torture [UNCAT] (2004: 5) described the regime as unacceptable, not least the lack of gender-specific policies and the disproportionate number of male guards.

A subsequent full inspection into the conditions at Hydebank Wood criticised specifically the "overuse of handcuffs" during routine transport, serious deficiencies in induction, routine strip-searching, "excessive" adjudication punishments, bullying, lack of constructive activities, unjustifiable lock-downs, minimal outdoor activity and inadequate resettlement policies (HMIP and CJINI 2008: 6). This institutional failure was emphasised three years later by the Inspectorates' findings that its previous recommendations had been ignored and "excessive use of cellular confinement as a punishment" had continued (HMIP and CJINI 2011: 5). Further, prison officers were considered "negative and punitive" and healthcare remained seriously deficient, particularly mental healthcare.

During this period Maghaberry underwent a further inspection. Treatment of the prison's diverse population—remand, short, medium and life sentences, sex offenders, politically-affiliated loyalist and republican prisoners—was criticised with fine defaulters in prison for days subjected to "the same security regime as someone serving a 10-year-sentence" (HMIP and CJINI 2009: v). Reflecting the four assessment criteria constituting a "healthy prison"—safety; respect and dignity; purposeful activity; resettlement—the regime was rated deficient. Of 155 recommendations made previously by the inspectors only 44 had been addressed. They concluded that as "one of the most expensive prisons in the United Kingdom" the "situation" could not "be permitted to continue" (HMIP and CJINI 2009: vii).

Political Devolution and Resistance to Change

As mentioned previously, while the 1998 Agreement provided the constitutional foundation for devolution of powers to a democratically elected Northern Ireland Assembly, all policing and criminal justice matters remained under direct control of the UK Government. In April 2010 a devolved Department of Justice was established providing the foundation for much-needed penal reform (Hillsborough Agreement 2010: para. 7). It prioritised a full review of conditions, management and oversight within prisons setting the foundation for exploration of custodial alternatives alongside urgent reform of women's imprisonment and young people's detention. An independent Prison Review Team [PRT] was appointed to address a series of serious concerns: ongoing conflict in Maghaberry; the replacement of Magilligan; a strategy for women prisoners; and reform of the young offenders' regime (PRT 2011a).

In February 2011 the PRT published a devastating interim report. It found the Prison Service "dysfunctional", revealing serious deficiencies in "management, leadership, vision, objectives, culture" (PRT 2011a: 2). Deep-rooted failings compromised prisoners' rights across all elements of operational practice: rehabilitation, healthcare, education, purposeful activities, physical environment, staff engagement, industrial relations and leadership. Previous severe critiques by the Inspectorates, monitoring boards and independent researchers had not been addressed. The PRT demanded "transformative change" in all regimes alongside a community-based programme of justice reinvestment offering alternatives to prison. A radical reform programme would require recruitment of appropriately trained staff at all levels, challenge the "security-dominated" mindset and introduce progressive regimes.

The PRT reiterated the World Health Organisation's commitment to "healthy" prisons, emphasising just and fair punishment processes inside prisons, security and safety of prisoners, and "respect for human dignity" consistent with "human rights" (PRT 2011a: 27). It detailed the depth of institutionalised malaise within the management and staffing of a prison estate unfit for purpose. Organisational deficiencies were stark: resistance to cultural change; operational inflexibility; ineffective engagement with outside professionals or prisoners; and endemic failure in the duty of care.

Announcing an "efficiency and effectiveness programme" of reform, the newly appointed Director General accepted that the "most vulnerable" prisoners had been failed, as had a "disaffected, demoralised and demotivated" workforce and management (NIPS 2011: 1). Reform would prioritise effective management, security, rehabilitation, external partnerships and professional training. Yet it was a commitment without substance recognised by the PRT whose final report was scathing in revealing negligible progress towards resolving the "endemic and systemic problems", particularly the obstructiveness of the Prison Officers' Association (PRT 2011b: 5–6). Systemic denial of prisoners' rights, prioritised for immediate action by the PRT, remained unaddressed. Publicly frustrated, the PRT condemned institutional intransigence, specifically a reluctance to initiate cultural transformation within the workforce.

Concluding its review the PRT presented 40 recommendations, the realisation of which was considered necessary to establish a progressive and effective prison system compliant with internationally agreed "human rights standards and ethical values" (PRT 2011b: 9). Fundamental reform would affirm rehabilitation as the primary objective of imprisonment emphasising personal development, purposeful activity, education, vocational training, social skills, independent living, reintegration and desistance from offending. Emphasising the need to progress alternatives to prison, the PRT identified three policy imperatives: supervised activity orders for fine defaulters; statutory time limits for remands; and community-based sanctions for those sentenced to three months or less (ibid.: 28).

The Review also prescribed major reform of the prison estate necessary to meet the requirements of a complex prison population. It included the closure of Magilligan. Also, as a matter of urgency, it proposed a purpose-built, small women's prison offering gender-appropriate programmes developed in partnership with statutory, voluntary and community organisations alongside integrated community-based mental healthcare support. The historical "neglect" of young offenders could be addressed by engaging and developing community-based multi-agency partnerships to service the prison as a "secure college".

Within months, however, Maghaberry received another negative inspection report (HMIP et al. 2012). Safety, respect and purposeful activity were rated "insufficient". The prison was considered "unsafe" with half the population sharing cramped cells, often confined for 20 hours a day. Hydebank Wood Young Offenders' Centre, was inspected soon after. While its regime had made some progress, "safety" and "respect" were "not sufficiently good", and "purposeful activity" was "poor". The inspectors criticised complacent, institutionalised negative attitudes towards violence, bullying, self harm, suicide and prisoner vulnerability. Staff were disengaged from and indifferent to the needs of young prisoners and lock-downs were frequent and unpredictable. There had been "significant slippage in the regime", education classes cancelled regularly and prisoners "too long locked in their cells" and limited "access to outside activities" (HMIP et al. 2013: 29).

An independent Prison Review Oversight Group, appointed by the Department of Justice, recognised worsening industrial relations across the prison estate, evident in deeply-ingrained resistance to change. It recorded serious breakdowns in relations between guards, management and the Director, warning that "the ability of the programme to deliver" had been compromised (Prison Review Oversight Group 2014: 19). Three years on from the PRT's uncompromising demand for "root and branch" reform, restrictive "custom and practice" remained entrenched within deeply institutionalised negative environments. Developing a human rights informed agenda had been a key PRT objective, evident throughout its comprehensive reports. Within two years, however, it had fallen from the political radar, replaced by the reformist rhetoric of humane containment. As soon became evident, the rhetoric masked harsh reality.

In its 2014–2015 annual report, Maghaberry's Independent Monitoring Board (2015) condemned four accommodation blocks as "unfit for purpose". It identified connections between poor "recreational and training opportunities", boredom and drug-taking. Drugs strategy meetings were poorly attended and lacked focus. Tensions within the prison fuelled bullying and provoked self-harm. Healthcare, particularly specialist mental health provision, was at breaking-point and low staff retention pre-empted constant crisis management. Remand prisoners were locked down often for 23 hours each day, impacting further on mental ill-health particularly regarding vulnerable prisoners. During the previous 12 months three prisoners had taken their own lives.

In the wake of the IMB's critical review the regime received a comprehensive, unannounced inspection. The outcome was unprecedented in its criticisms. Based on extensive experience inspecting prisons in England and Wales, the Chief Inspector of Prisons condemned Maghaberry as "Dickensian"—the "most dangerous" prison he had inspected (BBC 2015). His assessment was endorsed by Northern Ireland's Chief Inspector of Criminal Justice who considered the prison "unsafe and unstable", gripped by a "downward spiral". Treatment of "men in despair was inadequate" and "several self-inflicted deaths" had occurred (HMIP et al. 2015: 5–6). In a petulant media response the NIPS Director General downplayed these damning findings. The Northern Ireland Assembly Justice Minister affirmed that that all criticisms made by the Inspectorates had been addressed.

Within months, profoundly concerned, the Inspectorates revisited Maghaberry unannounced. They found conditions for vulnerable prisoners—those with "learning difficulties, mental health issues, addiction problems and personality disorders"—had worsened (HMIP et al. 2016a: 5). Violence levels remained high, access to illicit drugs and diversion of prescription drugs were "pervasive" and the investigation of staff assaults on prisoners were inadequate. Most significantly, "mental health provision had deteriorated" and required "urgent attention" (ibid.: 14). Half the prison population were confined to cells throughout the day. Such parlous conditions generated and exacerbated mental ill-health. Most unusually in September 2016 the Inspectorates returned yet again. They concluded: "much needs to be done in order for Maghaberry Prison to be a safe, secure, respectful and rehabilitative custodial setting" (HMIP et al. 2016b: 19).

As argued above, securing human rights compliant principles and ensuring their application was essential in progressing conflict transformation in Northern Ireland. Yet, submissions to the PRT, successive inspection reports and independent research revealed the systemic denial of prisoners' rights and the institutionalised resistance to addressing this deficit. The PRT considered prisoners' rights as essential to reforming the management and operation of the prisons but Inspectorates neither conduct their inspections nor contextualise their findings within a rights framework. Calibrating the 'health' of penal institutions implies rights' assessment yet compliance with internationally agreed standards remains absent. While accepting imprisonment is retributive, the focus remains reformative humane containment, personal rehabilitation and community reintegration.

In progressing the transition to peace, the organisation tasked with the promotion of human rights was and remains the Northern Ireland Human Rights Commission [NIHRC]. Exemplified by the women in prison research, its extensive powers provide unique access to information and documents not in the public domain and entry into places of detention. However, since publishing its second report on women's imprisonment in 2007 the NIHRC has not conducted further primary research within prisons. Given the severity of the PRT's critique of systemic human rights abuses, it is inexplicable that it has not engaged its powers of entry to investigate the specific and generic conditions exposed by the Inspectorates' reports. Despite failing to engage in primary investigations, it submitted recommendations regarding overcrowding, women, suicide, medication, bullying and solitary confinement to the United Nations Committee against Torture. The following year it "advised the Department of Justice to consider the introduction of effective community sentences" as an alternative to custody (NIHRC 2016: 28). Further, the Northern Ireland Children's Commissioner [NICCY] has not examined conditions under which children are incarcerated.

The Limits of Penal Reformism and the Case for Abolition

The above analysis of Northern Ireland's operational regimes—and the institutional failure to address systemic rights abuses revealed by independent reviews and inspections—raises profound concerns about the limits of penal reform. In progressing transition from war to peace the expectation was that devolved government powers alongside institutional reform across criminal justice agencies would provide a unique opportunity to overhaul the penal system, in the words of the PRT, "root and branch". It was the PRT's primary objective to secure a rights-based prison service. That this did not happen is not simply lack of vision or understanding but a direct consequence of the contradictions inherent in penal reform discourses. It demonstrates the clash between regressive penological ideology and progressive rehabilitative alternatives.

Embedded within the criminological tradition and resonating throughout popular discourse on prisons, are four distinct, reactionary principles: *incapacitation* in removing the 'offender' from the community; *punishment* commensurate with the crime committed; *retribution* or 'repayment' to the victim and community; *deterrence* of others. Alongside these overarching punitive principles prisons are expected, counter-intuitively, to deliver programmes of *reform* and *resettlement*. Based on in-depth observational research, however, Sim (2009: 4) demonstrates that such initiatives have no "institutionalised presence in the everyday, working lives of prison officers or the landing culture that legitimates and sustains their often regressive ideologies and punitive practices". Rather, prisons are "invisible places of physical hardship and psychological shredding" (ibid.). Mind numbing routines operating behind high walls and closed doors institutionalise "populations of incomplete and wounded lives" (Quinney 2006: 270). As Richard Quinney concludes, the consequences are "pervasive–economic, social, psychological, and spiritual" and the "injuries caused by the prison shared by all" (ibid.). Yet, the pains of confinement and the violence of incarceration are inflicted in 'our' name, financed through the public purse. Within marginalised communities incarceration infects, and often destroys, familial, social, political and emotional relationships.

Penal reformism has its roots in the nineteenth century dawn of the 'New Prison' and its over-claimed commitment to creating opportunities for rehabilitation. While the worst excesses of incarceration were ended, prisons remained sites of condemnation, punishment and retribution. This clash of ideologies plays out daily behind prison walls—on landings, in exercise yards, regularly extending to healthcare provision. The 'worthy' prisoner is the compliant prisoner. A further tension, well-illustrated by the evidence discussed earlier, is the presumption that human rights and civil liberties shared by citizens in the community can be extended to places of detention within a framework of internationally agreed rules and conventions. Yet custodial institutions operate regimes of forfeiture. It is assumed that prisoners' loss of liberty will be accompanied by a commensurate loss of rights.

Further, what happens outside prison walls is crucial. Given the political and cultural investment in prisons and the unquantifiable social and economic impact of penal regimes on families and communities, informed debate regarding transparency and accountability is notably absent. While media-fuelled popular discourse demands ever-longer sentences served in ever-expanding prisons little consideration is given to the social and societal consequences of incarceration in harsh, damaging regimes. This dominant discourse remains condemnatory and retributive, baulking at any hint of penal reform, cynically pitting the rights of prisoners against the losses of victims. As this chapter demonstrates, even the mildest reform agenda—consistent with internationally agreed standards and measures—is resisted by managers and guards committed to retaining their institutional power, safe in the assumption that they will receive unquestioning public support.

Reflecting on the longevity and durability of the inhumane prison suggests a counsel of despair—that pursuing a carceral rights-based agenda is wasted energy. This is not necessarily so. Applied to specific cases, it can provide limited scope for delivering change. Exposing individual or collective violations of prisoners' rights occasionally initiates mild reforms in policy and practice. As noted above, the potential for ensuring that prisons are rights-compliant exists through independent monitoring boards and inspection teams with capacity to make assessments founded on human rights principles. Moore and Scraton (2014: 228) note that these external bodies "provide a valuable and significant presence in the current penal climate", their interventions raising "critical questions about individual cases and institutionalized practices that otherwise would remain hidden from external scrutiny". Implementation of their recommendations, however, is not mandatory. While their presence suggests comprehensive institutional accountability, it is a veneer masking the operational autonomy evident in the routine management and administration of regimes.

In conducting inspections it is not evident that operational policies and practices are assessed against criteria rooted in internationally agreed human rights standards and obligations. As discussed earlier, inspectorates rank regimes under four broad "expectations"—prisoner safety, respect for human dignity, purposeful activity, and resettlement (HMIP 2018: 8). While this framework affirms respect for international human rights standards, assessment criteria are imprecise in reporting egregious breaches of prisoners' rights. A more explicit assessment of rights compliance would require a fifth, discrete category. While not rejecting the potential of rights discourse and rights implementation in facilitating reforms that benefit the daily lives of prisoners, the Northern Ireland research reveals the strength of professional, political and institutional resistance to change. It limits the potential of monitoring, inspection and reviews to deliver rights compliant prisons.

Consequently, however "well-intentioned", a reform agenda "facilitates a politics of incorporation in which places of detention become 'rights-compliant', their managers and staff gain rights, management and protection diplomas and independent monitors annually report their visits and inspections" (McCulloch and Scraton 2009: 11). The assumption being that, in developing a calculus applied through independent monitoring agencies for inspecting and assessing rights compliance, operational regimes can be humanised. This underscores the liberal reformist proposition that rights compliance can deliver a 'healthy', 'humanitarian' context protecting prisoners' mental and physical well-being while enabling their 'rehabilitation'. In contrast, and as this article demonstrates, institutionalised authoritarian routines and practices within prison and the imposition of discretionary authority remove from the prisoner her/his capacity for self-determination. The routine imposition of non-negotiable, institutional authority denies rights with impunity.

Routine rights violations remain endemic, "hidden beneath the veneer of mission statements, glossy brochures and internet virtual tours" (McCulloch and Scraton 2009: 11). Consequently, critical researchers face a significant dilemma. Committed to confronting the abuse of power in the moment there is little option other than to appeal to rights' protections in the knowledge, as prisoners regularly comment, that just outcomes are rarely delivered. While important to disclose rights violations, particularly when revealed repeatedly by independent inspectorates, persistent institutional failure to establish and deliver rights-based policies and practices demonstrates an inherent deficit in implementation. In most advanced liberal democracies punitive regimes have managed liberal reformist critiques through political incorporation. This enabled a new era of punishment to emerge and consolidate masked by apparently adaptive alternatives.

In his analysis of USA penal expansion Rothman (1980: 9) demonstrates how "progressive" reformism led to "innovations that appeared to be substitutes for incarceration". Located within punitive ideology and practice, however, they "became supplements to incarceration" (ibid.). Without a shift in the retributive mind-set pre-eminent within professional and popular discourses, "innovations often became add-ons with probation services extending the authority of the state and parole expanding the terms of incarceration" (ibid.: 12). Thus reformists' "grand hopes of transforming" jails were lost. Progressive reformism found itself positioned, literally, "up against [ever higher] walls" (ibid.: 158).

Sharing this critique and abandoning penal reformism, in 2005 the pioneering Oakland-based organisation Critical Resistance republished the Prison Advocacy Project's 1976 abolitionist campaign handbook (Critical Resistance 2005). Detailing a century of academic research and political activism, it notes Frank Tannenbaum's (1938) call to "destroy the prison, root and branch" and David Greenberg's (1970) conclusion that the "problem of prisons" cannot be resolved by "drastic prison reform" but only through abolition. Elsewhere, Erving Goffman (1968) presented his definitive analysis of the dehumanisation of the 'self' inflicted by the penitentiary and Nils Christie (1981) detailed of how penal regimes function to destroy personal dignity and self-worth.

Yet across liberal democratic states the dehumanisation and damage inflicted by incarceration persists virtually unchallenged, reflecting a broad "acceptance that millions of people should spend part or all of their lives in cages" (Gilmore 2007: 243). At the heart of the "anti-prison movement" is the proposition, clearly evident in the discussion earlier in this chapter, that "frameworks that rely exclusively on reforms produce the stultifying idea that nothing lies beyond the prison" (Davis 2003: 103). Securing community-based alternatives to breach the school to prison pipeline, challenging the criminalisation of working-class young men and women and initiating programmes of decarceration are essential components in liberating communities from pains of confinement. Of course, some individuals require removal from their communities for their own or others' safety, but not in the ideological conceptualisation and physical manifestation of 'prison'. Yet, despite the intellectual and common-sense persuasiveness of the abolitionist argument, incarcerating men, women and children for ever-longer periods within "human warehouses" (Simon 2007: 142), particularly in the USA, shows little sign of abating.

In a consistently punitive climate Davis (2003: 103) argues that the "major challenge" for abolitionists is to campaign for "more humane environments" for men, women and children currently incarcerated "without bolstering the permanence of the prison system". It is imperative to monitor and actively support prisoners' rights, social justice and the principles of "reparation and reconciliation" while simultaneously seeking a "constellation of alternatives" to incarceration—thus establishing an agenda that challenges the popular discourse of "retribution and vengeance" (ibid.: 107). As this chapter demonstrates, however, penal reformism in isolation inevitably reinforces and legitimates the politics of incarceration. It is instructive that the outworking of reformism has contributed to clearing the ground on which ever-expanding prisons are now under construction.

Central to a critical analysis of rights, whether in prison or the community, is their contextualisation within prevailing social, political and economic relations and the State's role in ensuring their reproduction. Within the advanced capitalist democracies discussed here, the structural conditions and social consequences of marginalisation are starkly evident in communities blighted by persistent poverty, long-term structural unemployment, poor housing, ever-diminishing welfare support, prescribed and illicit drug dependency and under-funded schools. On these hard streets exclusion is material and its social consequences evident in endemic illness, low life expectancy and self-inflicted death. It is from within impoverished communities and neighbourhoods that prisons recruit their captives. This reality, albeit relatively small-scale, is evident throughout the North of Ireland. Its relatively low rate of imprisonment compared to England disguises the prevalence of community-based punishments administered by paramilitaries and vigilante groups. As earlier sections of this chapter demonstrate, economic marginalisation, social exclusion and political disenfranchisement underpin systemic denial of all forms of rights whether in the community or in the prison.

In their operational policies and practices, an inescapable reality is that prisons remain sites of continuing immiseration and exploitation, their growth driven by financial investment in so-called humane containment rather than a commitment to resolving the systemic denial of social and economic rights within marginalised communities. Effective challenges to the privations inflicted by punitive ideologies and manifested in the stark reality of bricks and steel that separate prisoners from their communities cannot be achieved by penal reform. 'Making better prisons' is a mantra shackled by the same decontextualised appeal to 'making better prisoners'. Each assumes that the best interests of complex individuals and the best interests of their communities can be realised in sites of confinement, isolation, deprivation and dehumanisation.

Critical prison research, including that developed by prisoners inside (see the excellent *Journal of Prisoners on Prisons*), has been comprehensive and revelatory in exposing the routine deprivations and brutalisation of harsh regimes in which physical coercion presides over intellectual reason. In this harsh environment of threat and counter-threat there is little potential to normalise creative exchanges or humanise social interaction. As places built politically and ideologically on the premises and promises of punishment, retribution and deterrence, prisons impose regimes dedicated to eliminating the personal and social capacities of those locked behind the door. Institutionally resilient to the rights of prisoners, they stifle agency, break potential, numb creativity and inflict pain.

> I talked with [Tommy] on the landing. The guard introduced him as a 'model prisoner'. Serving 20 years for a first–serious–offence; visited weekly by wife and three children. He said: 'I've done my highers in here, and a degree and a higher degree and all. I love studying and feel I've made something of myself. I've exhausted all the prison has to offer but I still have five to eight years to do. I asked the Governor what I might do next. He replied: "Son, you've done well, keep your head down, blend with the paintwork"'. (Fieldnotes, Scotland)

The challenge for critical analysts of the carceral state, familiar with the depth of suffering and mental ill-health inflicted within punitive, isolating and demeaning regimes, is to support immediate humanitarian initiatives in prisons while developing and progressing abolitionist strategies.

Acknowledgements Many thanks to Lizzy Stanley for her important, generous comments on the first draft and to Deena Haydon for her constant support and critical reflection. In memory of Ciara McCulloch.

Note

1. In June 2004, women prisoners were transferred from Mourne House, Maghaberry to one of Hydebank Wood's five houses. In 2015 the site was rebranded as Hydebank Wood Secure College and Women's Prison.

References

BBC. (2015). *Maghaberry Prison "Most Dangerous" Ever Visited Says Chief Inspector*. [Online]. Available http://www.bbc.com/news/uk-northern-ireland-34733832. Accessed March 20, 2018.

Boyle, K., Hadden, T., & Hillyard, P. (1975). *Law and the State: The Case of Northern Ireland*. London: Martin Robertson.

Christie, N. (1981). *Limits to Pain*. Oxford: Oxford University Press.

Critical Resistance. (2005). *Instead of Prisons: A Handbook for Abolitionists*. Oakland, CA: Prison Education Action Project/Critical Resistance.

Davidson, G., McCallion, M., & Potter, M. (2003). *Connecting Mental Health and Human Rights*. Belfast: NIHRC.

Davis, A. (2003). *Are Prisons Obsolete?* New York: Seven Stories Press.

Gilmore, R. W. (2007). *Golden Gulag: Prisons, Surplus, Crisis, and Opposition in Globalizing California*. Berkeley: University of California Press.

Gil-Robles, A. (2005). *Report on Visit to the UK 4–12 November 2004*. Strasbourg: Office of the Commissioner for Human Rights.

Goffman, E. (1968). *Asylums: Essays on the Social Situation of Mental Patients and Other Inmates*. Harmondsworth: Penguin.

Greenberg, D. (1970). *The Problem of Prisons*. Philadelphia: National Peace Literature Service.

Harvey, C. (2003). On law, politics and contemporary constitutionalism. *Fordham International Law Journal, 26*(4), 996–1014.

Hillsborough Agreement. (2010). *Agreement at Hillsborough Castle: 5 February 2010*. Belfast: Northern Ireland Office.

Hillyard, P. (1987). The normalization of special powers: From Northern Ireland to Britain. In P. Scraton (Ed.), *Law, Order and the Authoritarian State* (pp. 279–312). Milton Keynes: Open University Press.

Hillyard, P., Rolston, B., & Tomlinson, M. (2005). *Poverty and Conflict in Ireland: An International Perspective*. Dublin: Institute of Public Administration and Combat Poverty Agency.

HM Inspectorate of Prisons [HMIP]. (2003). *Report on a Full Announced Inspection of HM Prison Maghaberry, 13–17 May 2002*. London: HMIP.

HM Inspectorate of Prisons [HMIP]. (2018). *Guide for Inspectors, January 2018*. London: HMIP.

HM Inspectorate of Prisons [HMIP], & Criminal Justice Inspection Northern Ireland [CJINI]. (2005). *Report on an Unannounced Inspection of the Imprisonment of Women in Northern Ireland, Ash House, Hydebank Wood Prison, 28–30 November 2004*. London: HMIP.

HM Inspectorate of Prisons [HMIP], & Criminal Justice Inspection Northern Ireland [CJINI]. (2008). *Report on an Announced Inspection of Ash House, Hydebank Wood, 29 October–2 November 2007*. London: HMIP.

HM Inspectorate of Prisons [HMIP], & Criminal Justice Inspection Northern Ireland [CJINI]. (2009). *Report on an Unannounced Full Follow-Up Inspection of Maghaberry Prison, 19–23 January 2009*. Belfast: CJINI.

HM Inspectorate of Prisons [HMIP], & Criminal Justice Inspection Northern Ireland [CJINI]. (2011). *Report on an Unannounced Short Follow-Up Inspection of Hydebank Wood Young Offenders Centre, 21–25 March 2011*. Belfast: CJINI.

HM Inspectorate of Prisons [HMIP], Criminal Justice Inspection Northern Ireland [CJINI], & Regulation and Quality Improvement Authority [RQIA]. (2012). *Report on an Unannounced Inspection of Maghaberry Prison, 19–23 March* Belfast: CJINI.

HM Inspectorate of Prisons [HMIP], Criminal Justice Inspection Northern Ireland [CJINI], Regulation and Quality Improvement Authority [RQIA], & The Education and Training Inspectorate [ETI]. (2013). *Report on an Announced Inspection of Hydebank Wood Young Offenders' Centre, 18–22 February 2013*. Belfast: Department of Justice.

HM Inspectorate of Prisons [HMIP], Criminal Justice Inspection Northern Ireland [CJINI], Regulation and Quality Improvement Authority [RQIA], & The Education and Training Inspectorate [ETI]. (2015). *Report on an Unannounced Inspection of Maghaberry Prison, 11–22 May 2015*. Belfast: Department of Justice.

HM Inspectorate of Prisons [HMIP], Criminal Justice Inspection Northern Ireland [CJINI], Regulation and Quality Improvement Authority [RQIA], & The Education and Training Inspectorate [ETI]. (2016a). *Overview of Initial Findings of a Report on an Announced Inspection of Maghaberry Prison, 4–15 January 2016*. Belfast: CJINI.

HM Inspectorate of Prisons [HMIP], Criminal Justice Inspection Northern Ireland [CJINI], Regulation and Quality Improvement Authority [RQIA], & The Education and Training Inspectorate [ETI]. (2016b). *Report on an Announced visit to Maghaberry Prison to Review Progress Against the Nine Inspection Recommendations made in 2015, 5–7 September 2016*. Belfast: CJINI.

Independent Commission on Policing for Northern Ireland [ICP]. (1999). *A New Beginning: Policing in Northern Ireland*. London: HMSO.

Independent Monitoring Board [IMB]. (2015). *Independent Monitoring Board, Annual Report 2014–2015, Maghaberry Prison*. Belfast: IMB.

Kilkelly, U., Moore, L., & Convery, V. (2002). *In Our Care: Promoting the Rights of Children in Custody*. Belfast: Northern Ireland Human Rights Commission.

McCulloch, J., & Scraton, P. (2009). The violence of incarceration: An introduction. In P. Scraton & J. McCulloch (Eds.), *The Violence of Incarceration* (pp. 1–18). London: Routledge.

McEvoy, K. (2001). *Paramilitary Imprisonment in Northern Ireland: Resistance Management and Release*. Oxford: Oxford University Press.

McKeown, L. (2001). *Out of Time: Irish Republican Prisoners Long Kesh 1972–2000*. Belfast: Beyond the Pale.

McKittrick, D., Kelters, S., Feeney, B., Thornton, C., & McVea, D. (1999). *Lost Lives: The Stories of Men, Women and Children Who Died as a Result of the Northern Ireland Troubles*. Edinburgh: Mainstream Publishing.

Moore, L., & Scraton, P. (2014). *The Incarceration of Women: Punishing Bodies, Breaking Spirits*. London: Palgrave Macmillan.

Northern Ireland Affairs Committee. (2004). *The Separation of Paramilitary Prisoners at HMP Maghaberry, Second Report of the Session 2003–04*. HC 302-1. London: The Stationery Office.

Northern Ireland Affairs Committee. (2007). *The Northern Ireland Prison Service, First Report of the Session 2007–08*. HC 118-2. London: The Stationery Office.

Northern Ireland Human Rights Commission [NIHRC]. (2016). *The 2016 Annual Statement: Human Rights in Northern Ireland*. Belfast: NIHRC.

Northern Ireland Prison Service [NIPS]. (2011). NIPS SEE Programme Launch—Director General's Speech, 28 June. Belfast: NIPS

O'Dowd, L., Rolston, B., & Tomlinson, M. (1980). *Northern Ireland: Between Civil Rights and Civil War*. London: CSE Books.

Owers, A. (2004). Prison inspection and the protection of human rights. *European Human Rights Law Review, 2*(2), 105–116.

Prison Review Oversight Group. (2014). *Second Annual Report*. Belfast: Prison Review Oversight Group.

Prison Review Team [PRT]. (2011a). *Review of the Northern Ireland Prison Service: Conditions, Management and Oversight of All Prisons. Interim Report February 2011*. Belfast: Department of Justice Northern Ireland.

Prison Review Team [PRT]. (2011b). *Review of the Northern Ireland Prison Service: Conditions, management and Oversight of All prisons. Final Report October 2011*. Belfast: Department of Justice Northern Ireland.

Quinney, R. (2006). The life inside: Abolishing the prison. *Contemporary Justice Review, 19*(3), 269–275.

Rolston, B., & Tomlinson, M. (1986). Long-term imprisonment in Northern Ireland: Psychological or political survival? In B. Rolston & M. Tomlinson (Eds.), *The Expansion of European Prison Systems* (pp. 162–183). Belfast: The European Group for the Study of Deviance and Social Control.

Rothman, D. J. (1980). *Conscience and Convenience: The Asylum and Alternatives in Progressive America.* Berkeley: University of California Press.

Scraton, P., & Moore, L. (2005). *The Hurt Inside: The Imprisonment of Women and Girls in Northern Ireland.* Belfast: Northern Ireland Human Rights Commission.

Scraton, P., & Moore, L. (2007). *The Prison Within: The Imprisonment of Women at Hydebank Wood: 2004–2006.* Belfast: Northern Ireland Human Rights Commission.

Sim, J. (2009). *Punishment and Prisons: Power and the Carceral State.* London: Sage.

Simon, J. (2007). *Governing Through Crime.* Oxford: Oxford University Press.

Standing Advisory Commission on Human Rights. (1977). *Second Annual Report (HC130).* London: HMSO.

Steele, J. (2004). *Review of Safety at HMO Maghaberry.* Belfast: Safety Review Team to Secretary of State for Northern Ireland.

Tannenbaum, F. (1938). *Crime and the Community.* New York: Columbia University Press.

UN Committee Against Torture [UNCAT]. (2004). *Consideration of Reports Submitted by States Parties Under Article 19 of the Convention. Conclusions and Recommendations of the Committee Against Torture, United Kingdom of Great Britain and Northern Ireland, Crown Dependencies and Overseas Territories.* CAT/C/CR/33/3. [Online]. Available http://undocs.org/CAT/C/CR/33/3. Accessed March 22, 2018.

10

Reconceptualising Custody: Rights, Responsibilities and 'Imagined Communities'

Margaret S. Malloch

Introduction

While there has been much reflection and concern with human rights in prison, the depiction of women's prisons as something 'other than' punishment has often resulted in a concealment of the punitive basis of custody as applied to women (e.g. Carlen 1983, 2008; Hannah-Moffat 2001; Carlen and Tombs 2006). At the same time, while the rights of prisoners (as underpinned by human rights priorities) are intended to mitigate the punitive practices of the state, they have become increasingly blurred by a growing emphasis on 'reintegration' and 'rehabilitation'. For Cohen (1985), the dispersal of control mechanisms from the prison into the community (integral to concepts of rehabilitative through-care and re-integrative practices) not only blurs boundaries between these spaces but conceals the nature of this expansion of control. The rehabilitative discourse that underpins women's

M. S. Malloch (✉)
Faculty of Social Sciences, University of Stirling, Stirling, Scotland, UK
e-mail: m.s.malloch@stir.ac.uk

© The Author(s) 2018
E. Stanley (ed.), *Human Rights and Incarceration*, Palgrave Studies in Prisons and Penology, https://doi.org/10.1007/978-3-319-95399-1_10

imprisonment makes it a paradox around which the nature of punishment and the significance of wider economic, social and cultural inequalities that drive punitive practices might usefully be considered.

This chapter is inspired by developments in Scotland, reflecting progressive work internationally, which simultaneously aim to reduce the number of women in prison and improve the experiences of those who are imprisoned. The chapter draws upon the recently introduced concept of 'community custody', and highlights the ambiguity that emerges from ongoing attempts to connect the community and prison as spaces of punishment. It thus explores what recent shifts towards discourses of 'need' might mean for women prisoners specifically (but with resonance for both men and women more generally) when disconnected from considerations of equality in the broader sense. The notion of equality that is embedded in the mainstream concept of human rights is based on an individualised notion of equal treatment or equity, rather than a recognition of the structural underpinnings of carceral systems.[1]

The emphasis on social need, as responded to by punishment systems, creates the impression of 'benevolent space' which draws on notions of individual misfortune and the adoption of a philanthropic intervention. When discussing the issue of human rights in prison and how to attain them, this concept of 'need', and how it is defined and responded to, encounters problems when attempts are made to breach the gap between the prison and the 'community' (in terms of dominated and dominating spaces). Thus the chapter highlights the structural significance of penal power and the symbolic dissonance between prison and the community in respect of human rights in the context of the imprisonment of women.

A confusion of aims and objectives has become increasingly prominent given recent attempts to embark on a 'radical' transformation of imprisonment in Scotland where prisons are being revamped and conditions inside prisons improved across the country, in marked contrast to increasing evidence of a crisis in the penal estate south of the border. Noting international developments to reorganise penal estates for women, this chapter explores the relevance of a human rights framework in the repositioning of custodial spaces. It considers the links between human rights and social justice in relation to women and explores the relationship between mainstream rights and critical rights thinking. Finally, it reflects on how critical rights thinking and practices can facilitate progressive change.

Penal Reforms for Women

The history of penal reform in many western countries is characterised by good intentions leading to unintended consequences. For many scholars, this reflects a failure to consider the ability of the prison to co-opt and circumvent these good intentions according to its own institutional logics (e.g. Correctional Services Canada 1990; Rafter 1990; Hannah-Moffat 2001; Malloch and McIvor 2013; Moore et al. 2017). The result has often been to reinforce the legitimacy of punishment as a response to wider social problems while innovative 'alternatives' become extensions of the prison system.

Over the years, a number of enquiries and reports have been produced[2] which have recognised the general inappropriateness of sending many women to prison and made the case for gender-appropriate alternatives. In England and Wales, concerns about the circumstances of women in prison and the impact of imprisonment on them led to the commission of the Corston review of "women with particular vulnerabilities in the criminal justice system". This reported in 2007, making a range of recommendations to reduce the number of women in prison and to restructure the remaining penal estate (see Moore et al. 2017). Corston (2007), like others previously (e.g. Social Work and Prison Inspectorates 1998, reporting on Scotland) was of the view that her proposed penal reforms would result in a significant reduction in the number of women imprisoned and that, as a consequence, the female prison estate (as it existed at the time of her report) would require radical restructuring. While the *Corston Report* focused particularly on England, it also had implications for other UK jurisdictions and it reflected similar and parallel work in Northern Ireland and Scotland where the plight of women in prison—and the need for action—had been highlighted over previous decades.[3]

The *Corston Report* (2007) provided a blueprint which set out the importance of addressing the specific "vulnerabilities" of women within the prison specifically and the criminal justice system more generally (see also All Party Parliamentary Group on Women in the Penal System 2015). This report—as well as the Commission for Women Offenders in Scotland (see below)—placed an emphasis on needs and equity as key concepts governing the imprisonment of women. Both highlight the importance of addressing women's 'needs' during the process of punishment and providing equity in penal measures.

Nevertheless, subsequent recommendations frequently direct their attention to delivering improved services in/through the criminal justice system, despite the widespread recognition that women's imprisonment is inextricably linked to circumstances and conditions outside the prison. Across other international jurisdictions, similar developments have been evident (Hannah-Moffat 2008). The extent to which recommendations from inquiries and commissions have been accepted by national governments and incorporated into practice is questionable. As one example, deaths of women in prison continue to be a significant cause for concern (Prisons & Probation Ombudsman 2017) and appear to be on the increase despite the recommendations set out by a number of official reports (e.g. Social Work Services and Prison Inspectorates for Scotland 1998; Prisons & Probation Ombudsman 2003; Corston 2007).

The Scottish Context

The experience of women in prison in Scotland had received considerable media and public attention during the 1990s and early 2000s when a series of tragic deaths occurred in Scotland's national prison for women, HMP Cornton Vale. This resulted in a series of official reports and concerted action by penal reformers, service-providers and policy-makers to reduce the imprisonment of women. For policy-makers in Scotland, the development of community provisions which could offer alternatives to custody were considered a priority.[4]

The most recent report into women in the criminal justice system in Scotland, the Commission for Women Offenders (2012) echoed many of the recommendations of the *Corston Report* and specifically called for the closure of the national prison for women which it denounced as being "unfit for purpose". This call was widely welcomed and agreed to by the Scottish Government. The Scottish Prison Service (SPS) swiftly developed plans to build a new 'state of the art' institution for women, intended to meet the needs of most imprisoned women in one location. Although acknowledging the benefits of an enhanced environment for women, there was widespread dissatisfaction (from community based service providers, academics and penal reformers) at the construction of such a large prison which, it was claimed, would result in more rather than fewer women being imprisoned. Following a concerted public campaign to halt the development of this 300–350 bed prison (see Malloch 2016 for details), the Cabinet Secretary for Justice agreed to revise SPS plans for a restructured penal estate and indicated that, instead, a new approach to women would be "radical and ambitious", reflecting the vision of the Commission for Women Offenders (2012). Again, these revised developments were led by the SPS who organised a series of forums across Scotland aimed at informing the plans for a reconfigured penal estate. This culminated in an international symposium and a subsequent 2015 report *From Vision to Reality: Transforming Scotland's Care of Women in Custody* (SPS 2015). Confusingly, the developments for this radical and ambitious approach were held firmly under the auspices of the SPS who maintained the leading role in taking plans forward. There was certainly much good will to improve the system for women. However, in the preparatory discussions and developing plans, there emerged evidence of an increasingly blurred boundary between prison services and community provisions. This was not along the lines of an abolitionist approach to the imprisonment of women (it was made clear by the SPS organisers that this was not for debate at the international symposium), but instead a new penal imaginary was projected: that of 'community custody'.

Setting out the vision of the reshaped prison estate for women, the Cabinet Secretary for Justice announced, on 22 June 2015, that a new small national prison with 80 places would be created, alongside five smaller community-based custodial units each accommodating up to 20 women across Scotland.[5] These custodial units were intended to provide women with access to intensive support for issues such as alcohol, drugs, mental ill-health and domestic abuse trauma. It was intended that the units would be located in areas which would support the maintenance of family contact. The vision was for an individually-focused, 'recovery-based' approach to women of all ages (Lidell Thomson Consultancy 2015)[6]; the attempted creation of benevolent space within the prison system reflected international attempts to enhance the use of custody for women. Plans for these community-custody units are ongoing and, at present, the location sites have been identified for some but not all of the units. Much work is being carried out to develop the practical, physical structures of the units although there are ongoing concerns that unless services are established in local communities, women will continue to be processed through the criminal justice system to access resources and, ultimately, the numbers sentenced to custody are unlikely to be reduced significantly. As identified elsewhere (see Carlen 2008, 2013; Malloch and McIvor 2013), if services (including support for problems such as poverty, substance use, refuge from violent and abusive relationships) are absent in communities, but help is available in prison (with the punitive element of incarceration assuaged by terms such as 'community custody') then sentencers will continue to send women to prison.

This "radical and ambitious" approach introduced in Scotland may sound resonant of developments in Canada in the early 1990s (Hannah-Moffat 2001, 2008; Hannah-Moffat and Shaw 2000; Hayman 2006). Here, the report *Creating Choices* (Correctional Services of Canada 1990) outlined plans to close the national prison for women (Kingston Prison) and to hold women in five community-based institutions across Canada, including an Aboriginal healing lodge. However, the Canadian government was subsequently criticised for not providing the necessary funds for the introduction of these community-based services; leading to an imbalance in funding which prioritised support for the institutions to the detriment of the community infrastructures surrounding them (Hannah-Moffat and Shaw 2000).

While the history and legacy of these Canadian developments have been explored elsewhere (notably Hannah-Moffat and Shaw 2000;

Hayman 2006), they share a number of challenges with efforts to transform the women's prison estate in Scotland, notably: (i) the challenging relationships between the prisons and the communities in which the new prisons for women were to be sited[7]; (ii) inquiries which highlight the inextricable social, political and economic circumstances (and in the case of Canada, the legacy of colonial policies) outside the prison which impact on experiences within it[8]; and (iii) increasing security features beyond those originally intended (see also Malloch 2013). As attempts to develop the new institutional system in Scotland have proceeded, the significance of human rights and the potential consequences of penal reforms have come to the fore.

Human Rights Discourse

Ongoing international developments intended to divert individuals from custody or provide alternatives to imprisonment (see Cohen 1985) have led to an increasing emphasis on punishment and/or detention in the community. This area is also governed by international standards and norms. For example, the *International Covenant on Civil and Political Rights* (1996) (Article 9 and Article 14) and the UN *Standard Minimum Rules for Non-custodial Measures (Toyko Rules)* (1990) set out the conditions under which UN Member States should develop measures within their legal systems intended to reduce the use of imprisonment, and to rationalise criminal justice policies, "taking into account the observance of human rights, the requirements of social justice and the rehabilitation needs of the offender". The *Tokyo Rules* indicate that non-custodial measures should be used in accordance with the principle of minimum intervention and that they should "be part of the movement towards depenalization and decriminalization instead of interfering with or delaying efforts in that direction" (United Nations 1990: para. 2.7).

In 2010, the United Nations developed specific *Rules for the Treatment of Women Prisoners and Non-custodial Measures for Women Offenders (Bangkok Rules)*. Until the introduction of these Rules, the particular concerns of women had rarely featured in human rights discourse; other than in relation to the general prohibition of discrimination, requirements of care for pregnant women, mothers and babies in custody, the separation of male and female prisoners and gender staffing requirements.[9] The *Bangkok Rules* encouraged the development and use of non-custodial and gender-specific policies and practices. They covered a number of issues including accommodating women close to their homes where possible, acknowledging vulnerability and responding to various gendered needs.

Recognising the potentially harmful effects of imprisonment, the *Bangkok Rules* emphasised the importance of alternatives to custody and prioritised non-custodial measures to women who have come into contact with the criminal justice system. The *Rules* encourage Member States to adopt legislation to establish alternatives to imprisonment and to give priority to the financing of such systems. Under Section 3 of the Rules (on Non-custodial measures), the importance of appropriate responses to women is outlined, including gender-specific options for diversionary measures and pretrial and sentencing alternatives. The need to take account of histories of victimisation and women's caretaking responsibilities is also highlighted.

The *Bangkok Rules* recognise that women in contact with the criminal justice system must be provided with appropriate resources to address their most common problems. Examples of this include: therapeutic courses and counselling for victims of domestic violence and sexual abuse; suitable treatment for those with mental disability; educational and training programmes to improve employment prospects; and, "gender-sensitive, trauma-informed, women-only substance abuse treatment programmes" (United Nations 2010, Rule 62). Such initiatives, which have clearly informed aspirations for a reformed penal estate for women in Scotland, are recognised as positive developments which can eliminate or mitigate the harms caused by prison sentences. They also recognise the legitimacy of nation states to provide criminal justice disposals outside the prison; wherever possible, these resources should be directed to the community where it is envisioned that a range of support and opportunities will be available.

Benevolent Spaces

The difficult circumstances of women prior to imprisonment are features of the lives of women in the justice system internationally: poverty, family issues and victimisation characterised by high levels of problematic substance use and experiences of poor mental health. Rates of self-harm and attempted/realised suicide are disturbingly high. It is such circumstances that led Carlton and Segrave (2011) to argue that the "pains of imprisonment" are not distinct to the prison itself but for many women the pains exist before, during and after imprisonment. Baldry (2010) has described this as a disadvantaged or liminal space where women are located from an early age. This 'space' consists of an environment with inadequate housing, abuse, poor schooling and time spent in care resulting in cumulative hardships which are exacerbated by the criminal justice system.

In many ways, the penal treatment of women is often indistinguishable from 'welfare treatment' with punitive impact in both spheres. Carlen (2013) argues that the shift from a welfare state to a security state is characterised by the use of risk scores to determine the extent to which human and legal rights should be respected (in light of assessments of potential risk). And in highlighting this, she points to the unequal structures of society within which concepts of rehabilitation have no relevance for the rich, but characterise the injustice directed at the poor. Indeed 'criminal justice' supports the maintenance of an unjust social order. Recognition of the intersectionality of class, ethnicity and gender relations becomes evident as the basis for overlapping structural inequalities that determine and shape processes of criminalisation and disadvantage.

Social, political and economic influences are crucial in determining processes of criminalisation and punishment, and also impact on the ways in which both criminalisation and punishment are subsequently experienced by the individuals and communities on whom they are directed. Prisoners are drawn disproportionately from disadvantaged and marginalised communities (Houchin 2005) for whom rehabilitation has almost rhetorical significance. While this is acknowledged by Scottish Government policy-makers (Scottish Government 2017), attention to improving the prison estate is unlikely to impact on the circumstances which feature within the communities from which most prisoners originate. Thus, while a discursive focus is directed towards meeting woman's needs (see Fraser 2013), consideration of women's 'rights' are often absent from discussions in penal contexts.[10] This reflects the 'therapeutic' approach that is such a consistent feature of discourse surrounding penal service design for women, where health models regularly form the basis of a 'trauma-informed approach'. As Fraser (2013) notes more generally, the relationship between needs and rights is a controversial issue in contemporary theory. Concerns that rights claims work against radical social transformation by encapsulating notions of 'bourgeois individualism' are countered by those like Fraser who argues for the translation of justified needs claims into social rights. She suggests (2013: 82), "in a context devoid of poverty, inequality and oppression, formal liberal rights could be broadened and transformed into substantive rights, say, to collective self-determination". This raises important questions around the significance of collective rights (recognised within Indigenous communities in Latin America and aboriginal communities elsewhere) but rarely considered within a westernised model of individual rights. The collective rights of women and the application of rights within communities requires some attention; the notion of community-custody brings these issues to the fore.

Attempted reforms, including the concept of community custody, emerged from good intentions, aimed at reducing the number of women in prison and facilitating better integration into communities.[11] However, there is rarely any meaningful sense of what 'community' is or what the wider implications in terms of human rights might be, both inside and outside the prison. It is this shift in discourse—from 'punishment' to 'needs'—that has been highlighted as particularly troublesome in relation to justice for women.

Recognition of the needs of many women in the justice system is indeed, very important. Services aimed at providing support are crucial. Relatedly, the focus given to supporting trauma and addiction, meeting health needs and developing life-skills via training and contact with families is also important in many respects. However, introducing such resources in a penal context, with the aim of addressing the potential 'risk' of reoffending weighs such interventions towards 'responsibilities' of individuals with the expectation that counteracting such deficits will resolve imbalance and result in a return to law-abiding citizenship. This assumes that individuals who break the law can be 'fixed' by changing their cognitive behaviour. However as Dryden and Souness (2015) show in their study of women's services across Scotland, women who had been referred to criminal justice interventions did not display faulty cognitive processes, rather, the problems underpinning their involvement with the criminal justice system appeared more related to their actual lived circumstances of extreme disadvantage.

Individual Rights Versus Community Entitlement

For advocates, the role of human rights in supporting a shift toward democratic legitimacy can only be partial, limited and narrow if more structural concerns are not acknowledged. The hope that penal and criminal justice institutions are capable of reforming themselves has not been borne out by history. As examples, Bell (2014) details the absence of a human rights ethos within many criminal justice institutions, the UK government's opposition to human rights legislation, and the failure to comply with rulings from the European Court of Human Rights on prisoner voting.

Given the limitations of penal institutions to develop a cultural environment grounded in the application of rights, the likelihood of revising the structure of penal estates may continue to operate with a rights deficit, concealed by an over-riding discourse of responses to 'needs'. Similarly, while recognising the importance of 'community' in supporting reductions in imprisonment, countervailing factors are evident. Attempts to shift focus from the prison to the community fail to denote on what theoretical/ideological basis of 'community' these developments are based. Community can be conceived of as a conceptual ideal, spatial entity or political signifier (Lacey and Zedner 1995). As Bauman (2001: 3) notes "'Community' is nowadays another name for paradise lost—but one to which we dearly hope to return, and so we feverishly seek the roads that may bring us there".

Community as a concept has been problematised within sociology and criminology. It is both vague and open to misinterpretation, and the application of the term to actual lived experience is often widely contested.[12] As I. M. Young (2011) states, critics of welfare capitalist society often proffer an alternative domination—and oppression-free vision of society in an ideal of community. She explores this notion, drawing out the significance of moral theory and the potential of a community based on needs and solidarity in contrast to the liberal concept of community in terms of rights and entitlements. Within criminal justice, community is often used to refer to punishment outside the prison (community punishment, community payback, community corrections) and rather than being portrayed for what it *is*, there has been more attention to what it *is not* (i.e. not-prison). There appears to be an implicit assumption that in order for women to access support and services, location in 'the community' is a good thing[13] and that 'community custody' would be a way of joining up some of the dots that are reflective of the currently fractured process that appears to characterise many women's propulsion through the criminal justice system. Community spaces are presented as the locus where individual problems can be addressed.

Under-Resourced Communities

There have been many insights into the ways in which communities are affected by crime and punishment although these have limited impact on theoretical considerations of punishment. Mauer and Chesney-Lind (2002) and Leonard (2015) highlight the ways in which incarceration policies in the United States impact on communities in terms of cutting into public spending and the opportunities of those who remain in these communities. Internationally, there is evidence to suggest that the majority of prisoners come from a small number of geographical areas (Houchin 2005; Wacquant 2008, 2009; Leonard 2015). Despite a reduction in experiences of crime and victimisation in Scotland, and internationally, these reductions are not experienced equally across communities.

While the risk of being a victim of crime has fallen overall, it is unchanged in the most deprived areas (Leonard 2015). Overall, it is estimated that in Scotland, for example, less than five per cent of adults experience 58% of all crime with those living in the most deprived areas at greater risk of being a victim of crime, civil law problems (including with neighbours, debt and housing), hospitalisation or death from alcohol or drug related causes, imprisonment and criminalisation (Scottish Government 2017). There are parallels in relation to health, where inequalities in health are noticeable across the UK.[14]

Poverty and hunger remain features of the lives of the most disadvantaged within society (see All Party Parliamentary Group on Hunger and Food Poverty 2014). Recent social policy changes in areas of welfare reform in the UK (including significant cuts to benefits, tax credits, pay and pensions since 2010) have impacted negatively on those who are already disadvantaged and this has had a disproportionate impact on women who are more likely to be dependent on welfare benefits than men. The majority of lone parents (92%) are women and 95% of lone parents who claim income support are women (Engender 2015). The criminalisation of many women in the UK and internationally is associated with material disadvantage, poverty, unemployment, psychological distress, addiction, victimisation and abuse (Loucks 1997). Thus the impact of inequality is significant.

This has two main consequences for a human rights framework in the interstice between prison and community that 'community custody' is paradoxically presented as a panacea for. Firstly, an individual model of rights within institutional spaces cannot address the factors that contribute to imprisonment, sustain processes of criminalisation and continue to exert impact following imprisonment and into communities post-release. Secondly, this has implications for the siting of community custody units which, if they are to be near the majority of prisoners' home addresses, are likely to be in already deprived areas, begging the question of how the existing absence of resources in these areas will then be addressed. A continual theme across international literature is the concern about moving 'punishment' into communities that are already lacking in resources. As Pate (2013) notes in Canada the new prisons for women were built in areas where there was limited access to the services that women required, resulting in the development of such services within the prisons themselves. This also caused resentment for those outside prison fuelling public concerns that resources were provided in prisons that were not available in the community (see Hannah-Moffat and Shaw 2000). The emphasis on human rights tends to proffer individualised solutions which focus on the individual, where the emphasis on 'rights' and 'responsibilities' is also focused.

Human Rights and Social Justice

Access to 'justice' and the resources (redistribution, recognition, participation) that influence how structural forces operate on the individual both create and restrict opportunities to social, political, economic and civil engagement (Fraser 2007). Although communities often appear to be fragmented and dislocated entities, it may be that the concept of community as being in opposition to individualistic approaches, may have the potential to provide a source of "active, mutual responsibility" where needs are "woven together from sharing and mutual care" (Bauman 2001: 150). This has the potential to raise broader issues of (social) equality that need to be considered in transformative penal programmes. The basis for this goes beyond the confines of criminal justice systems. For example, the Secretary General of the Council of Europe (2015) highlights the importance of pursuing the attainment of conditions in which, among other things, the right to health, the right to social security, the right to social and medical assistance and the right to benefit from social welfare services may be effectively realised. At a time when there is a growing number of people in Europe deprived of dignity because of their exclusion from society, specific importance should be attributed to the protection against poverty and social exclusion (Secretary General of the Council of Europe 2015: 78).

Fundamental reform requires imaginative alternatives but also a radical change in structures of power and the rethinking of dominant cultures, both institutionally and politically. As Bloch (1986 [1961]:

xxix) argued, "There can be no true installation of human rights without the end of exploitation, no true end of exploitation without the installation of human rights". Similarly, Douzinas and Gearey (2005: 101) assert "… there can be no freedom or dignity without economic equality". This fits with a 'utopian' vision by recognising the need for structural change rather than individual conformity. Opportunities to collectivise experience and opportunities to challenge existing structures and normative views of 'crime' have the potential to shift focus away from crime to much more comprehensive and broader visions of justice. But moving outside the criminal justice system and exploring the resurrection of concepts of 'community' in terms of local autonomy, self-governance and mutual aid requires a different language and different frameworks of 'rights'.

In the absence of 'community' itself, community when discussing penal disposals is generally taken to mean 'non-prison' yet the very retention of 'custody' suggests the retention of incarceration—this is a real oxymoron. It is also an imaginary concept, a policy built on 'imaginary communities'.[15] Inevitably, visions of a just and equitable society raise questions around material and social inequalities, private ownership and power relations (see Malloch and Munro 2013). Similarly, recognition of the intersectionality of class, ethnicity and gender relations becomes evident as the basis for overlapping structural inequalities that determine and shape processes of criminalisation and cumulative disadvantage. Fundamental reform requires imaginative alternatives but also a radical change in structures of power and the rethinking of dominant cultures, both institutionally and politically. Addressing structural injustices requires a different way of seeing 'community' and a different language in which to discuss it. Opportunities to collectivise experience and to challenge existing structures and normative views of crime have the potential to shift the focus away from this to much more comprehensive and broader visions of justice. This would require attention to addressing economic inequality, the collective rights of women and the inclusion of excluded communities in the distribution of resources and access to social and political decision-making.

Conclusion

Addressing inequality is as important as upholding individual rights, but what, if any, emancipatory potential can human rights have? For Douzinas and Gearey (2005: 101), "The first task of freedom as liberation from oppressive determinations is therefore to eliminate economic deprivation". Reflecting on Bloch's *Principle of Hope*, they claim that human rights will be at the heart of socialism. Like Bloch, they hold out a hope that human rights can create new imaginings in the struggle against injustice, claiming that:

> … their promise exists hidden beyond conventions, treaties and bills in a variety of inconspicuous cultural forms. Human rights, based as they are on the fragile sense of personal identity and the--impossible--hope of social integrity, link integrally the individual and the communal. (ibid.: 105)

Critical criminology requires going beyond the limitations of a mainstream approach to crime and justice and, as well as critiquing penal solutions within a social, political and economic analysis, requires the presentation of new visions for a 'just' society (Cohen 1985; Hudson and Ugelvik 2012). While there is a long tradition of re-imagining justice within a critical context, this has been evident more recently in discussions around the potential for radical imaginings (e.g. Barton et al. 2011; Young J. 2011; Malloch and Munro 2013; Bell and Scott 2016) aimed at reinvigorating debates around the necessity of penal abolitionism (Moore et al. 2017). Certainly, there remains a tension around the potential for achieving radical change and the legitimation of the existing system; evident in the creation of apparently benevolent spaces within which women are incompatibly both punished and rehabilitated. A central problem to moving beyond current conceptual frameworks is the centrifugal pull of criminal justice and penal systems around which alternatives are developed, thus failing to challenge the 'ontological reality' of crime (Hulsman 1986). These challenges and paradoxes remain features of current developments in the Scottish penal context and have resulted in an ongoing oscillation between hope (for improvements in responses to women as law-breakers) and fear (that the criminal justice system remains the go-to solution for social distress created and experienced in and by communities).

Challenges to systems of harm require significant social, political and economic change capable of addressing wider social conditions; hence Bloch's argument for the inextricable connection between human dignity and economic liberation which requires human rights. Radical reform thus requires the development of socially just and thereby transformative solutions, rather than simply enhancing the operation of criminal justice interventions. For Bloch (1986 [1961]: xxx) differences between social utopias and their aim of happiness, and theories of natural law with their focus on dignity, must be brought together. He says "This much is certain: There is just as little human dignity without the end of misery as there is happiness without the end of all old and new forms of subjugation". This will require the reimagining, not of different forms of custody or enhanced penal systems, but of better societies where resources are targeted at structural inequality. While human rights may be central to such processes, wider collective obligations are also required to achieve these transformations.

Notes

1. Chesney-Lind (2002: 91) describes the impact of equality in punishment as "vengeful equity" in terms of its gendered impact. She notes: "This is the dark side of the equity or parity model of justice--one that emphasises treating women offenders as though they were men, particularly when the outcome is punitive, in the name of equal justice".
2. The list is considerable but for indicative examples see, Bloom et al. (2003), Canadian Human Rights Commission (2003), Corston (2007), Commission on Women Offenders (2012), All Party Parliamentary Group on Women in the Penal System (2015).
3. See for example Social Work Services and Prisons Inspectorates for Scotland (1998), Scraton and Moore (2007).
4. See Malloch and McIvor (2013) for a collection of papers on international developments.

5. Corston (2007: 86) had also called for small custodial units that would gradually replace the women's prison system as her wider initiatives came into play—and it was suggested that eventually, these units would be removed from the prison service to be taken over by specialists in working with women. Similar aims were held by Correctional Services Canada in the development of the Healing Lodges which, for those built on Aboriginal land, were intended to be handed to community control and administration at a future date.

6. In a presentation to the Scottish Association for the Study of Offending, Rona Hotchkiss (SPS operational lead for the development of the women's custodial estate), outlined plans for: "minimal visible security" where women will be held in "optimum security conditions for their individual needs, risks and strengths"—most will be serving short-term sentences (Robertson 2016). Plans for these units include the potential for dedicated space for visiting experts and workers, residential facilities designed like small flats, opportunities for children to visit and to stay overnight and for an environment where women will be "able to wander about, confined only within the perimeter of the building and only at the times that are appropriate".

7. The healing lodge, which was located in Nekaneet land and had been intended to connect Aboriginal women with their communities and traditions, instead took on the features of Correctional Services rather than the Nekaneet custom and culture, on whose land it was built.

8. In February 2017 the Standing Senate Committee on Human Rights launched a 'comprehensive study' into the human rights of federal prisoners notably 'vulnerable or disadvantaged' groups to include Indigenous people, visible minorities, women and those with mental health issues.

9. For example the UN *Standard Minimum Rules for the Treatment of Prisoners (Nelson Mandela Rules)*; *European Prison Rules*; European Committee for the Prevention of Torture and Inhuman or Degrading Treatment or Punishment, which also established standards for the gender-specific health care of women.

10. Although the Commission on Women Offenders team included a secondment from the Equality and Human Rights Commission attached to the Commission, with oral evidence provided by representatives from the Scottish Human Rights Commission.

11. Although see Anthony (2013) for a discussion of changing conceptions about the impact of community as a site for reintegrating Indigenous People.

12. Lacey and Zedner (1995: 305) note that it was the governments (of Thatcher and Reagan) that "exploited the appeal to community most wholeheartedly" yet "simultaneously pursued socio-economic policies which directly or indirectly attacked the very infrastructures which might be thought to make references to community meaningful". By the late 1980s, as Lacey and Zedner (1995: 310) state, "community" in terms of criminal justice was associated with "the diffusion of responsibility for both crime prevention and the management of crime".

13. 'Community' is referred to 257 times in the Commission on Women Offenders (2012) report (a report of 109 pages).

14. For example after adjustment for differences in deprivation, premature mortality (<65 years) in Scotland is 20% higher than in England and Wales (10% higher for deaths at all ages); similarly, the excess for Glasgow compared with Liverpool, Manchester and Belfast has been shown to be approximately 30% for premature mortality, and around 15% for deaths at all ages (Scottish Public Health Observatory 2016).

15. This reimagining and re-visioning has affinities with the work of Anderson whose definition of a nation was of an *imagined and political* community. A nation was imagined because "the members of even the smallest nation will never know most of their fellow members, meet them, or even hear of them, yet in the minds of each lives the image of their communion" (Anderson 2006: 6).

References

All Party Parliamentary Group on Hunger and Food Poverty. (2014). *Feeding Britain: A Strategy for Zero Hunger in England, Wales, Scotland and Northern Ireland*. London: The Children's Society.

All Party Parliamentary Group on Women in the Penal System. (2015). *Report on the Inquiry into Preventing Unnecessary Criminalisation of Women*. London: Howard League.

Anderson, B. (2006). *Imagined Communities*. London: Verso.

Anthony, T. (2013). *Indigenous People, Crime and Punishment*. London: Routledge.

Baldry, E. (2010). Women in transition: From prison to .... *Current Issues in Criminal Justice, 22*(2), 253–267.

Barton, A., Corteen, K., Scott, D., & Whyte, D. (Eds.). (2011). *Expanding the Criminological Imagination*. Abingdon: Routledge.

Bauman, Z. (2001). *Community: Seeking Safety in an Insecure World*. Cambridge: Polity Press.

Bell, E. (2014). There is an alternative: Challenging the logic of neoliberal penality. *Theoretical Criminology, 18*(4), 489–505.

Bell, E., & Scott, D. (Eds.). (2016). *Justice, Power and Resistance. Foundation Issue: Non-Penal Real Utopias*. London: EG Press.

Bloch, E. ([1961] 1986). *Natural Law and Human Dignity* (D. J. Schmidt, Trans.). Cambridge: MIT Press.

Bloom, B., Owen, B., & Covington, C. (2003). *Gender Responsive Strategies: Research, Practice and Guiding Principles for Women Offenders*. Washington, DC: National Institute of Corrections.

Canadian Human Rights Commission. (2003). *Protecting Their Rights*. Ottawa: Canadian Human Rights Commission.

Carlen, P. (1983). *Women's Imprisonment: A Study in Social Control*. London: Routledge & Kegan Paul.

Carlen, P. (2008). *Imaginary Penalities*. Cullompton: Willan Publishing.

Carlen, P. (2013). Against rehabilitation: For reparative justice. In K. Carrington, M. Ball, E. O'Brien, & M. Juan (Eds.), *Crime, Justice and Social Democracy: International Perspectives* (pp. 89–104). London: Palgrave Macmillan.

Carlen, P., & Tombs, J. (2006). Reconfigurations of penality. *Theoretical Criminology, 10*(3), 337–360.

Carlton, B., & Segrave, M. (2011). Women's survival post-imprisonment: Connecting imprisonment with pains past and present. *Punishment & Society, 13*(5), 551–570.

Chesney-Lind, M. (2002). Imprisoning women: The unintended victims of mass imprisonment. In M. Mauer & M. Chesney-Lind (Eds.), *Invisible Punishment: The Collateral Consequences of Mass Imprisonment* (pp. 79–94). New York: The New Press.

Cohen, S. (1985). *Visions of Social Control*. Cambridge: Polity Press.

Commission on Women Offenders. (2012). *Commission on Women Offenders: Final Report*. Edinburgh: Scottish Government.

Correctional Services of Canada [CSC]. (1990). *Creating Choices*. Canada: CSC.

Corston, J. (2007). *The Corston Report: A Report by Baroness Jean Corston of a Review of Women with Particular Vulnerabilities in the Criminal Justice System*. London: Home Office.

Douzinas, C., & Gearey, A. (2005). *Critical Jurisprudence: The Political Philosophy of Punishment*. Oxford: Hart Publishing.

Dryden, R., & Souness, C. (2015). *Evaluation of Sixteen Women's Community Justice Services in Scotland*. Edinburgh: Scottish Government.

Engender. (2015). *A Widening Gap: Women and Welfare Reform*. Edinburgh: Engender.

Fraser, N. (2007). Reframing justice in a globalizing world. In T. Lovell (Ed.), *(Mis)recognition, Social Inequality and Social Justice: Nancy Fraser and Pierre Bourdieu* (pp. 17–35). London: Routledge.

Fraser, N. (2013). *Fortunes of Feminism*. London: Verso.

Hannah-Moffat, K. (2001). *Punishment in Disguise: Penal Governance and Federal Imprisonment of Women in Canada*. Toronto: Toronto University Press.

Hannah-Moffat, K. (2008). Re-imagining gendered penalities: The myth of gender responsivity. In P. Carlen (Ed.), *Imaginary Penalities* (pp. 193–217). Cullompton: Willan Publishing.

Hannah-Moffat, K., & Shaw, M. (2000). *An Ideal Prison? Critical Essays on Women's Imprisonment in Canada*. Halifax: Fernwood Publishing Company.

Hayman, S. (2006). *Imprisoning Our Sisters: The New Federal Women's Prisons in Canada*. Montreal: McGill-Queen's University Press.

Houchin, R. (2005). *Social Exclusion and Imprisonment in Scotland*. Glasgow: Glasgow Caledonian University.

Hudson, B., & Ugelvik, S. (Eds.). (2012). *Justice and Security in the 21st Century*. Abingdon: Routledge.

Hulsman, L. (1986). Critical criminology and the concept of crime. *Contemporary Crises, 10*(1), 63–80.

Lacey, N., & Zedner, L. (1995). Discourses of community in criminal justice. *Journal of Law and Society, 22*(3), 301–325.

Leonard, E. (2015). *Crime, Inequality and Power*. London: Routledge.

Lidell Thomson Consultancy. (2015). *Consultation Report: The Future of the Female Custodial Estate*. Edinburgh: Scottish Government.

Loucks, N. (1997). *Research into Drugs and Alcohol, Violence and Bullying, Suicides and Self-injury and Backgrounds of Abuse* (Occasional Papers Report No. 1/98). Edinburgh: Scottish Prison Service.

Malloch, M. (2013). A healing place? Okimaw ohci and a Canadian approach to Aboriginal women. In M. Malloch & G. McIvor (Eds.), *Women, Punishment and Social Justice* (pp. 79–91). Abingdon: Routledge.

Malloch, M. (2016). Justice for women: A penal utopia? *Justice, Power and Resistance*, Foundation Volume, 151–169.

Malloch, M., & McIvor, G. (Eds.). (2013). *Women, Punishment and Social Justice*. Abingdon: Routledge.

Malloch, M., & Munro, B. (Eds.). (2013). *Crime, Critique and Utopia*. London: Palgrave Macmillan.

Mauer, M., & Chesney-Lind, M. (2002). *Invisible Punishment*. New York: The New Press.

Moore, L., Scraton, P., & Wahidin, A. (Eds.). (2017). *Women's Imprisonment and the Case for Abolition: Critical Reflections on Corston Ten Years On*. London: Routledge.

Pate, K. (2013). Women, punishment and justice: Why you should care. In M. Malloch & G. McIvor (Eds.), *Women, Punishment and Social Justice* (pp. 197–205). Abingdon: Routledge.

Prisons & Probation Ombudsman. (2003). *The Death in Custody of a Woman and the Series of Deaths in HMP/YOI Styal, August 2002–2003*. London: Home Office.

Prisons & Probation Ombudsman. (2017). *Learning Lessons Bulletin: Fatal Incidents Investigations. Issue 13. Self-inflicted Deaths Among Female Prisoners.* [Online]. Available https://www.ppo.gov.uk/document/learning-lessons-reports. Accessed February 16, 2018.

Rafter, N. (1990). *Partial Justice: Women, Prisons, and Social Control* (2nd ed.). New Brunswick: Transaction Publishers.

Robertson, A. (2016). They will not look like prisons. *Holyrood*, February 5. [Online]. Available https://www.holyrood.com/articles/feature/they-will-not-look-like-prisons. Accessed March 23, 2017.

Scottish Government. (2017). *Justice in Scotland: Vision and Priorities*. Edinburgh: Scottish Government.

Scottish Prison Service [SPS]. (2015). *From Vision to Reality: Transforming Scotland's Care of Women in Custody*. Edinburgh: SPS.

Scottish Public Health Observatory. (2016). *Excess mortality in Scotland and Glasgow*. [Online]. Available http://www.scotpho.org.uk/comparative-health/excess-mortality-in-scotland-and-glasgow. Accessed February 16, 2018.

Scraton, P., & Moore, L. (2007). *The Prison Within: The Imprisonment of Women and Girls at Hydebank Wood*. Belfast: Northern Ireland Human Rights Commission.

Secretary General of the Council of Europe. (2015). *State of Democracy, Human Rights and the Rule of Law in Europe*. Strasbourg: Council of Europe.

Social Work Services and Prisons Inspectorates for Scotland. (1998). *Women Offenders—A Safer Way*. Edinburgh: Scottish Office.

UN General Assembly. (1990). *United Nations Standard Minimum Rules for Non-Custodial Measures [Tokyo Rules]*. A/RES/45/110. Adopted December 14, 1990.

UN General Assembly. (2010). *United Nations Rules for the Treatment of Women Prisoners and Non-Custodial Measures for Women Offenders [Bangkok Rules]*. A/RES/65/229. Adopted December 21, 2010.

Wacquant, L. (2008). *Urban Outcasts*. Cambridge: Polity.

Wacquant, L. (2009). *Punishing the Poor*. Durham: Duke University Press.

Young, I. M. (2011). *Justice and the Politics of Difference*. Princeton: Princeton University Press.

Young, J. (2011). *The Criminological Imagination*. Malden, MA: Polity.

11

'Stone Walls Do Not a Prison Make': Bare Life and the Carceral Archipelago in Colonial and Postcolonial Societies

Harry Blagg and Thalia Anthony

Introduction

Human rights under international law classically extend western notions of citizenship by affording individual rights within a sovereign and exclusive, Westphalian nation state. However, citizenship under conditions of settler colonialism is an artifact of whiteness. Since colonisation, Indigenous peoples have remained excluded from the white public realm and subject to strategies consistent with the "logic of elimination": "to replace Indigenous society with that imported by the colonisers" (Wolfe 1999: 27). In turn, the prison needs to be understood as an instrument of sovereign elimination rather than simply a

H. Blagg (✉)
Centre for Indigenous Peoples and Community Justice, Law School,
University of Western Australia, Crawley, WA, Australia
e-mail: harry.blagg@uwa.edu.au

T. Anthony
Faculty of Law, University of Technology Sydney, Ultimo, NSW, Australia
e-mail: Thalia.Anthony@uts.edu.au

© The Author(s) 2018
E. Stanley (ed.), *Human Rights and Incarceration*, Palgrave Studies
in Prisons and Penology, https://doi.org/10.1007/978-3-319-95399-1_11

site of disciplinary power. While much critical western scholarship has remained focused on paradigm shifts and cultural movements of transition between relatively discrete epochs (see Garland 2001), a 'contrapuntal' reading (following Edward Said [1993]), conversely stresses the pervasive continuities between technologies of control for Indigenous peoples. Instead of ruptures and breaks, a postcolonial critique focuses on repetition, the "re-opening" of history and the tendency for "temporal overlay" (Williams, cited in Collits 2005). Geeta Chowdhry (2007: 105) suggests that the aim of the contrapuntal reading is "to not privilege any particular narrative but reveal the 'wholeness' of the text, the intermeshed, overlapping, and mutually embedded histories of metropolitan and colonised societies and of the elite and subaltern".

Contrapuntal readings disrupt the linear flow of western historical time by recuperating the lost and subordinated time of the 'Other', and bringing to consciousness their histories of struggle, resistance and refusal. Things consigned to the deep past by settler modernity (frontier wars, genocide, forced assimilation), remain ever contemporary in Indigenous consciousness and memory. In the postcolony, western and Indigenous cultures become "entangled" (Mbembe 2001) and "intertwined" (Said 1993), continuously morphing rough hybrids. Within a human rights frame, a contrapuntal reading refutes individual rights as being in conflict with collective rights; instead, the rights of the collective are integral to the rights of the individual (De Feyter and Pavlakos 2008). For Indigenous peoples, the collective is not merely a group but a sovereign order that challenges the sovereignty and "territorial integrity" of the state (Watson 2011a: 621, 632; 2015: 39). We recognise that we contribute to the maintenance of colonial domination if we impose individual over collective rights, or collective rights that are devoid of political currency, as this elides the distinctiveness of Indigenous sovereignty.

This chapter offers a contrapuntal reading of Australian prisons as sites of settler colonial repression and Indigenous resistance. It sets out to unsettle taken-for-granted assumptions regarding the nature of the prison derived from Euro-American theory. We encourage what Paul Ricoeur (1970: 356) called a "hermeneutics of suspicion" when weighing up the applicability of western critical scholarship to postcolonial institutions, not because they are flawed in relation to the discursive arenas they set out to critique, but because they are univocal, partial and limited in time and place. A cardinal weakness lies in the tendency to generalise from the experience of the social formations of Euro-America, taking as given, for example, that the periodisations and patterns of social change typical of Euro-modernity (which include hegemonic forms of power, 'Fordism' and 'Post-Fordism', and so on) provide a master pattern for the development of social relations on the postcolony. We contend that Indigenous rights depend not simply on the abolition of prisons, but a challenge to 'the Camp' that subordinates every aspect of their lives. This is only realisable through reimagining the role of Indigenous sovereignty within, or adjacent to, the settler colonial nation state. This requires a paradigm shift in how we conceive not only individual rights, but the position of the state in relation to Indigenous nations and peoples.

Settler colonial policies towards Indigenous peoples have tended to rest on extreme, punitive action and a large degree of open coercion, unmitigated by the need to shape consent or create political consensus. There was no gilded age of welfare-correctionalism or liberal democracy for Indigenous people. Indigenous people have never shared in the bounties of civil citizenship. This chapter details the experiences of Indigenous children in the Northern Territory of Australia in youth prisons. We argue that their experiences of torture inside these prisons is not inalienable but one aspect of a constellation of power relations between the settler sovereign and the Other, which is reduced to its bare bones under the ongoing racist policy of the Northern Territory Intervention in Australia.

We refer to transcripts from 2016 to 2017 Royal Commission into Child Protection and Youth Detention in the Northern Territory (hereafter 'Royal Commission') to reveal how the racist policies towards Indigenous people manifests in the racist treatment of Indigenous children in prisons as part of the same continuum. It is against this background that we must frame discussion about Indigenous people and imprisonment and treat with suspicion its standing as an *exceptional* state of un-being, outside of 'normal' social relationships: in the colony the exception is the norm. While we support penal abolitionism as an ultimate objective, we maintain that this can only be meaningful within a decolonising process that also decolonises other sites of exception and indistinction for Indigenous people. This recognises the rights to self-determination as stipulated, for instance, in the United Nations Declaration on the Rights of Indigenous Peoples. Nevertheless, it also suggests that a self-determination framework must challenge the western nation state, rather than assume its cooperative capacity. After all, it is the nation state that promotes the Camp and is antithetical to Indigenous nationhood.

Bare Life and the Colonial Prison

Following Agamben (1998), we argue that the settler state is incapable of providing anything more than 'bare life' to Indigenous people, on either the 'inside' or the 'outside'. Indeed, our pivotal argument is that the 'in and out' dichotomy loses explanatory coherence in the settler colonial context. It cannot be taken as given that the experience of being 'inside' diverges radically from that of being 'outside' for Indigenous prisoners, or that regimes of control are more oppressive on one side of the fence than on the other. The violations of Indigenous human rights occur not only on the inside but also in broader society. We imagine control in the postcolony as an archipelago of intersecting camps founded on what Sylvester (2006) calls "bare life biopolitics". The prison serves as one link within a chain of camps. In the words of Wacquant (2001: 97), it is part of a "carceral continuum" where state and charitable interventions take on a prison character, and where prisons adopt a social services role for the vulnerable. Foucault's (1977, 1984) influential thesis: that the prison became the model for multiple sites of knowledge/power in modernity, requires recalibration in the postcolony; where the Camp, not the penitentiary, serves as the template for institutional control over the colonised 'Other'.

Colonial binaries function to marginalise the experience of Indigenous people. Social statuses that would normally be viewed—through a Eurocentric lens—as discrete (expressed in the binary of 'free' [in the community] or 'un-free' [in prison]), need to be redefined to accommodate the fluidity of, and arbitrariness of, confinement in the settler colonial prison camp. Oppressive controls are *routinised* and *ubiquitous*, and they dynamically intersect with a cluster of camps, bordered zones, detention facilities, exclusionary places, reserved for those who cannot be accorded normal 'freedom'.

In our research we have heard Indigenous voices flip over the inside/outside dichotomy, describing instances where being inside is safer, less precarious and more secure (culturally and physically) than being outside; or, at least, where there is little to choose between them. John Pratt (1994: 303) observes that the "less eligibility" principle of the English Poor Law—the notion that life on the inside should always be less desirable than on the outside—undergirded penal ideologies from the nineteenth century onwards, and, like other institutions of the imperial country, it was crated up and shipped to the colony to provide a coarse moral foundation for colonial correctionalism. The thing is, though, that it became impossible to make bare life in the prison noticeably *less desirable* than bare life in other state institutions and in families crushed beneath multiple forms of colonial violence, including the stealing of land, being forced into indentured labour, epistemic violence, being classified and subject to regimes of moral and physical hygiene, the violent disavowal of their humanity, and the brutal kidnapping of their children. Of course, the settler colonial regime was less interested in the 'Other's' body than it was in their land: settler colonial governmentality has combined both body disciplining and body exterminating practices where Indigenous peoples are concerned. Settlers wanted Indigenous people gone.

The colonial and postcolonial prison is merely the consolidated signifier of repressive order. Repressive colonial power is also refracted through repetitive and spectacular pageantry, through which humiliation and abjection that inscribe difference into everyday life were performed (Fanon 1986; Ceasare 2000). Because colonial power is more concerned with imposing order than shaping consent, it relies heavily on repressing Indigenous rights across civil society. One consequence of this is that "sovereign power, justice, and order in the postcolonial states were from the outset partial, competing, and unsettled" (Blom Hansen and Stepputat 2005: 4). The lack of hegemonic stability generated the need for multiple sites where sovereign power could be displayed

(Brown 2014: i). Therefore the settler colonial prison lacks *singularity* in its display of repression.

The inner-world of the colonial prison mirrored this disparity: it was not a homogenous site of punishment, but was spatially differentiated according to race. Racial hierarchies were safeguarded through the creation of different regimes for whites and 'Others': "the European body maintained its privileged status even in confinement" (Arnold 1994: 170): For instance, in the colonial era, Roebourne prison in the remote north west of Australia—designed by British architect G. Temple-Poole and opened in 1886—was of an octagonal design with a central 'inspection house' and inmates stationed around the perimeter, in classic Benthamite fashion. However, colonial realities bent the octagon out of shape, until it became a microcosm of colonial hierarchy. White prisoners were housed close to the inspection house in relative comfort. "Asiatics" were housed in the next section, and finally Aboriginal prisoners were kept chained 24 hours a day in a long section of their own (beyond the panoptic gaze). They were chained when they were taken out to do heavy work developing colonial infrastructure, they were also chained by the neck when being taken hundreds of kilometres from their homes by police, even as witnesses (Harman and Grant 2014). The Roebourne prison demonstrates how the carceral system adapted to the requirements of colonial rule. The interior spacing of prisons in Western Australia still reflect racial difference; Koori prisoners in southeast Australia told Blagg et al. (2005: 154) that, "if you're black you're down the back (and on your back)".

Foucault and Biopower

Foucault (1978: 143) theorised "biopower" or "biopolitics" as the proliferation of techniques designed to safeguard the life of the nation and eliminate its opponents. The pre-modern sovereign is superseded by *governmentality* that regulates life through the dispersed microphysics of power. *Governmentality* boosts the capacity of the modern state to move beyond its own legal limitations by creating extra-legal spaces governed not by law but by directing individual and collective biological life through social and scientific engineering, expert administration, and everyday technologies of the self (Foucault 1979).

For Foucault, disciplinary power dispenses with punishment as spectacle and achieves conformity through the routinisation of institutional discipline and control. The target soul becomes the disciplined subject of bourgeois society burdened by the anguishes of personal responsibility (continued contemporaneously by internalised strategies of responsibilisation that affect compliance with the law). Furthermore, according to Foucault, the techniques of bio-power are not necessarily negative, but often "productive" (Foucault 1978: 85–86).

Yet as Gregory (2004: 3) cautions, Foucault's spacings are all "spacings *within* Europe" (emphasis in the original). Colonial power could not impose its spatial grids evenly across the colonial geography. The west simply could not, or would not, reproduce biopower on anything like the scale it did 'at home'; in particular, it did not institute 'positive' bio-power for the colonised 'Other' that Foucault, correctly, views as part of the hegemonic contract between classes in the west under liberal democratic modernity. This meant a greater reliance on crude spectacle and brute force.

In Australia, spectacular public executions and floggings were administered to Aboriginal people years after such practices had been deemed cruel and unusual for Europeans (Finnane and Macguire 2001). In the colony, as we shall see in greater detail later, there were different "legal geographies" in play (Harvey 1985), modern disciplinary techniques (including the Panopticon and the reformatory) sat side by side with crude displays of physical violence. Here, prison was but one of range of sites where various colonial techniques of subordination and control were deployed. Aboriginal people (those who survived the genocide) were evicted from traditional lands and interned and concentrated in a variety of ways. Food was a key mechanism through which the settler state exercised control over the native population, at a time when Aboriginal peoples were being denied access to their traditional food sources. Rowse (2002: 5) describes how rationing became a cheap and productive means of controlling and managing an increasingly dispossessed Indigenous population: a technique, he argues, transferrable "across a diversity of institutions: the scientific party, the pastoral lease, the mission enclave, the police station, the welfare settlement". Another enclave of subordination was exploitation as workers on cattle stations (Gray 2007; Anthony 2003, 2004, 2007/2008). The prison complements these sites of enclosure. Aboriginal people became habituated to involuntary, collective confinement in a ubiquitous array of institutions, all employing roughly the same disciplinary techniques—separation of gender, splitting up of family, rationing of food, standardised time and work discipline, scripts of racial inferiorisation. These inter-linked spatialities were intended to create docile Indigenous bodies.

In *Discipline and Punish*, Foucault (1977) talks of the similarity of techniques between systems (such as factories, schools, prisons), through the structuring of time and the ordering of space. Power was not replicated but mirrored. Factories weren't simply *like* prisons, they were, in all but name, prisons: labour was coerced rather than 'free'. In north Australia's cattle industry, Indigenous people were indentured to white cattle station owners. The power ascribed to Aboriginal Protectors under the Protection Acts were assumed by pastoralists who had stolen Aboriginal land to use it for their enterprises. These pastoralists and their managers flogged and beat Aboriginal people (as punishment for absconding or disobeying orders), made them work without pay and controlled their movement (Anthony 2004). But when Aboriginal labour was no longer essential for the cattle industry's profitability from the 1960s, they did not enjoy the freedom to leave. Rather, they were detained on government settlements until the 1970s where they continued to be subject to the government's coercive welfare powers (Anthony 2007).

Gazing back at colonial power, Indigenous peoples saw a dense, connected and relatively integrated system of authority based on whiteness, incorporating everyone from the policeman to the local shopkeeper (Huggins 1987/1987: 14). Every white man was a potential policeman, gaoler, protector, supervisor and chastiser. Lay Justices of Peace (the local Chamber of Commerce enrobed) in rural Australia, literally held the power of life or death when serving on Western Australia's Courts of Native Affairs (Auty 2000, 2005). The fact that death sentences on Indigenous offenders—by the local shopkeeper or publican—were always commuted by the Supreme Court matters little: it was designed, as they say, to send a message.

The Camp

The fact that Indigenous peoples did not have borders, standing armies, or exercise sovereignty within the European world view, meant that Europeans saw Indigenous peoples as existing beyond the frontiers of established civilisation and regarded them simply as 'savages'. They were governed through the routinisation of the "state of emergency"—the suspension of legal rights—as a normal feature of daily life and law (Agamben 1998). Mbembe (2003: 24) establishes:

> … colonies are zones in which war and disorder, internal and external figures of the political, stand side-by-side or alternate with each other. As such, the colonies are the location par excellence where the controls and guarantees of judicial order can be suspended--the zone where the violence of the state of exception is deemed to operate in the service of "civilization".

Geographical separation and the forced settlement of Indigenous peoples in camps of various kinds is a hallmark of the state of exception and the creation of bare life. Franz Fanon (1986) recognised that colonial rule required the separation of coloniser and colonised into radically incommensurate zones. This spacialisation and compartmentalisation of life and bare life ensures that racially worthy life, the life of the settler, is nurtured through forms of biopower that builds hospitals, sanitation, education and employment: while the unworthy life of the native is the target of necropower—doomed to servitude and violence and considered disposable. Indigenous people have been forced *en masse* into spatial zones of exclusion. This was enacted through the physicality of reserves, missions, cattle stations and government settlements *and* the legal zone of exceptional laws imposed under Aboriginal protection acts and other exclusions by virtue of Indigenous status. In both realms, Indigenous people were trapped in a constellation of discriminatory laws that applied exclusively to them. The Camp is more than spaces of confinement; it is the subjection to power that eludes boundaries, which make it all the more powerful.

It was the 'camp', rather than the modern penitentiary or reformatory (the privileged site for disciplining the 'penitent soul' in

Euro-modernity), that provides the paradigm for Indigenous incarcer-ation. Rather than the prison being the exemplar of disciplinary power that spills over into other disciplinary sites (hospitals, factories, asy-lums, clinics, army barracks etc.), it is the Camp that informs enclosures across a range of institutions and the dispersal of technologies of disci-pline (across prisons, detention centres, ration stations, police lock-ups, pastoral stations, mobile work camps, missions, domestic servitude, and so on). Here the distinction between Foucault and Agamben becomes clearer: Foucault's prison remained within the normal judicial order, while Agamben's camp is outside the normal order and is governed by "martial law and the state of siege" (Agamben 1998: 20). The follow-ing sections shows how coercive tactics on Aboriginal children in the Northern Territory was both the norm and the exception, permeating youth prisons ('detention centres') and child removals from Aboriginal families.

Zones of Exception for Indigenous Children: Bare Life in Youth Prisons

The zone of exceptionalism in youth prisons ('detention centres') in the Northern Territory is marked by torture and brutality inflicted on Indigenous children by guards. That treatment of Indigenous children is not mere diversion from legal rights available in policy and proto-cols, it is a violation of their humanity (see Bauman 1997). Evidence of this cruelty in detention emerged with the televising of CCTV footage by the Australian Broadcasting Corporation in July 2016. This stirred national concern for the abuses and the lack of accountability, and pre-cipitated a Royal Commission into the detention and protection of chil-dren in the Northern Territory. While this Commission ran adversarial proceedings, and gave greater credence to the views of non-Indigenous people and staff working in the system, it nonetheless painted a clear picture of the abusive policies and practices to Indigenous people and children both inside and outside prison walls. It also developed a range of recommendations to challenge these harms.

The guards committed brutal acts on Indigenous children without opprobrium, and in clear sight of CCTV cameras, their peers and seniors. Detention centre managers and relevant ministers kept children in cells that were oppressive, filthy concrete cages and some detention centres were simply reclaimed adult prisons that were no longer deemed fit for adult prisoners (Hamburger 2016; Middlebrook 2017). Indigenous boys and girls were arbitrarily placed in segregation cells for 23 hours per day, treated like "dogs", denied food, water and basic hygiene and stripped naked by guards; they were reduced to bare life (AB 2017; AD 2016; Voller 2016). Their cells smelt like sewage, were dark, dirty and lacking airflow and oppressively muggy (De Souza 2017: 1678–1679; Hunyor 2017: 1487; Voller 2016: 680).

The guards, their superiors and the state flagrantly breached the *Youth Justice Act* (NT), Australia's administration of Juvenile Detention Rules. They violated international human rights conventions such as: the United Nations *Convention Against Torture* (CAT) which protects against torture, cruel, inhumane or degrading treatment or punishment; the *Convention on the Rights of the Child* (CRC); and the *International Covenant on Civil and Political Rights* (ICCPR) that "requires detainees be treated with humanity and respect for their inherent dignity of the human person". There were also breaches of the *Convention on the Elimination of all Forms of Racial Discrimination* and the *United Nations Declaration on the Rights of Indigenous People*.

Violations under these provisions also included that Indigenous children in prisons had restricted contact with other people, including family, peers, and even the guards would not respond to their cries for help (AD 2016: 615; Voller 2016: 681). They would be sent thousands of kilometers away from country, home and everyone familiar to them and sometimes housed with adults in adult prisons. Officers tormented Indigenous children by telling them their "family did not really care" about them and refused phone contacts and visits as punishment (Voller 2016: 688). They were also not allowed to attend funerals and sorry business when family passed on. This resulted in dislocation from family, community and culture. The guards would swear at the children, calling them "stupid black cunts", "camp dogs", "oxygen thieves", "waste of space", "little black poofters" and "fucking sluts", including in conjunction with physical abuse and threatening acts (Fattore 2017: 1000; Zamolo 2017: 1396; Kelleher 2017: 1547; Tobin 2017: 1782–1783). The guards and teachers in prisons would prohibit the Indigenous children from speaking in language and ridiculed them for not speaking English properly (Coon 2017: 2725–2726; Tasker 2017: 1113; Voller 2016: 714).

The Royal Commission heard evidence of guards bashing Indigenous children, smashing their heads against prison walls and floors (Turner 2017: 923; BY 2017: 1204; AU 2017: 8; Voller 2017: 2666; Hamburger 2016: 384; Engels 2017: 3578; Kelleher 2017: 1573; Middlebrook 2017: 3365). Violence in youth prisons included gassing children using chemical weapons such as CS gas—o-chlorobenzylidene malononitrile—which burnt children's eyes and throats. Use of toxic gases are prohibited under the *Chemical Weapons Convention*. Dylan Voller (2016: 708) described its effect:

> I thought I was going to die. My heart was racing because of the tear gas. My eyes were burning. I couldn't hardly see properly … My heart was racing because I didn't know what was going to happen next.

In Darwin, Indigenous children were shackled to restraint chairs with their hands, arms, ankles and waists mechanically restrained while hoods were placed on their head and tightly tied around their necks for hours. Voller (2016: 712) expressed to the Royal Commission the panic attacks and breathing difficulties he experienced on the chair: "My body just shut down". He feared for his life because he viewed that there was "no responsible person there" to draw the line when his pain became too great: "I was defenceless at that time. Felt like there was nothing I could do … I was telling them the whole time that it was hurting … They didn't care".

The fear and shame endured by Indigenous children in detention was not only in highly violent episodes, but also in everyday activities such as taking a shower and going to the toilet. Voller (2016: 684) told the Commission it was "scary" having an officer "watching you going to the toilet or when you are having a shower". Children were strip-searched and pat searched naked on a regular basis. This included young Indigenous girls who were forcibly stripped by up to six male officers who would cut off their clothes for non-compliance. AN (2017: 9) described one occasion:

> A large group of guards picked me up ... and threw me face down ... They then used the Hoffman knife to cut off all my clothes including my bra and underwear. I was fully naked and I felt real shame with all those men in the room.

These conditions and systematic abuse maintained Indigenous children in a state of 'bare life' (Agamben 1998). They were punished beyond the boundaries of juridical punishment and their rights were eroded to the point that they were no longer regarded as rights-bearing humans but as a nuisance to be controlled and contained. This view was highly politicised to give state practices in youth detention, and state sovereignty itself, its *raison d'être* (reason for existence) (see Agamben 1998). The Northern Territory Government described the children in detention as "the worst of the worst" and "ratbags" (Elferink 2017: 3139). The Chief Minister, Adam Giles (2017: 3280) said publicly that if he were Prisons Minister he would dig:

> a big concrete whole and put all the bad criminals in there. Right, you're in the hole, you're not coming out, start learning about it. I might break every United Nations Convention on the rights of the prisoner, but get in the hole.

These public proclamations enabled the government to define and control and boundaries of exclusion and inclusion. Ultimately, however, sovereign power is vested in the guards in Northern Territory youth detention centres. The Royal Commission heard testimony that guards had the power to give and take life, with little oversight or accountability. These power relations did not end at the prison gate, but penetrated the walls of youth detention, where the Camp on the outside replicated power relations between the sovereign and the Indigenous other inside prisons.

The Camp Outside Prison Walls in the Northern Territory

Evidence provided to the Royal Commission, especially by Indigenous people with lived experience, reveal how the Camp transcends prison walls and subjects the Indigenous Other to zones of exceptionalism in which they are subjected to damaging interactions with police and welfare officers (Anderson 2016; Havnen 2017). The disempowerment of communities and growing numbers of suicides among Indigenous young people in the Northern Territory is part of the ongoing legacy of the Northern Territory Intervention (hereafter 'the Intervention') since 2007[1] (Gibson 2017). The Intervention restricted the rights of Indigenous people living in 73 prescribed communities and town camps across the Northern Territory. These included rights to social security, to alcohol, to computers (due to restrictions on viewing pornography) and to manage their land. Police were given extended powers to enter houses and seize property without a warrant; medical staff could force Indigenous girls to take contraceptives, and Federal government business managers seized control from Indigenous community councils. These restrictions and powers were exclusively applied to Indigenous people and were extraordinary laws. The Intervention, and its controls, turned communities into prisons where Indigenous homes become cells.

Alayawarre woman and Chairperson of the Lowitja Institute for Aboriginal and Torres Strait Islander Health Research, Pat Anderson, gave evidence to the Royal Commission that the experience of Indigenous youth in detention was not *sui generis* (unique, or distinct to that environment). Rather, it was a continuum of the experience of Indigenous children and adults under the Intervention policy. She states that the racist legislation and accompanying ideology that Indigenous people were a problem has produced a "general moral decay" that "has allowed children being put in hoods and restraint chairs" (Anderson 2016: 168). She stated that the "disempowerment" and "appalling" treatment of Aboriginal people living under the Intervention culminated in the torture of Aboriginal children at Don Dale Detention Centre.

The policies and practices of the Intervention were an extension of nineteenth and twentieth century *Aboriginal Protection Acts* and the Stolen Generations (the systemic removal of Indigenous children) which sought to assimilate and subordinate Indigenous Australians and control their movements, residence, culture, language, money and family (Gibson 2012: 66). The Intervention was directed to removing Aboriginal people from country, forcibly acquiring Aboriginal land as leasehold, making it more difficult to practice culture on country (including due to policing surveillance), diluting bilingual education, abolishing self-governing Aboriginal councils, circumscribing the functions of Aboriginal-owned Night Patrols, and taking Aboriginal children out of the care of their families and communities. These policies were implemented with punitive force: if Aboriginal children missed school their parents' income would be entirely managed by the state or cut off; if Aboriginal families were impoverished their children could be taken; if alcohol was found in a car that car would be confiscated, and if communities refused to lease their land their housing needs would not be met (see Anthony 2010; Anthony and Blagg 2013). There were no legal rights for Indigenous people under this regime, only bare life.

Indigenous children who had been forcibly taken from their parents by the state, since the Intervention, told the Royal Commission stories about their fear, loneliness and trauma. Some were removed to residential institutions or (mostly white) foster parents who were located thousands of kilometers from their country and home. Siblings were usually separated and children were given no explanation or warning about their removal and separation (DB 2017; AI 2017; DM 2017; DF 2017). They were denied visits to their home and family while in state care (CJ 2017). Some children were moved around to over 20 state care placements (DM 2017). One child explained the feelings of removal: "my heart was just crashing to pieces" (DG 2017: 5). Another young person, DB (2017: 2), said:

I was scared and crying and I knew I was being taken away from Mum and Dad. It was a terrible day and the worst experience of my life.

The main desire expressed by children in state care was their wish to go home (CL 2017). They wanted to return to their family who they "grew up with" and this denial made them feel like the "odd one" (DB 2017: 5). One young person said, the foster carers were not related and "they treated me differently and I didn't belong there" (ibid.). A common response, therefore, was for Indigenous children to run away in search of their family. But they were often pulled up and punished by their foster carers, including by being belted (DM 2017). Other children self-harmed in response to the trauma and pain from being taken from their parents (DG 2017). Young people told the Royal Commission stories of abuse, the denial of food and the shame of being watched in the shower while in state care (DM 2017; DF 2017; DG 2017; DO 2017). As DG (2017: 8) put it, being taken from families makes it "really hard [for children] … to live in their life". These emulate the stories of children in detention, but these children need not come under the juridical realm of punishment to experience segregation and confinement.

Indigenous children taken by the state were not made to feel like real children. This was a sad irony since the protection of children from abuse was the *casus belli* (motivation) for the Intervention. One child stated: "I like welfare to actually--actually look at their self and think of their self just like they would treat their own child. Doesn't matter what colour you are" (DG 2017: 8). Children instead were treated harshly and lost their family and sense of belonging. One young person stated, "I don't have a relationship with my mum or dad. I haven't seen my brothers in years. … I feel like I had to make my family for myself, and the kid shouldn't have to do that" (CJ 2017: 9). The effect of the removals was described lucidly by one child:

> The decision to remove us from our Mum and Dad destroyed our family. I know that my brothers and sisters have also all suffered because of it. I notice with Dad that whenever I talked about the past or about what happened my brothers and sister are doing he puts his head down and looks real upset. I know he feels broken because of what happened. (DB 2017: 16)

The state of exception goes beyond judicial or administrative decision-making in the Northern Territory, it is based on a range of non-judicial constructs around morality, race, ethnicity, dangerousness and difference. The notion of the Camp is better suited to settler colonial enclosure than the prison. Indeed, the segregationist practices have been felt across the Northern Territory—whether it is segregation to another land, family or detention centre—and the restriction of rights are not contained to prisons—they are the experience of all Indigenous people in the Northern Territory.

The Colonial Matrix of Power

The prison must be situated within what postcolonial writers Anibal Quijano (2007) and Walter Mignolo (2011: 8–9) call the "colonial matrix of power". Although, as attested in this edited collection, rights-based approaches can bring into sharp relief the wrongs committed by state institutions, and particularly prisons, and provide a framework for moving forward, they are incapable of redressing power relations that underpin the derogation of rights across institutions and inherent in the dispossession of Indigenous people of their land. This is because rights maintain and uphold the sovereignty of the state, even when they are intent on promoting Indigenous self-determination. Watson (2011b: 508) contends that the United Nations Declaration on the Rights of Indigenous Peoples:

> Poses no threat to the sovereignty of nation-states and no possibility of the recognition of indigenous peoples' sovereignty. It fails to enable or open up space for a dialogue on coexisting sovereignties--that is, state and aboriginal sovereignties.

In its very nature, settler colonialism was less interested in the 'souls' of Indigenous people than it was in their land. Without land and sovereignty, rights for Indigenous people will never be fully realised and ideologies and practices that dehumanise Indigenous people will persevere in various guises; most patently in systems of law and order, control and punishment. This is because all institutions are bent towards fulfilling the manifest destiny of European settler colonisation: uprooting native social order and implanting white social order (Wolfe 2006). Settler colonialism differs from other brands of colonialism in that it embraces not simply the exploitation but the wholesale appropriation of land, as though it were always/already the property of the European, awaiting 'discovery'. This ontology of settlement, according to Patrick Wolfe (ibid.), has an inherently eliminatory logic; though it is, he insists, not inevitably genocidal. Settlement requires the "extinguishment" of Indigenous rootedness in land, not always the extinguishment of the people themselves: genocide remains one among a range of strategies, including forced assimilation, dispossession, enforced mobility and concentration in places of confinement (ibid.: 393). The necessity of violence runs through settler colonisation globally.

Settler colonial desire to uproot Indigenous owners and replace them in the soil—transplanting the Global North into the Global South—was legitimised via a particularly rich and thematically nuanced repertoire of self-exculpatory and self-aggrandising narratives, including biblical-scale themes of redemption and renewal, promised lands flowing with milk and honey, and such like. Such narratives obscured the crimes of land theft and the necessary denial of Indigenous sovereign law. As Lisa Ford (2010: 2) suggests, the eradication of Indigenous law became the "litmus test of settler statehood".

Indigenous people were, paradoxically, both subject to white law and exempted from its protections. Colonialism claimed sovereignty while denying Indigenous peoples citizenship. Or as Morgensen (2011: 53) notes: "Western law incorporates Indigenous peoples into the settler nation by simultaneously pursuing their elimination". Although, it would be more accurate to say that Indigenous people were incorporated directly into the state of exception as bare life, rather than into law as such (Thobani 2007).

For this to occur, Indigenous people had to be governed in a state of legal exception. They had to be placed in zones that applied only to them. The zones were not uniformly marked by a religious mission, a penal prison, a state-administered reserve or an over-policed long grass, bush camp or urban block (see Jones 2016)—they were all of these things. What ties together these dispersed sites is what Diken and Laustsen (2002: 291) refer to as the "logic of camp", as the "zone of indistinction": "notions of inside and outside … tend to disappear into a zone of indistinction", the Camp was the "prototypical" zone of indistinction. The "logic" of the Camp has spread outwards into society. For Indigenous people, settler-colonisation has seen the legal normalisation of the state of exception. Unsettling this camp requires more than a legal human rights framework, it requires recognition of Indigenous people as the original and sovereign owners of the land and affording them a central role in protecting their rights as a people.

Conclusion: Pain, Shame and Resistance

Rather than seeing imprisonment in the colony, then, as an unusual event, where someone is excised from, or cast out of, society (albeit temporarily), prison remains but one of a network of routine and quotidian sites of colonial subordination and resistance, for those beyond redemption. *For many Aboriginal people prison involves pain but not shame.* It does not carry the same stigma within the Aboriginal domain to be incarcerated in a white gaol (Blagg 2016; Cunneen et al. 2013). It does not have the same consequences of having one's children removed. One's status in Aboriginal society is not threatened by involvement in the white criminal justice system, for many it has become a normal 'rite of passage' (Beresford and Omaji 1996). This is not to diminish the derogation of rights that imprisonment involves, but to emphasise that prison is not necessarily an exceptional experience but common to many state-enforced Indigenous experiences in settler colonial societies.

For whites, by contrast, the circulation of cultural capital is restricted to membership of civil society: one goes into 'deficit' when excised from society. In the board game Monopoly (as in life) a stint in gaol means temporary disenfranchisement from the community of players. This is not the case for Indigenous people, whose status does not rest on acceptance, or abjection, by white society.

The contrapuntal reading of the prison views it as but one institution of involuntary confinement amongst many: and not necessarily the most destructive when compared to the damage to the Aboriginal collective by other sites of indistinction such as missions, residential schools and orphanages that were deliberately designed to destroy Aboriginal family life. 'Kill the Indian in the Child' was the saying in

Canada: 'Kill the Indian, Save the Man' in the USA, as a justification for child removal to so-called residential schools where Indigenous children were forcibly, often violently and abusively, 'assimilated'. The torture of Aboriginal children and young people in the Northern Territory detention system—which is clearly an Aboriginal youth prison system in all but name—continues colonial practices of extreme violence against Aboriginal resistance. It is only with the displacement of the dominant colonial institutional fabric that the rights that are the basis of aboriginal resistance, such as the rights to sovereignty, can be realised.

Note

1. The key legislative measure to enact the Intervention was the *Northern Territory National Emergency Act 2007* (Cth).

References

AB. (2017). Statement. In the matter of a Royal Commission into the child protection and youth detention systems of the Northern Territory, 1 March. [Online]. Available https://childdetentionnt.royalcommission.gov.au/NT-public-hearings/Documents/evidence-2017/evidence23march/Exh-139-001.pdf. Accessed March 13, 2018.

AD. (2016). Transcript of proceedings. In the matter of a Royal Commission into the child protection and youth detention systems of the Northern Territory, 9 December. [Online]. Available https://childdetentionnt.royalcommission.gov.au/NT-public-hearings/Documents/transcripts-2016/Transcript-9-December-2016.pdf. Accessed March 13, 2018.

Agamben, G. (1998). *Homo Sacer: Sovereign Power and Bare Life* (D. Heller-Roazen, Trans.). Stanford: Stanford University Press.

AI. (2017). Transcript of closed court proceedings. In the Matter of a Royal Commission into the child protection and youth detention systems of the Northern Territory, 21 June. [Online]. Available https://childdetentionnt.royalcommission.gov.au/NT-public-hearings/Documents/transcripts-2017/Transcript-21-June-2017-closed-court-session-1.pdf. Accessed March 13, 2018.

AN. (2017). Statement. In the matter of a Royal Commission into the child protection and youth detention systems of the Northern Territory, 17 February. [Online]. Available https://childdetentionnt.royalcommission.gov.au/NT-public-hearings/Documents/evidence-2017/evidence24march/Exh-159-001.pdf. Accessed March 13, 2018.

Anderson, P. A. (2016). Transcript of proceedings. In the matter of a Royal Commission into the child protection and youth detention systems of the Northern Territory, 12 October. [Online]. Available https://childdetentionnt.royalcommission.gov.au/NT-public-hearings/Documents/transcripts-2016/Transcript-12-October-2016.pdf. Accessed March 13, 2018.

Anthony, T. (2003). Postcolonial feudal hauntings of northern Australian cattle stations. *Law Text Culture, 7*, 277–307.

Anthony, T. (2004). Labour relations on northern cattle stations: Feudal exploitation and accommodation. *Australian Review of Public Affairs, 4*(3), 117–136.

Anthony, T. (2007). Reconciliation and conciliation: The irreconcilable dilemma of the 1965 "equal" wage case for Aboriginal station workers. *Labour History, 93*(11), 15–34.

Anthony, T. (2007/2008). The feudal thread in the Indian and Australian colonial colonies: A comparative approach. *Journal of the Oriental Society of Australia, 39/40*(1), 50–70.

Anthony, T. (2010). Governing crime in the intervention. *Law in Context, 27*(2), 90–113.

Anthony, T., & Blagg, H. (2013). STOP in the name of who's law? Driving and the regulation of contested space in central Australia. *Social & Legal Studies, 22*(1), 43–66.

Arnold, D. (1994). The colonial prison: Power, knowledge and penology in nineteenth-century India. In D. Arnold & D. Hardiman (Eds.), *Subaltern Studies VIII: Essays in Honour of Ranajit Guha* (pp. 148–187). New Delhi: Oxford University Press.

AU. (2017). Transcript of closed court proceedings. In the matter of a Royal Commission into the child protection and youth detention systems of the Northern Territory, 23 March. [Online]. Available https://childdetentionnt.royalcommission.gov.au/NT-public-hearings/Documents/transcripts-2017/Transcript-23-march-2017-Closed-court.pdf. Accessed March 13, 2018.

Auty, K. (2000). Western Australian courts on native affairs 1936–1954—One of "our" little secrets in the administration of "justice" for Aboriginal people. *University of New South Wales Law Journal, 23*, 148–172.

Auty, K. (2005). *Black Glass: Western Australian Courts of Native Affairs 1936–54*. Fremantle: Fremantle Arts Centre Press.

Bauman, Z. (1997). The work ethic and prospects for the new poor. *Arena Journal, 9,* 57–76.

Beresford, Q., & Omaji, P. (1996). *Rites of Passage: Aboriginal Youth, Crime and Justice*. Perth: Fremantle Press.

Blagg, H. (2016). *Crime, Aboriginality and the Decolonisation of Justice* (2nd ed.). Sydney: The Federation Press.

Blagg, H., Morgan, N., Cunneen, C., & Ferrante, A. (2005). *Systemic Racism as a Factor in the Over-Representation of Aboriginal People in the Victorian Criminal Justice System*. Report to the Equal Opportunity Commission and Aboriginal Justice Forum, Melbourne.

Blom Hansen, T., & Stepputat, F. (2005). *Sovereign Bodies: Citizens, Migrants, and States in the Postcolonial World*. Princeton: Princeton University Press.

Brown, M. (2014). *Penal Power and Colonial Rule*. Oxon: Routledge.

BY. (2017). Transcript of proceedings. In the matter of a Royal Commission into the child protection and youth detention systems of the Northern Territory, 16 March. [Online]. Available https://childdetentionnt.royal-commission.gov.au/NT-public-hearings/Documents/transcripts-2017/Transcript-16-March-2017.pdf. Accessed March 13, 2018.

Césaire, A. (2000). *Discourse on Colonialism* (J. Pinkham, Trans.). New York: Monthly Review Press.

Chowdhry, G. (2007). Edward Said and contrapuntal reading: Implications for critical interventions in international relations. *Millennium: Journal of International Studies, 36*(1), 101–116.

CJ. (2017). Statement. In the matter of a Royal Commission into the child protection and youth detention systems of the Northern Territory, 31 May. [Online]. Available https://childdetentionnt.royalcommission.gov.au/NT-public-hearings/Documents/evidence-2017/evidence31may/Exh-474-000.pdf. Accessed March 13, 2018.

CL. (2017). Transcript of closed court proceedings. In the atter of a Royal Commission into the child protection and youth detention systems of the Northern Territory, 2 June. [Online]. Available https://childdetentionnt.royalcommission.gov.au/NT-public-hearings/Documents/evidence-2017/evidence2june/Exh-486-000.pdf. Accessed March 13, 2018.

Collits, T. (2005). *Postcolonial Conrad: Paradoxes of Empire*. London: Routledge.

Coon, L. (2017). Transcript of proceedings. In the matter of a royal commission into the child protection and youth detention systems of the

Northern Territory, 21 April. [Online]. Available https://childdetentionnt. royalcommission.gov.au/NT-public-hearings/Documents/transcripts-2017/ Transcript-21-April-2017.pdf. Accessed March 13, 2018.

Cunneen, C., Baldry, E., Brown, D., Brown, M., Schartz, M., & Steel, A. (2013). *Penal Culture and Hyperincarceration: The Revival of the Prison.* Farnham: Ashgate.

DB. (2017). Statement. In the matter of a Royal Commission into the child protection and youth detention systems of the Northern Territory, 26 June. [Online]. Available https://childdetentionnt.royalcommission.gov.au/ NT-public-hearings/Documents/evidence-2017/evidence26june/Exh-577-000.pdf. Accessed March 13, 2018.

De Feyter, K., & Pavlakos, G. (Eds.). (2008). *The Tension Between Group Rights and Human Rights: A Multidisciplinary Approach.* Oxon: Hart Publishing.

De Souza, L. J. M. (2017). Transcript of proceedings. In the matter of a Royal Commission into the child protection and youth detention systems of the Northern Territory, 22 March. [Online]. Available https://childdetentionnt. royalcommission.gov.au/NT-public-hearings/Documents/transcripts-2017/ Transcript-22-March-2017.pdf. Accessed March 13, 2018.

DF. (2017). Transcript of closed court proceedings. In the matter of a Royal Commission into the child protection and youth detention systems of the Northern Territory, 30 June. [Online]. Available https://childdetentionnt. royalcommission.gov.au/NT-public-hearings/Documents/evidence-2017/ evidence30june/Exh-653-000.pdf. Accessed March 13, 2018.

DG. (2017). Transcript of closed court proceedings. In the matter of a Royal Commission into the child protection and youth detention systems of the Northern Territory, 22 June. [Online]. Available https://childdetentionnt. royalcommission.gov.au/NT-public-hearings/Documents/transcripts-2017/ Transcript-22-June-2017-Closed-Court-Session-1.pdf. Accessed March 13, 2018.

Diken, B., & Laustsen, C. B. (2002). Zones of indistinction: Security, terror, and bare life. *Space and Culture, 5*(3), 290–307.

DM. (2017). Recording played to the commission. In the matter of a Royal Commission into the child protection and youth detention systems of the Northern Territory, 22 June.

DO. (2017). Recording played to the commission. In the matter of a Royal Commission into the child protection and youth detention systems of the Northern Territory, 19 June.

Elferink, J. W. (2017). Transcript of proceedings. In the matter of a Royal Commission into the child protection and youth detention systems of the

Northern Territory, 27 April. [Online]. Available https://childdetentionnt. royalcommission.gov.au/NT-public-hearings/Documents/transcripts-2017/ Transcript-27-April-2017.pdf. Accessed March 13, 2018.

Engels, K. (2017). Transcript of proceedings. In the matter of a Royal Commission into the child protection and youth detention systems of the Northern Territory, 9 May. [Online]. Available https://childdetentionnt. royalcommission.gov.au/NT-public-hearings/Documents/transcripts-2017/ Transcript-9-May-2017.pdf. Accessed March 13, 2018.

Fanon, F. (1986). *Black Skin, White Mask*. London: Pluto Press.

Fattore, J. (2017). Transcript of proceedings. In the matter of a Royal Commission into the child protection and youth detention systems of the Northern Territory, 14 March. [Online]. Available https://childdetentionnt. royalcommission.gov.au/NT-public-hearings/Documents/transcripts-2017/ Transcript-14-March-2017.pdf. Accessed March 13, 2018.

Finnane, M., & McGuire, J. (2001). The uses of punishment and exile: Aborigines in colonial Australia. *Punishment and Society, 3*(2), 279–298.

Ford, L. (2010). *Settler Sovereignty: Jurisdiction and Indigenous People in America and Australia, 1788–1836*. Cambridge: Harvard University Press.

Foucault, M. (1977). *Discipline & Punish: The Birth of the Prison* (A. Sheridan, Trans.). London: Allen Lane.

Foucault, M. (1978). *History of Sexuality: An Introduction* (R. Hurley, Trans.). New York: Random House.

Foucault, M. (1979). Governmentality. *Ideology and Consciousness, 6*(5), 21.

Foucault, M. (1984). Truth and power. In P. Rainbow (Ed.), *The Foucault Reader* (pp. 51–75). New York: Pantheon Books.

Garland, D. (2001). *The Culture of Control*. New York: Oxford University Press.

Gibson, P. (2012). Return to the ration days: The Northern Territory intervention—Grassroots experience and resistance. *Ngiya: Talk the Law, 3*, 58–107.

Gibson, P. (2017). 10 impacts of the NT intervention. *NITV SBS*, 21 June. [Online]. Available http://www.sbs.com.au/nitv/article/2017/06/21/10-impacts-nt-intervention. Accessed October 10, 2017.

Giles, A. (2017). Transcript of proceedings. In the matter of a Royal Commission into the child protection and youth detention systems of the Northern Territory, 28 April. [Online]. Available https://childdetentionnt. royalcommission.gov.au/NT-public-hearings/Documents/transcripts-2017/ Transcript-28-April-2017.pdf. Accessed March 13, 2018.

Gray, S. (2007). The elephant in the drawing room: Slavery and the "stolen wages" debate. *Australian Indigenous Law Review, 11*(1), 30–53.

Gregory, D. (2004). *The Colonial Present*. Oxford: Blackwell.

Hamburger, R. K. (2016). Transcript of proceedings. In the matter of a Royal Commission into the child protection and youth detention systems of the Northern Territory, 6 December. [Online]. Available https://childdetentionnt.royalcommission.gov.au/NT-public-hearings/Documents/transcripts-2016/Transcript-6-December-2016.pdf. Accessed March 13, 2018.

Harman, K., & Grant, E. (2014). Impossible to detain ... without chains'? The use of restraints on Aboriginal people in policing and prisonsxs. *History Australia, 11*(3), 157–176.

Harvey, D. (1985). The geopolitics of capitalism. In D. Gregory & J. Urry (Eds.), *Social Relations and Spatial Structures. Critical Human Geography*. London: Palgrave.

Havnen, O. (2017). Transcript of proceedings. In the matter of a Royal Commission into the child protection and youth detention systems of the Northern Territory, 21 March. [Online]. Available https://childdetentionnt.royalcommission.gov.au/NT-public-hearings/Documents/transcripts-2017/Transcript-9-May-2017.pdf. Accessed March 13, 2018.

Huggins, J. (1987/1988). "Firing on in the mind": Aboriginal women domestic servants in the inter-war years. *Hecate, 13*(2), 5–23.

Hunyor, J. (2017). Transcript of proceedings. In the matter of a Royal Commission into the child protection and youth detention systems of the Northern Territory, 20 March. [Online]. Available https://childdetentionnt.royalcommission.gov.au/NT-public-hearings/Documents/transcripts-2017/Transcript-20-March-2017.pdf. Accessed March 13, 2018.

Jones, R. (2016). Stories from the long grass: The daily struggle to survive for Darwin's growing number of homeless Indigenous people. *ABC News*, 12 October. [Online]. Available http://www.abc.net.au/news/2015-06-29/darwins-homeless-longrassers-tell-of-struggle-to-survive/6570440. Accessed October 16, 2017.

Kelleher, B. (2017). Transcript of proceedings. In the matter of a Royal Commission into the child protection and youth detention systems of the Northern Territory, 21 March. [Online]. Available https://childdetentionnt.royalcommission.gov.au/NT-public-hearings/Documents/transcripts-2017/Transcript-9-May-2017.pdf. Accessed March 13, 2018.

Mbembe, A. (2001). *On the Postcolony*. Berkeley: University of California Press.

Mbembe, A. (2003). Necropolitics. *Public Culture, 15*(1), 11–40.

Middlebrook, K. (2017). Transcript of proceedings. In the matter of a Royal Commission into the child protection and youth detention systems of the

Northern Territory, 28 April. [Online]. Available https://childdetentionnt. royalcommission.gov.au/NT-public-hearings/Documents/transcripts-2017/ Transcript-28-April-2017.pdf. Accessed March 13, 2018.

Mignolo, W. (2011). *The Darker Side of Western Modernity: Global Futures, Decolonial Options*. Durham: Duke University Press.

Morgensen, S. L. (2011). The biopolitics of settler colonialism: Right here, right now. *Settler Colonial Studies, 1*(1), 52–76.

Pratt, J. (1994). Understanding punishment: Beyond "aims and objectives". *Current Issues in Criminal Justice, 5*(3), 301–308.

Quijano, A. (2007). Coloniality and modernity/rationality. *Cultural Studies, 23*(2/3), 168–178.

Ricoeur, P. (1970). *Freud and Philosophy: An Essay on Interpretation*. New Haven: Yale University Press.

Rowse, T. (2002). *White Flour, White Power: From Rations to Citizenship in Central Australia*. New York: Cambridge University Press.

Said, E. (1993). *Culture and Imperialism*. London: Vintage.

Sylvester, C. (2006). Bare life as a development/postcolonial problematic. *The Geographical Journal, 172*(1), 66–77.

Tasker, D. J. (2017). Transcript of proceedings. In the matter of a Royal Commission into the child protection and youth detention systems of the Northern Territory, 15 March. [Online]. Available https://childdetentionnt. royalcommission.gov.au/NT-public-hearings/Documents/transcripts-2017/ Transcript-15-March-2017.pdf. Accessed March 13, 2018.

Thobani, S. (2007). *Exalted Subjects*. Toronto: University of Toronto Press.

Tobin, E. (2017). Transcript of proceedings. In the matter of a Royal Commission into the child protection and youth detention systems of the Northern Territory, 24 March. [Online]. Available https://childdetentionnt. royalcommission.gov.au/NT-public-hearings/Documents/transcripts-2017/ Transcript-24-March-2017.pdf. Accessed March 13, 2018.

Turner, J. (2017). Transcript of proceedings. In the matter of a Royal Commission into the child protection and youth detention systems of the Northern Territory, 13 March. [Online]. Available https://childdetentionnt. royalcommission.gov.au/NT-public-hearings/Documents/transcripts-2017/ Transcript-13-March-2017.pdf. Accessed March 13, 2018.

Voller, D. (2016). Transcript of proceedings. In the matter of a Royal Commission into the child protection and youth detention systems of the Northern Territory, 12 December. [Online]. Available https://childdetentionnt.

royalcommission.gov.au/NT-public-hearings/Documents/transcripts-2016/
Transcript-12-December-2016.PDF. Accessed March 13, 2018.

Voller, D. (2017). Transcript of proceedings. In the matter of a Royal Commission into the child protection and youth detention systems of the Northern Territory, 20 April. [Online]. Available https://childdetentionnt. royalcommission.gov.au/NT-public-hearings/Documents/transcripts-2017/ Transcript-20-April-2017.pdf. Accessed March 13, 2018.

Wacquant, L. (2001). Deadly symbiosis: When ghetto and prison meet and mesh. *Punishment & Society, 3*(1), 95–134.

Watson, I. (2011a). Aboriginal(ising) international law and other centres of power. *Griffith Law Review, 20*(3), 619–640.

Watson, I. (2011b). The declaration on the rights of indigenous peoples: Indigenous survival—Where to from here? *Griffith Law Review, 20*(3), 507–514.

Watson, I. (2015). *Aboriginal Peoples, Colonialism and International Law: Raw Law*. Oxon: Routledge.

Wolfe, P. (1999). *Settler Colonialism and the Transformation of Anthropology: The Politics and Poetics of an Ethnographic Event*. London: Cassell.

Wolfe, P. (2006). Settler colonialism and the elimination of the native. *Journal of Genocide Research, 8*(4), 387–409.

Zamolo, C. L. (2017). Transcript of proceedings. In the matter of a Royal Commission into the child protection and youth detention systems of the Northern Territory, 20 March. [Online]. Available https://childdetentionnt. royalcommission.gov.au/NT-public-hearings/Documents/transcripts-2017/ Transcript-20-March-2017.pdf. Accessed March 13, 2018.

12

Indigenous Rights, Poetry and Decarceration

Tracey McIntosh

Then the dispossessed
Disappear
Behind the wire
Concentrated as one blemished body
Where the truth of that dispossession is
Destroyed
Till only the crim remains

In the face of the manifold injuries wrought by the mass incarceration of Indigenous people in the settler states we must call on all our faculties to critically engage, analyse and offer ways forward that recognise as a starting point the right of Indigenous sovereignty. In drawing on our past we must be able to imagine our futures.

T. McIntosh (✉)
Wānanga o Waipapa, Faculty of Arts, University of Auckland,
Auckland, New Zealand
e-mail: t.mcintosh@auckland.ac.nz

© The Author(s) 2018
E. Stanley (ed.), *Human Rights and Incarceration*, Palgrave Studies in Prisons and Penology, https://doi.org/10.1007/978-3-319-95399-1_12

To imagine is to draw on our creative, intellectual, emotional, cultural and spiritual energies to create a just society where social harm is diminished, where community safety is enhanced, where victims and perpetrators are not constantly reproduced. The carceral logic we presently live with creates cognitive restriction: it suppresses our ability to think beyond the prison or even think that there is a beyond, beyond the prison.

We must envisage and work towards the end of prisons. We must have a gaze that goes beyond our immediate circumstances, that does not normalise our present as some enduring blueprint for our future; that is not tied to short electoral cycles or succumbs to a social myopia and collective apathy that renders us incapable of recognising our ability to be agents of transformative change. We must go beyond merely describing our world and seek to change it. This necessitates a generational gaze that demands a better future: a just future for those who will come. As a Māori woman, I believe that one of our greatest strengths comes from our commitment to mokopunatanga[1]: a recognition that our focus must be on the lives of our grandchildren and of their grandchildren. We must work with conviction and a revolutionary confidence towards a flourishing future where the shadow of the prison no longer distorts and corrupts one's life chances, or where the inter-generational reach of the prison is so long.

In reflecting on the notion of human rights and Indigenous rights and their relationship with a politic of decarceration I wish to consider the words of Maia,[2] a young Māori woman, who is presently incarcerated. Her poetry is not only an attempt for her to make sense of her personal situation but it is also part of a politic of collective transformative change. In this she follows Audre Lourde (2009: 356), who in her essay "Poetry is not a Luxury" noted:

> Poetry is not only dreams and visions; it is the skeleton architecture of our lives, it lays the foundation for a future of change, a bridge across our fears of what has been before … Poetry coins the language to express and charter this revolutionary demand, this implementation of that freedom.

Maia's poem was written in response to Maya Angelou's famous poem *Caged Bird* (1983). The following stanza from Angelou's poem powerfully conveys the domains of the caged and the free. Having already expressed the insouciance of the free bird who accepts as his due the bounty of food delivered by each fresh dawn, Angelou's stanzas masterfully move from the free bird to the caged bird underscoring the fact that the free bird's status of freedom is an unremarked, unconscious *natural* state. The free bird takes his liberty for granted as he does his right to be in and name his world.

> But a caged bird stands on the grave of dreams
> his shadow shouts on a nightmare scream
> his wings are clipped and his feet are tied
> so he opens his throat to sing. (Angelou 1983: 16–17)

Devoid of the rights inherent to his nature, particularly to fly unencumbered, the caged bird has a deep recognition of his profound unfreedom. The past is a haunting and the present a torment. Yet the caged bird intimates knowledge of the ways of the free even when he has not been permitted to experience them. His life is a life confined where all is blurred beyond the bars of the cage. In the final stanza the song of the caged bird captures the deep desire to know a world beyond confinement and isolation, and a recognition that a new consciousness will emerge across time. There is a belief that his song of loss and protest will be heard and enacted upon. His song imagines freedom, recognises the right to freedom and anticipates a state of freedom.

Maia on reading Angelou's poem for the first time a number of years ago experienced a sense of deep recognition and her own poetic written response was immediate. Given that her formal education was interrupted early, I have constantly been amazed and envious of her ability to express herself so spontaneously. In her poem, she moves from the third person, depicting the woman prisoner as the caged bird, to the first person as she perceives the force of her 'song' as it relates to her life narrative:

> A time to be caged and a time to be numb
> Her beauty in songs unheard of by some
> A cry of joy? Or purely from pain
> She'll wake up and sing again
> No doubt of how her voice will be heard

Whether she sings or shouts she is still a caged bird
Sung with volume as days pass her by
But how will she know what is beyond the sky?
Is it to be happy why the caged bird sings?
Unaware of what her life may bring
Or is it a greater power that locks her cage
Someone with fury or someone with rage
…..

The joys of the songs of freedom and flying
Are caged in sorrow and belong in dying
Soft warmth of sun, born in mists of rain
Sung herself to sleep to try to hide her pain
…..

Now I know why I sang and what pulled me through
I questioned the system but they had not a clue
Coz deep in mai heart it had a beat
The wind blew hard but I got back on mai feet
I can sing through the pain and all that they dealt
I would rather be caged than to have never have felt
Then the cage grew old and fell apart
It gave me a journey--a journey of heart

Here there is the realisation of her resilience in spite of a system that ensured that she would understand confinement well before her first actual experience of incarceration. A recognition that hers was a life characterised by violence and enforced borders and where the state was an intimate other and often a perpetrator of harm (see Stanley 2016).

Maia acknowledges elsewhere in her poetry the great remorse for her actions that led to her incarceration. She is also aware as a *tūturu* (real, authentic) Māori women that her prison life is overwhelmingly shared by other Māori women whose backgrounds, in too many cases, are indistinguishable from her own. Often she normalises the devastating homogenous ethnic uniformity of prison due to her learnt familiarity with the outcomes of "racialized oppression" (Ross 1998: 15). Her experience is specific to her but it is also a part of a collective Indigenous experience. While prisons are not Indigenous institutions and had no equivalent in traditional Indigenous society, in contemporary settler states prisons are populated, indeed over-populated, by Indigenous peoples (Jackson 2017).

Maia's lived experience, and the fact that she is an expert of her own condition, demonstrates the need to bring both lived experience and creative energies into our work. Maia demands that we imagine a world without prisons even while she finds it nearly impossible to contemplate given the place they have played in the lives of everyone she knows. Dian Million (2013: 3) a Tanana Athabascan scholar, believes that "when victims of state violence speak their truth in the presence of their oppressors, a new story will emerge, a reconciled national history".

The work of Angela Davis reinforces the inevitability, permanence and, paradoxically, invisibility of prison as features of our social lives. She argues that the invisibility of incarceration and the ability to forget prisons and those populations that inhabit them is because of the degree of difficulty for us to envision, to imagine "a social order that does not rely on the threat of sequestering people in places designed to separate them from their communities and families" (Davis 2003: 10). It is however not a pursuit of the impossible. Linda Tuhiwai Smith (2016), in response to recognising the burden of negative social indicators, said that rather than bearing the paralysing burden of their weight we must seek the pursuit of the possible. Our incarceration rates and the prison system are not part of our natural world. The prison is part of our social world: it is socially constructed and just as it has been made it can be unmade. We can pursue the possible.

Over the last nine years I have gone into a women's prison as a volunteer on a weekly basis and delivered a creative writing programme as well as offered educational support. My research work focuses particularly on Māori hyper-incarceration, global Indigenous incarceration and strategies to inform decarceration. My intent here is not to recite a litany of statistics to illustrate that Māori are over-represented in every step of the criminal justice system and to demonstrate that this over-representation increases at every step of that system. This is both a social and statistical fact. As is noted elsewhere (McIntosh and Workman 2017; Stanley and Mihaere, this volume) the gross disproportionate number of Māori who are imprisoned is one of the most well-known social statistics in New Zealand. The ubiquity of this knowledge in New Zealand has meant that it has become normalised and naturalised and regarded as an intractable problem that is not amenable to change. Nevertheless, I take it as a given that there is a recognition of the devastation that the prison plays in the lives of *whānau* (extended family), communities and the nation. It has resulted in an increasing unjust society where the shadow of the prison colonises our landscapes and for far too many people colonises their future (McIntosh and Radojkovic 2012: 39).

The Māori experience of colonisation is paralleled by struggles of Indigenous peoples in other settler states who have also been systematically brutalised and marginalised by state policies and practices, and where they continue to be over-represented in prison populations (Webb 2011). Stormy Ogden (2009: 355), a Yokurts and Pomo woman who was incarcerated in the Californian Prison system on what is her ancestral land, asserts that Indigenous incarceration "is an extension of the history and violent mechanisms of colonization". In her essay on incarceration in California, she includes a poem that speaks to the dispossession of Indigenous peoples of their lands and culture and the racism of neo-colonial incarceration practices:

> We have been degraded to criminal status in our homeland
> and become a people incarcerated.
> What was my crime, why 5 years in prison?
> Less than $2,000 of welfare fraud
> What was my crime?
> Being a survivor of molestation and rapes
> What was my crime?
> Being addicted to alcohol and drugs
> What was my crime?
> Being a survivor of domestic violence
> What was my crime?
> Being an American Indian woman.
> (ibid.: 359–360)

Is then a human rights discourse or an Indigenous rights framework a useful vehicle to pursue a policy and praxis of decarceration? Certainly, a right's discourse is never far from someone's mind who is living under conditions of incarceration. Rights and particularly loss of rights are invoked regularly and the observance of a particular right is often contested between people who are imprisoned and agents of the state. Interpretation of particular rights are sites of conflict within a prison but they also provide a framework and a conduit to identify and respond to concerns. I have seen how a recognition of a human right can be empowering for individuals and groups of people who are imprisoned. An individual who is experiencing a long lag or who has frequently churned through the system becomes much more sensitive to both human rights and regulatory rights and often demonstrates expert knowledge of particular rights and is able to provide counsel to both the incarcerated and those who work within the system.

It is impossible to underestimate the impact of human rights on the experience of prison life in the settler states. The following excerpts from the International Centre for Prison Studies' [ICPS] *Prison Digest* gives a few examples of infractions that affect Indigenous prison populations:

> United Nations officials have expressed concern at the number of Maori in New Zealand prisons … Maori make up more than 50 per cent of the prison population despite comprising around 15 per cent of the general population, while more than 65 per cent of women prisoners are Maori.

> Living conditions at Roebourne Regional Prison in Western Australia have been described as 'intolerable and inhumane' in a report by the Inspector of Custodial Services … the situation is exacerbated by the holding of six prisoners in cells which have been designed for four.

> In Canada … a report by two lawyers from the Federal Office of the Correctional Investigator … highlights the appalling state of a prison housing mainly Inuit prisoners … some prisoners had to sleep on mattresses on concrete floors due to a lack of beds. (cited in Bennett 2016: 329)

Human rights monitoring can apply pressure at an international level. There is the potential of both shaming governments and the possibility of generating positive action and reform. Peter Bennett notes that issues surrounding the legitimacy of detention affect huge numbers of people, often the most marginalised groups "those very people whom human rights seek to protect" (Bennett 2016: 325). A human rights framework recognises that people are sent to prison *as* punishment not *for* punishment. Deprivation of liberty is the punishment. This basic premise of our punishment regime is often ignored or wilfully misunderstood by proponents of more punitive reforms. Human rights monitoring can offer a corrective measure to this.

A human rights framework starts from the basic principle of recognition of the dignity and value of the individual. The fact of being incarcerated does not release authorities from their duty to ensure the prisoner is ensured of her right to be treated with dignity. Moreover international instruments remind us that due to the nature of incarceration it is itself a reason for special protection. The European Court of Human Rights asserts "that persons in custody are in a vulnerable position and the authorities are under a duty to protect them". Under the *International Covenant on Civil and Political Rights* (1966), we are obligated to ensure that "all persons deprived of their liberty shall be treated with humanity and with respect for the inherent dignity of the human person" (Article 10.1).

The case for the value of human rights in ensuring the protections of prisoners and creating the framework for legislative and regulatory change has been well made by other contributors to this book. They have also noted the limitations of a human rights framework in confronting the reality of incarceration. In reflecting on these limitations I would like to explore both the possibility of Indigenous rights with its focus on collective rather than individual rights and the pernicious effects of a totalising rights discourse for Indigenous peoples.

In looking for a framework that would support decarceration, a human rights legal framework is likely to be found wanting. While the aims of human rights are noble, they seek to improve incarceration rather than question its right of existence. The prison is seen to be part of the normative social landscape even if its existence is to be regretted.

States are to be held to account and reminded that the treatment of prisoners is the test of a civilised nation. Bennett (2016: 324) notes:

> That the state becomes subject to the ultimate moral test by the way it treats those subjected to one of its most severe sanctions, the deprivation of liberty with its potential violations of inhuman treatment and torture.

These are significant aspirations, and their application has promoted progressive societal change. However, in underscoring the right of prisons to exist, human rights legislation focuses on mitigating the pains of imprisonment and responding to violations in an attempt to improve conditions for prisoners. The explicit acceptance of the prison severely limits our ability to think of alternatives to detention as a form of punishment. Indeed, it may reinforce prison as *the* punishment. It may even support legislative and popular cognitive restriction in this regard.

The acceptance of prison as an inevitable component of our social worlds may be likened to the acceptance of war as part of normative human experience. This is underscored by the existence of rules of war. Throughout history societies have developed a form of 'warrior's code' that reveals and mirrors their most intensely held values. Values worth dying for and perhaps, more significantly, values perceived as worth killing for. From the first *1864 Geneva Convention* to the updated *1949 Convention*, international treaties have formed the core of laws of war (Fried 2000: 16–17). These laws are not about human rights as such. They are more about the maintenance of a discourse of civilisation in times of conflict. It is an attempt to both normalise and legitimise war within a moral framework that accepts human suffering as the norm. These codes seek to control the excesses of war and render illegitimate the offensive war, they do not countenance or even believe possible the elimination of war. They do however, presuppose that war will only occur when the many other options, including state to state diplomacy, have been exhausted.

Similarly we may ask what role, if any, do human rights frameworks play in questioning the over reliance of prisons as an obscene mechanism of managing complex social problems such as poverty, racism, structural and lateral forms of violence? How does it help us move away

from the "continued reliance on primarily retributive, individual, punitive, criminal legal responses to interpersonal violence and other forms
of socially harmful conduct"? (McCloud 2015: 1232).

Jennifer Hendry and Melissa Tatum (2016) note that Western legal
systems have for the last 200 years promulgated the liberal notion of
individual rights and freedom that have shaped and informed legal
frameworks globally. They are based upon the claim that these rights
and freedoms are universal to all individuals and that these rights "are
a vehicle for justice, perhaps even *the* vehicle for justice" (ibid.: 352).
They question these claims particularly as they relate to Indigenous
justice:

> The concept of rights has become so embedded in legal discourse, so nor-
> malized in contemporary legal practice, and so synonymous with justice,
> that it is all too easy to forget that a rights-based approach is not the only
> option available for addressing conflicts between the state and its citizens
> and, moreover, to accept it as such without any real critical engagement.
> (ibid.)

A significant issue is that the Western liberal-democratic state notion
of sovereignty (based on popular sovereignty) and the legitimacy of the
nation-state is largely enshrined in human rights legislation and is at
odds with notions of Indigenous sovereignty. Chris Cunneen and Juan
Tauri (2016) note that the Western nations see their source of political legitimacy through popular consent and support; a view that is at
odds with the Indigenous view of colonial and neo-colonial processes.
They note that settler states see their criminal justice systems informed
by universal principles of the rule of law that are fair and just; whereas,
many Indigenous peoples believe "that settler colonial criminal justice
systems are ineffective in their operation and oppressive in their outcomes" (ibid.: 13).

While human rights privilege individual rights, Indigenous rights
clearly focus on the collective and, in doing so, may be better aligned to
address the issue of the mass incarceration of Indigenous peoples. Sheryl
Lightfoot (2016: 190) writes that "Indigenous rights aim to eradicate
the discursive, normative and material remnants of the colonial
project". She further notes:

[The] adoption of the Indigenous Rights Declaration (2007) represents the first time that a broad set of collective rights was accepted within the human rights consensus. By constituting Indigenous rights in both individual and collective terms, global Indigenous politics creates a type of politics distinctive from other rights movements. Indigenous rights battle two sets of violences simultaneously: (1) discrimination/marginalisation and (2) the dispossession and assimilation of Indigenous peoples. Individual human rights could only address the first; collective rights standards were essential to beginning to address the second. (ibid.: 199)

For Moana Jackson, Māori understandings of sovereignty have been made subservient to the sanction and control of the settler legal system. Māori notions of sovereignty are informed by the ideals of authority and *rangatiratanga* (chieftainship and the right to exercise authority, self-determination). He details:

The tangata whenua [people born of the land, Indigenous peoples, hosts] status of the Māori is synonymous with what the 18th and early 19th century law called Aboriginal Rights, and which many jurisdictions and the United Nations now refer to as Indigenous Rights. In a general sense those rights are the traditional rights exercised by Indigenous peoples prior to European contact: they are the inherent ancestral rights which they employed to preserve social harmony and to maintain balance with the natural and supernatural worlds. In the exercise of those rights, such societies developed social, cultural, religious, and legal philosophies which were applied through a network of interdependent kin relationships. (Jackson 1988: 270)

However, the settler states sought to control Indigenous lives and to dispossess them of all resources, in what Cunneen and Porter (2017: 669) have called a process of "*immiseration*". Similarly, Luana Ross (1998: 14) notes that the subordination of Indigenous justice through warfare, genocidal practice and dispossession meant "[T]he system of justice was changed into a shadow of itself. Attempts were made to make Natives like white people, first by means of war and, when the gunsmoke cleared, by means of laws". Jackson recognises that [neo]colonising powers do not take challenges to their authority lightly. He asserts that "those who take power unjustly defend it with injustice" (New Zealand Herald 2009). He speaks of the settler states having a history of misremembering and misnaming. The Māori wars and land wars of the nineteenth century were:

> "sovereignty wars", which more aptly recognises them as colonising wars to take power. To properly name them in that way is recognition that, in the end, any remembering of the pity of war is necessarily a political and historical act as well as a deeply human one. It requires an honest and even moral reckoning with the past, and a context which explains why certain things happened, and the consequences which flowed from them. (Jackson 2016)

The *UN Declaration on the Rights of Indigenous Peoples* (UNDRIP) clearly has articles that can be invoked in thinking of alternatives to Indigenous incarceration. Article 3 speaks to the critical right to self-determination whereby Indigenous peoples may "freely determine their political status and freely pursue their economic, social and cultural development". Article 18 asserts that "Indigenous peoples have the right to participate in decision-making in matters that affect their rights as well as maintain and develop their own decision-making institutions". The *American Declaration on the Rights of Indigenous Peoples* adopted by the Organization of American States [OAS] in June 2016 declares in Article VI under Human Rights and Collective Rights that:

> Indigenous peoples have collective rights that are indispensable for their existence, wellbeing and integral development as peoples. In this regard, the states recognize and respect the right of the indigenous peoples to their collective action; to their juridical, social, political and economic systems or institutions …

While these Declarations privilege collective rights and speak explicitly of the right of Indigenous peoples to their own institutions, and being involved in everything that affects their development as a people, there is still nothing that explicitly challenges the existence of prisons.

Cunneen and Tauri (2016: 13) note that the process of reasserting Indigenous collective rights will require major institutional change to criminal justice agencies, particularly as the criminal justice system has been the site where "Indigenous rights have been ignored, in particular rights to self-determination, self-government and authority over the maintenance of social order". The willingness for major cultural criminal justice change has been mixed across the settler states. While there have been examples of shifts that could be seen as being responsive to Indigenous peoples (such as sentencing circles, and marae based youth courts) these still align firmly with state structures that accommodate Indigenous aspirations rather than truly face up to what a history of dispossession and institutional racism has produced. The assertion of Indigenous sovereignty that has never been ceded threatens to reveal what Audra Simpson has described as the "settlement secret", the secret of Indigenous sovereignty (cited in Razack 2015: 52). Sherene Razack notes that "settlers must always forget the source of their state's existence, the dispossession of sovereign nations (and the obliterations of human beings it requires). Forgetting requires the disappearance of the Native, since the settler never leaves" (ibid.: 62). Moana Jackson (2016) claims that even the term settler is a problem as it "misrepresents the reality of dispossession". The prisons are sites of both forgetting and the legitimation of the rights of the settler state. Jackson (2008: 3) states that colonisation is "in fact the history that has never left us":

It has always been about indigenous peoples being a threat whenever they have questioned their dispossession or whenever the colonisers wanted to keep them in a position of political powerlessness and economic equality. The real or perceived 'threat' has always been met with violence, either through military or paramilitary action or the more subtle but no less violent use of personal, collective and legal denigration. (ibid.: 2)

Often, prison administrator and state ministry responses to Indigenous over-representation rely on a broader discussion to increase culturally responsive programmes within the prison. This type of talk seems to suggest that prisons are just a vehicle for delivering programmes and completely renders invisible the fact that prisons are not just about punishment, deterrence, rehabilitation and incapacitation. They hold a moral and symbolic role—they reflect the state of the world in which we live. Prisons are architectures of control and one of the clearest expressions of state power. Moreover, prisons diminish all of those who reside or work in them. In this short extract of *If I was*, David Groulx (2015: 24), an Ojibwe poet, writes of how the system produces cruelty and expectations of cruelty even in uncruel people:

> If I was the warden of this place the lights would always be on and
>   the furnace off
> If I was the warden
> …..
>
> If I was the screw the hole would be colder
> If I was a screw I'd be boss
> …..
>
> If I was the prisoner in this place I'd sleep when I dream
> of getting even
> …..
>
> If I was a prisoner in this place
> The warden and the screws
> would know my name
> and not my number

Maia, drawing on her experience as a young imprisoned women, asks us to imagine a cage that will grow old and fall apart. To seek an end of imprisonment as the primary means of addressing social, economic and political problems means a need to dramatically reduce reliance on incarceration and to build the social institutions and conceptual frameworks that would render incarceration unnecessary. Decarceration is not a simple call for the immediate tearing down of all prison walls, but entails an array of alternative non-penal regulatory frameworks and a commitment to mauri ora, to human flourishing.

What counts as a just response to criminalised conduct turns crucially on the sociological, historical, and institutional settings in which punishment actually unfolds and has historically unfolded. The challenge, then, is to address the structural issues of limited opportunities, unemployment, marginalisation, poverty, to re-think how we conceptualise crime, punishment, justice and, ultimately, how we understand ourselves.

For this to happen it must first be an act of imagination, informed by research, informed by the experiences of victims and perpetrators and a recognition that too often these are not discrete or separate groups. It must be fuelled for a desire for greater levels of safety and reduction of social harm. Most critically, it must be focused on ensuring better lives for all our mokopuna and their mokopuna.

Notes

1. Mokopuna is the Māori term for grandchild or descendant. Mokopunatanga refers to the practice of considering how our practices and decision-making impacts on future generations, for our grandchildren's grandchildren.
2. Maia is her chosen pseudonym. She gives this extract as a koha or gift to the readers of this chapter. Other poems that Maia has written can be found on the Radio New Zealand website (Gay 2017).

References

Angelou, M. (1983). *Shaker, Why Don't You Sing?* New York: Random House.

Bennett, P. (2016). Prisons and human rights. In Y. Jewkes, J. Bennett, & B. Crewe (Eds.), *Handbook on Prisons* (pp. 324–339). London: Routledge.

Cunneen, C., & Porter, A. (2017). Indigenous peoples and criminal justice in Australia. In A. Deckert & R. Sarre (Eds.), *The Australian and New Zealand Handbook of Criminology, Crime and Justice* (pp. 667–682). Basingstoke: Palgrave Macmillan.

Cunneen, C., & Tauri, J. (2016). *Indigenous Criminology*. Bristol: Policy Press.

Davis, A. (2003). *Are Prisons Obsolete?* New York: Seven Stories Press.

Fried, J. (2000). War crimes violate the laws of war. In H. Kim (Ed.), *War Crimes* (pp. 13–23). San Diego: Greenhaven Press.

Gay, E. (2017). *Poetry Brings Peace Behind Bars*. [Online]. Available https://www.radionz.co.nz/news/national/321773/poetry-brings-peace-behind-bars. Accessed March 23, 2018.

Groulx, D. (2015). *These Threads Become a Thinner Light*. Penticton Indian Reserve: Theytus Books.

Hendry, J., & Tatum, M. (2016). Human rights, Indigenous peoples, and the pursuit of justice. *Yale Law and Policy, 34*(2), 351–386.

Jackson, M. (1988). *The Māori and the Criminal Justice System: He Whaipaanga Hou—A New Perspective*. Wellington: New Zealand Department of Justice Policy and Research Division.

Jackson, M. (2008). The constancy of terror. In D. Keenan (Ed.), *Terror in Our Midst?* (pp. 1–10). Wellington: Huia Publishers.

Jackson, M. (2016). *Moana Jackson: Facing the Truth About the Wars*. [Online]. Available https://e-tangata.co.nz/news/moana-jackson-facing-the-truth-about-the-wars. Accessed March 23, 2018.

Jackson. M. (2017). *Moana Jackson: Prison Should Never Be the Only Answer*. [Online]. Available https://e-tangata.co.nz/news/moana-jackson-prison-should-never-be-the-only-answer. Accessed March 23, 2018.

Lightfoot, S. (2016). *Global Indigenous Politics: A Subtle Revolution*. New York: Routledge.

Lourde, A. (2009). Poetry is not a luxury. In M. Damon & I. Livingston (Eds.), *Poetry and Cultural Studies: A Reader* (pp. 355–358). Chicago: University of Illinois Press.

McCloud, A. (2015). Prison abolition and grounded justice. *UCLA Law Review, 62*, 1156–1239.

McIntosh, T., & Radojkovic, L. (2012). Exploring the nature of the intergenerational transfer of inequalities experienced by young Māori people in the criminal justice system. In D. Brown (Ed.), *Indigenising Knowledge for Current and Future Generations* (pp. 38–48). Ngā Pae o te Māramatanga: Auckland.

McIntosh, T., & Workman, K. (2017). Māori in prison. In A. Deckert & R. Sarre (Eds.), *The Palgrave Handbook of Australian and New Zealand Criminology, Crime and Justice* (pp. 725–735). Basingstoke: Palgrave Macmillan.

Million, D. (2013). *Therapeutic Nations: Healing in an Age of Indigenous Human Rights*. Tucson: The University of Arizona Press.

New Zealand Herald. (2009). *Maori Resistance Not Terrorism—Moana Jackson*. [Online]. Available http://www.stuff.co.nz/national/30691/Maori-resistance-not-terrorism-Moana-Jackson. Accessed March 23, 2018.

Ogden, S. (2009). The prison-industrial complex in indigenous California. In R. Solinger, P. Johnson, M. Raimon, T. Reynolds, & R. Tapia (Eds.), *Interrupted Life: Experiences of Incarcerated Women in the United States* (pp. 355–360). Berkeley: University of California Press.

Organization of American States [OAS]. (2016). *American Declaration on the Rights of Indigenous Peoples*. AG/RES.2888 (XLVI-O/16). Adopted June 15.

Razack, S. (2015). *Dying from Improvement: Inquests and Inquiries into Indigenous Deaths in Custody*. Toronto: University of Toronto Press.

Ross, L. (1998). *Inventing the Savage: The Social Construction of Native American Criminality*. Austin: University of Texas Press.

Smith, L. T. (2016). *In Pursuit of the Possible: Indigenous Well-Being—A Study of Indigenous Hope, Meaning and Transformation*. [Online]. Available http://mediacentre.maramatanga.ac.nz/content/professor-linda-tuhiwai-smith. Accessed March 23, 2018.

Stanley, E. (2016). *Road to Hell: State Violence Against Children in Postwar New Zealand*. Auckland: Auckland University Press.

UN General Assembly. (1966). *International Covenant on Civil and Political Rights*. Adopted December 16.

UN General Assembly. (2007). *United Nations Declaration on the Rights of Indigenous Peoples*. A/RES/61/295. Adopted September 13.

Webb, R. (2011). Incarceration. In T. McIntosh & M. Mulholland (Eds.), *Māori and Social Issues*. Wellington: Huia Publishers.

Index

© The Editor(s) (if applicable) and The Author(s) 2018
E. Stanley (ed.), *Human Rights and Incarceration*, Palgrave Studies in Prisons and Penology, https://doi.org/10.1007/978-3-319-95399-1

Printed by Printforce, the Netherlands